D1578353

Also by Geoff Tibballs and published by Robson Books

Great Sporting Eccentrics

Great Sporting Mishaps

GEOFF TIBBALLS

Robson Books

First published in Great Britain in 1999 by Robson Books,
10 Blenheim Court, Brewery Road, London N7 9NT

British Library Cataloguing in Publication Data
A catalogue record for this title is available from the British Library

ISBN 1 86105 280 4

Set in Times by SX Composing DTP, Rayleigh, Essex
Printed and bound in Great Britain by
Creative Print & Design (Wales) Ltd

Contents

Introduction

We've all had sporting experiences we would rather not remember – the golf drive, struck low but sweet, which rebounded off the marker for the ladies' tee and whistled back past your right ear; the time you forgot how tired your legs were when attempting the obligatory jumping of the net at the end of a game of tennis so that you ended up in a tangled heap, looking more like a consignment of North Sea cod than a Wimbledon champion; and the race of your life in the over-40s half-marathon – a certain personal best – until a red setter began to show an unhealthy interest in your left leg.

Misfortune is never far away on the field of sport and for that we should be thankful because some sports need mishaps just to make them interesting. Until the authorities see sense and reintroduce the doom-laden judges with their scorecards and thick fur coats, ice skating is only worth watching for the falls. And think how much more entertaining it would be if a competitor actually fell *through* the ice! Who doesn't sit through the gymnastics in the hope that one of the muscular male competitors will end up with tears in his eyes after landing awkwardly on the pommel-horse? Or that someone will liven up the swimming by pulling the plug out during the 200 metres breaststroke? It's a question of fallibility. In Britain we don't seem to like our sporting heroes to be perfect. We look for signs of humanity. For example, Steve Davis would have been infinitely more popular if he'd ripped the baize once or twice.

Therefore this book is a tribute to all of those sports men and women who have found that, just when everything seems to be going according to plan, the fickle finger of fate can strike without warning to turn celebration into commiseration. Ask the Russian marathon runner who turned the wrong way on entering the stadium and saw a gold medal become bronze; the Irish jockey who didn't bother riding his horse out in a finish because he was mistakenly convinced that there was still a circuit to go; or the boxer who took a mighty swing at his opponent, missed, crashed out of the ring and succeeded only in knocking himself out.

While these particular wounds could be considered to have been self-inflicted, others were the result of sheer bad luck, such as the cricketer who was hit by a hang-glider while fielding in the deep; the French football team captain who accidentally swallowed the 5-franc piece which the referee tossed at kick-off; or the international golfer whose splendid drive collided in mid-air with a ball from a player on another hole and finished up in a pond.

Sadly a few mishaps have a tragic outcome but the vast majority are moments to be cherished. Sport wouldn't be the same without them. They're also a comfort when you next hit that ladies' tee marker . . .

Geoff Tibballs, 1999

1 Soccer

The Unluckiest Goalkeeper

Down the years many goalkeepers have claimed to be unlucky but more often than not it has just been a euphemism for incompetence. But Chic Brodie was something else. He really was unlucky. Brodie, who kept goal for Brentford with some distinction in the late 1960s, approached the 1970–71 season like any other, unaware that he would be involved in two bizarre incidents in the space of three months. The season was barely into its stride when Brodie and Brentford ventured north to take on Lincoln City in a Fourth Division fixture on 22 August. A high cross came over, Brodie hung on the crossbar to make sure that the ball drifted over the top and the next thing he knew the crossbar had snapped in half and he and two defenders were tangled up in the netting. The match was held up for forty-five minutes while repairs were carried out. Brentford lost 2–0.

But that was just for starters. On 28 November Brentford travelled to Layer Road to take on Colchester United. In the course of the game a stray mongrel dog wandered on to the pitch and clattered into Brodie on the edge of the penalty area, severely damaging the ligaments in the goalkeeper's knee. Brentford lost 4–0 but the injury to Brodie was more permanent. He didn't play again until February, and since he only managed another seven League games in total, the freak episode effectively ended his career. He did not harbour fond memories of the dog and was later quoted as saying: 'If I ever catch

up with that bloody animal, I'll blow its backside off with a shotgun.'
No room for misinterpretation there, then.

Sent Off for Flirting

In 1965 an East German junior soccer player was sent off for flirting
with the referee. The official, twenty-year-old Marita Rall, ordered
him off when he tried to arrange a date with her during the match.

Stanchion Stunners

It has been known for a perfectly good goal to be disallowed because
the ball hit the rear stanchion and rebounded back into play, leading
the referee to conclude that it must have hit the frame of the goal
instead. On 6 September 1980 in a match at Coventry, Crystal
Palace's Clive Allen sent a free-kick past home keeper Jim Blyth.
The ball struck the stanchion and bounced back into play but the
referee thought it must have hit the bar and waved play on. Palace
lost 3–1.

Similarly in 1993 at Firhill, Dundee United's Paddy Connolly
knocked a shot firmly between the posts where it hit the stanchion
and rebounded back into play. Accepting the inevitable, disconsolate
Partick Thistle defender Martin Clark picked the ball up and handed
it to his goalkeeper, only to discover that referee Les Mottram and
his linesman had failed to spot either the goal or the blatant handball
which followed. Despite this reprieve, Thistle still lost.

Yet probably the most famous stanchion drama concerned a goal
that should not have been given. Chelsea were leading visitors
Ipswich 1–0 in 1970 when, in the sixty-fifth minute, Alan Hudson
shot from 20 yards past Ipswich keeper David Best. The ball brushed
the side netting, hit the stanchion and spun back into play. In the
mistaken belief that the ball had gone between the posts, referee Roy
Capey awarded a goal. While the Chelsea players suppressed their
mirth, Ipswich protested vehemently and play was held up for two
minutes. Even the linesman tried to persuade Capey to disallow the

goal but the man in the middle was adamant that it was legitimate. It turned out to be a decisive score too as Chelsea won 2–1.

Fell Off Stretcher

Injured in the Second Division game with Chesterfield on 16 March 1996, Walsall midfielder Martin O'Connor was helped on to a stretcher. But as the two elderly St John Ambulance men carried him off the field, the one at the back slipped on the greasy pitch and fell over, sending O'Connor tumbling off the stretcher. Weighing up the situation, O'Connor sensibly decided it was safer to limp off under his own steam. He returned a few minutes later and scored in Walsall's 3–0 win.

Forced to Play in Street Clothes

In April 1896 Loughborough had to play a Second Division match at Newton Heath (the forerunners of Manchester United) in their street clothes after losing their kit. The game was played in pouring rain with the result that the Loughborough players had to travel home in their wet, muddy clothes. The farce had a tragic sequel when Loughborough's Jimmy Logan, who had been a hat-trick hero for Notts County in the 1894 FA Cup final, caught a chill after the Newton Heath game and died of pneumonia the following month.

Excuses for Absence

Brighton goalkeeper Perry Digweed didn't turn up for his team's Second Division home fixture with Bournemouth on 10 September 1988 because nobody remembered to tell him he was playing. In his absence, Brighton slipped up 2–1.

West Bromwich Albion striker Fabian de Freitas had a different excuse for his no-show against Crewe on the afternoon of Easter Monday 1999 – he thought it was an evening kick-off. With the time for handing in the team sheet rapidly approaching and still no sign of de Freitas, the club tried to phone him but couldn't get through because his girlfriend was on the line. Without him, Albion crashed 5–1.

But there was no doubting the commitment of Gillingham captain Mark Weatherley who trudged six miles through snow drifts to join his team for an FA Cup tie with Wigan in 1986. He arrived at the ground to find that the game had been called off.

Careless Hands

Voted Leicester City's 1995–96 Player of the Year for his safe hands, goalkeeper Kevin Poole was presented with a cut-glass rose bowl . . . which he promptly dropped.

Cricked Back in Anger

Frustrated after missing a good chance against Aberdeen in March 1991, Rangers' striker Mo Johnston picked up a lump of mud and hurled it down in annoyance. In the process he cricked his back, putting himself out of the next game.

Chelsea keeper Dave Beasant was ruled out of action for the opening weeks of the 1993–94 season after dropping a jar of salad cream on his big toe. Beasant had tried to catch the falling jar with his right foot but ended up severing the tendon. He didn't even manage to save the jar which shattered into pieces on the floor.

Taking a leaf out of Beasant's book, Liverpool striker Robbie Fowler was sidelined with a knee injury sustained by stretching to pick up the remote control for the TV.

A Volkswagen in the Centre Circle

A Nairobi League match being played on a college pitch at Kericho in 1975 was stopped when the college principal drove his

Volkswagen on to the pitch in a bid to have the game called off. It took the referee ten minutes to persuade him to leave. The game ended in a goalless draw.

The Phantom Whistler

Arsenal left-back Dennis Evans scored arguably the daftest own goal of all time, against Blackpool at Highbury in 1955. With seconds left and Arsenal coasting at 4–0, Evans heard a whistle and thought it was referee Frank Coultas blowing for full-time. Believing his day's work to be done, Evans casually flicked the ball into his own net where his goalkeeper, who had also assumed that it was the final whistle, was collecting his cap and gloves. But the whistle hadn't come from the referee at all – it had been blown by a spectator. So the referee had no choice but to award Blackpool a goal.

Referee Sent Himself Off

Football referee Melvin Sylvester knew there was only one penalty for fighting on the pitch. So when he lost his temper and threw a punch at one of the players, he sent himself off. Forty-two-year-old Mr Sylvester, a school caretaker and experienced referee, took over the running of the Andover and District Sunday League match between the Southampton Arms and Hurstbourne Tarrant British Legion in April 1998 when the appointed official was taken ill. All was going smoothly until Mr Sylvester, who also happened to be the manager of the Southampton Arms, reacted to what he claimed was a push by Hurstbourne player Richard Curd. 'I was sorely provoked,' said the referee. 'I punched him after he had pushed me from behind. He then swore. I just could not take any more – I blew my top.' Mr Sylvester then gave himself the red card and was substituted for the rest of the match by a spectator. Nursing a black eye, Richard Curd responded: 'I did nothing to provoke the situation at all. I never threw one punch and I only swore at the referee after he threw punches at me. I deny ever pushing him. We accidentally collided when I was chasing after the ball.'

A Smashing Time

To celebrate the installation of floodlights at their Gayfield ground in 1955, Arbroath staged a friendly with neighbours Dundee United. In the course of the game one of the lamps was smashed by a hefty clearance from an Arbroath player.

Bournemouth's first floodlit game was also accident-prone. It was a League match against Northampton in 1961 but the new lights failed just before kick-off and the match was delayed for an hour.

More recently, in August 1997, Derby County's first game at their new Pride Park stadium came to a premature finish after fifty-five minutes when the floodlights failed. The match was abandoned with Derby leading visitors Wimbledon 2–1.

Travel Problems

William Carr from the Owlerton club in Sheffield was selected to play in goal for England against Scotland in 1875. However, he missed the train down to London and by the time he arrived at the Kennington Oval ground the match had been under way for a quarter of an hour. Until then England had managed to keep a clean sheet but Carr proceeded to let in two goals as England were held to a 2–2 draw. He never played for his country again.

In 1889 Wales goalkeeper Sam Gillam arrived late for the international with Scotland at Wrexham even though he was a Wrexham player. Alf Pugh of Rhostellyn was allowed to keep goal until Gillam turned up – the first recorded use of a substitute. The game ended in a 0–0 draw.

Selection Headache

A deciding group match in the 1950 World Cup in Brazil saw the host nation pitted against Yugoslavia at the unfinished Maracaña stadium in Rio de Janeiro. While the builders had a day off, the two teams prepared for the key encounter but these preparations were thrown into confusion when, in the dressing room just before kick-off, Yugoslavia's influential forward Rajko Mitic stood up and banged his head on a protruding iron girder. Mitic was still having his head bandaged when the rest of the team took the field and by the time he was ready to join the action, Yugoslavia were already a goal down and on their way to a 2–0 defeat.

Players Called Back from the Bar

Following confusion over the competition rules, red-faced referee Martin Perry summoned the players of Clevedon Town and Witney Town back on to the pitch thirty minutes after the final whistle for a penalty shoot-out. The occasion was a first round Dr Martens Cup tie, played over two legs in October 1996. The first leg at Witney had ended in a 1–1 draw and the second leg at Clevedon also finished all square at 2–2 for a 3–3 aggregate. Referee Perry thought that away goals in extra-time counted double and declared Witney the winners but he then discovered that those rules did not apply to this competition and that the tie had to be decided by a penalty shoot-out instead. By that time the crowd had long gone and the players had showered and changed. Indeed, some were already in the bar. When they heard that the referee wanted them changed and back out on the pitch, they thought it was a wind-up. For the record, Witney won the shoot-out 4–2.

The Men Who Dropped the Cup

Charlton manager Jimmy Seed was so overcome with excitement after his team's triumph in the 1947 FA Cup final that he accidentally dropped the trophy and damaged the lid. With the Cup due to be paraded at a special civic reception, the club had to take it to a local garage to carry out emergency repairs.

In 1992 it was Liverpool's turn to lift the FA Cup and reserve team coach Phil Thompson's turn to damage the lid. Leaving the team's London hotel after the final, Thompson contrived to drop the lid and dented it so badly that it no longer fitted on the rim of the trophy.

Silent Protest Ruined by Goal

Furious at the financial state of their club, Portsmouth fans planned a ten-minute silent protest at the start of the First Division game with Huddersfield on 16 January 1999. However, their plans were wrecked when striker Steve Claridge put Pompey ahead after four minutes . . .

Injured During Celebrations

After scoring the winner for Arsenal against Sheffield Wednesday in the 1993 Coca-Cola Cup final – his first goal for the club – young midfielder Steve Morrow broke his arm when, in the post-match celebrations, skipper Tony Adams put him over his shoulder and accidentally dropped him.

Before he had even made his senior début, Chelsea's new signing, Celestine Babayaro, was ruled out for six weeks at the start of the 1997–98 season with a stress ankle fracture sustained during acrobatic celebrations to mark a goal in a reserve team friendly at Stevenage.

Brazilian fans mobbed their team with such enthusiasm after the 1970 World Cup final defeat of Italy that one of the Brazilian heroes, Roberto Rivelino, collapsed under the weight of the celebrations and had to be carried to the dressing room on a stretcher.

Immediately after putting his team ahead at Chester in March 1999, Plymouth Argyle's Dwight Marshall was injured by one of his own fans. The spectator ran on to the pitch to join in the goal celebrations but sent Marshall crashing to the ground. While Marshall was undergoing lengthy treatment, the fan was escorted away by police.

Coach Towed Away

En route to Chelsea for a League match on 1 December 1990, Spurs stopped for lunch at the Royal Lancaster Hotel. When they emerged from their meal ready to complete the journey to Stamford Bridge, they discovered that their coach had been towed away for being parked illegally. And in the coach was all their playing kit. A series of frantic phone calls tracked down the missing items but the kick-off had to be put back by ten minutes. Spurs were fined £20,000 for their late arrival and, to complete their day, they lost 3–2.

Gillingham's delayed arrival for a Fourth Division fixture at Barrow in 1961 had greater repercussions. It meant that the match started late and, with Barrow not having floodlights, the game had to be abandoned after seventy-five minutes because of bad light. Barrow were particularly peeved – they were leading 7–0 at the time.

Three Stockport County players got stuck in snow on the way to a Fourth Division game at Bury in April 1981, forcing the visitors to play the entire first half with only nine men. Maybe Bury felt sorry for them because they somehow allowed Stockport to claw out a 1–0 win.

Dover's Vauxhall Conference fixture at Woking on 20 April 1995 was called off after the Dover team coach was held up on the motorway for hours by a stray cow. When it became apparent that Dover wouldn't arrive until 9 p.m., the referee postponed the match.

Unleashed Bull on Fans

When fans invaded the pitch during a Cup tie at Raith Rovers in 1887, local businessman Robert Stark came up with a novel solution for this early outbreak of hooliganism. He simply unleashed a bull which he kept tethered in a field adjoining the ground. Not surprisingly, the sight of the rampaging beast encouraged the troublemakers to disperse swiftly.

Too Young

In 1989 the Herefordshire Football Association scrapped plans for a centenary dinner-dance when it was discovered that the association was actually only ninety years old. A total of 250 tickets had already been sold and FA Chief Executive Graham Kelly had been invited to attend.

A Kick in the Teeth

Arriving in Aberdeen for the second leg of a UEFA Cup preliminary round tie in 1994, Skonto Riga discovered that midfielder Alexey Semenov had left his boots back home in Latvia. Sympathetic to his plight, Aberdeen lent him a pair which he then used to score the goal which knocked the Scots out of the competition.

Another player who forgot his boots was Cardiff City's Stan Richards when reporting for duty at Maine Road in 1946 to make his international début for Wales against England. He was never capped again.

Police Raid

Nottinghamshire policemen who played against Lincolnshire Police at Scunthorpe in 1959 returned to their dressing room after the game to find that someone had been through their pockets and stolen their cash.

Medal Mix-up

At the end of the 1992 FA Cup final, Sunderland, beaten by

Liverpool, were mistakenly given the winners' medals and Liverpool were given the runners-up medals. The players exchanged medals afterwards.

In 1970 David Webb couldn't collect his medal after scoring the winning goal for Chelsea against Leeds United in the FA Cup final replay at Old Trafford. When the game ended, Webb had swapped shirts with a Leeds player and an official refused to allow him to go up to the directors' box because he thought Webb was a Leeds player. Webb was later given his medal in the dressing room.

Does Anyone Fancy a Game?

Faced with the prospect of being able to field only eight players for the GM Vauxhall Conference match with Maidstone United in November 1986, Northwich Victoria chairman Derek Nuttall asked over the club's public address system whether any of the 738 crowd fancied a game. To his amazement, there were three willing volunteers – Steve Garnett, Rick Parkin and Mark Fogg. With Northwich's injury crisis, they couldn't afford to be choosy, which was why they overlooked the fact that one of the trio had downed two pints and eaten a pork pie just before going to the ground. Yet despite taking the field with a team that included three spectators, Northwich managed to hold League leaders Maidstone to a 1–1 draw.

Mischievous Mascots

Club mascots have made some lurid headlines over the past few seasons. In September 1998 Scarborough apologised to Brentford after the Scarborough mascot, Sammy the Seagull, had mooned at visiting fans. Four months later, Swansea mascot Cyril the Swan was hauled before the Welsh FA to answer charges of trying to incite trouble during the club's November 1998 FA Cup tie with Millwall. Swansea commercial manager Mike Lewis was aware of a potential problem. 'Cyril is a mute swan,' he explained, 'so we must find a way around that at the meeting.' Despite character references from Lennie the Lion of Shrewsbury Town and Barclay the Bluebird of Cardiff City, Cyril had his wings clipped by the Welsh FA who, after a four-hour meeting, banished him to the back of the grandstand for future matches.

But the biggest story was the half-time punch-up between a wolf and three little pigs at Bristol City on 7 November 1998. Wolfie, mascot of visitors Wolverhampton Wanderers, was involved in an on-pitch brawl with the three pigs who were hosting a children's penalty shoot-out to promote double-glazing firm Coldseal. As the 15,000 crowd watched open-mouthed, tempers between the animals became frayed and one of the pigs was seen to aim a trotter at Wolfie. The Bristol City mascot, City Cat, tried to intervene but the bad feeling continued near the tunnel as the animals trooped off. In the end, they had to be separated by stewards. One of the pigs later accused Wolfie of giving him a cut lip. City fan David Singleton said: 'I could not believe what was going on. I thought it was a bit of fun at first but then it went a bit wrong when one of the pigs whacked Wolfie. It was the best half-time entertainment I've ever seen in twenty-two years watching football.' An Avon and Somerset police spokesman added: 'We were not involved but we understand there was a lot of huffing and puffing.'

Administrative Error

Birmingham City didn't take part in the 1921–22 FA Cup because the club forgot to post the entry form. They were not alone – Queen's Park Rangers did the same thing five years later. In 1932–33, Brighton of Third Division (South) remembered to enter the Cup but forgot to claim their exemption as far as the first round. So they went into the hat for the first qualifying round along with the likes of Courage Sports and Social FC, Leavesden Mental Hospital and Shoreham whom they beat 12–0.

Handball Sparked Mini Riot

With his Brazilian club San Lorenzo hanging on to a 2–1 lead against Estudiantes in the final minutes, defender Siminiota picked the ball up thinking that it had gone out of play. But referee Humberto Dellacasa decreed otherwise and awarded a penalty – his third of the game. The spot-kick was converted and in the resultant fracas two players were sent off for manhandling the referee who had to be escorted from the pitch by baton-wielding riot police.

This was positively mild compared to what happened towards the end of a 1971 South American (Libertadores) Cup tie between Argentinian champions Boca Juniors and Sporting Cristal from Peru. The match – in Buenos Aires – exploded into a mass brawl, forcing referee Alejandro Otero to call in the police. A total of nineteen players were arrested – three were taken to hospital, the other sixteen to the local police station. They were each given thirty days in jail although the sentences were later suspended.

Similar indiscipline prevailed at a 1993 Paraguayan League match between Sportivo Ameliano and General Caballero. Trouble flared after two Sportivo players were sent off. A ten-minute fight ensued, at the end of which referee William Weiler dismissed a further eighteen players, including the remainder of the Sportivo team. Understandably, the match was abandoned. Such are the joys of football in South America.

Locked in Loo

Spurs forwards Les Ferdinand and Ruel Fox missed the start of the second half of the club's game at Newcastle on 4 October 1997 after accidentally being locked in the toilet.

Explosive Encounter

Sheffield United's match with Oldham on 9 February 1984 was postponed when a wartime bomb was found near Bramall Lane.

An Invitation to Slaughter

Arbroath's record 36–0 drubbing of Bon Accord in a Scottish Cup tie in 1885 only happened because the Scottish FA invited the wrong team to take part in the competition. The invitation should have gone to Orion FC of Aberdeen but instead it went to Orion Cricket Club. Gamely the cricketers decided to give it a go and changed their name to Bon Accord. They had no pitch of their own – and so switched the tie to Arbroath – and no kit. Thus they arrived for the big match without shirts or boots. In the circumstances they probably got off lightly.

Another invitation which, with hindsight, should definitely have been declined was received by Wolverhampton Sunday League outfit Oxbarn Social Club in 1973. It offered them the chance to play in Germany against a team from Mainz. Eager to taste foreign travel, the lads from Oxbarn eagerly accepted, unaware that they would be playing crack German team SVW Mainz who, in turn, had thought they were inviting Wolverhampton Wanderers. The Oxbarn secretary didn't smell a rat until he walked into the magnificent Mainz stadium and heard that the opposition were on hefty win bonuses. By then it was too late to back out. Oxbarn lost 21–0.

The Wrong Kevin

With just five minutes left and England desperately needing a goal against Poland in the infamous 1973 World Cup qualifier at Wembley, Sir Alf Ramsey decided to send on Kevin Hector as substitute as a last throw of the dice. 'Kevin, get stripped,' ordered Ramsey on the bench. Misinterpreting his manager's request, Kevin Keegan began getting changed instead. Anxious to speed up the operation, reserve goalkeeper Ray Clemence even helped Keegan take off his tracksuit. It was only then that Ramsey realised that he was about to send on the wrong Kevin and clarified his orders. By the time Kevin Hector did finally get on to the pitch, there was only a minute and a half left and it was far too late for him to have any effect on the outcome of the match.

Cut Short by Fog

Colchester United's record crowd of 19,072 turned up to watch an FA Cup first round tie with Reading on 27 November 1948, only for the game to be abandoned after thirty-five minutes because of fog.

But at least the fans at Colchester got more for their money than those who braved the elements for Dundee United's Premier Reserve League game with Dunfermline Athletic at Arbroath in February 1998. The match was abandoned after just ninety seconds because of high winds.

Denture Search

Referee Henning Erikstrup was about to blow for full-time with Norager leading Ebeltoft 4–3 in a Danish League match in 1960 when his dentures suddenly fell out. As he scrambled around on the pitch in an effort to find them, Ebeltoft equalised. Despite vehement protests from Ebeltoft, Mr Erikstrup disallowed the goal, replaced his false teeth and promptly blew the final whistle.

Leicester City striker Alan Smith lost three teeth during his team's 2–2 draw with Stoke on 24 September 1983. They were retrieved from the pitch and replaced in hospital.

Fan Went Ape

In February 1992 a teenage Middlesbrough fan decided to get round a court curfew by disguising himself in a gorilla suit for a Rumbelows Cup replay against Peterborough United. But when 'Boro scored the only goal of the game, he forgot himself, threw the gorilla head into the air in celebration and was recognised by a police officer watching highlights of the game at home on TV later that evening.

The Three-Second Game

When Estonia failed to turn up for their World Cup qualifying tie with Scotland in Tallinn in 1996 – apparently they were finishing their lunch in a distant hotel – the resultant match was just about the shortest on record. Scotland lined up, kicked off and the referee blew the final whistle after just three seconds' 'play'. The fixture was subsequently replayed.

There had been a similar spectacle in Scottish football back in 1879. In that year's Scottish Cup final, Rangers drew 1–1 with Vale of Leven but were adamant that they'd had a perfectly good goal disallowed. Rangers' protests to the Scottish FA were dismissed and so they sulked and refused to turn up for the replay. Thus Vale of Leven kicked off, ran the ball into the unguarded goal and were declared the winners.

Girl Power

In May 1982 police were called to stop a fight at a girls' five-a-side tournament between two Croydon schools. The tournament had been organised by the Metropolitan Police.

Time Faults

Pressing for an equaliser against Argentina in a 1930 World Cup group match, French hopes were raised when winger Marcel Langiller was sent clear. But as Langiller homed in on goal, Brazilian referee Gilberto de Almeida Rego blew the final whistle. As puzzled looks became the order of the day, it was soon apparent that the referee had lost track of the time and had blown six minutes early. The game was restarted and the missing time played but France never came as close again and were knocked out of the competition.

With Southampton leading 4–1 at Millwall in a Southern League match in November 1898, referee Mr Saywell accidentally blew for time nine minutes early. As the fans headed across the pitch on their way home, Mr Saywell realised his error and tried to get the game restarted. But the playing area couldn't be cleared of people and so the score stood.

Kit Blew Away

Checking in at their seafront hotel in readiness for their game at Brighton in November 1989, Newcastle United began unloading the team kit from the coach. But as they did so, a sudden gust of wind caught hold of the trolley on which the kit baskets were being transported and sent it spinning off along the promenade where it was involved in a head-on collision with a number 67 bus. As elderly passengers removed jock-straps from their heads, the United staff set about repairing the damage. Newcastle proceeded to antagonise the Brighton public still further by defeating the local team 3–0.

A Game of No Halves

In September 1997 referee Jeff Arnold was banned for five years by the Devon Football Association for presiding over a football match which never took place. Mr Arnold submitted a fictitious report on Woodland Fort's 2–0 'victory' over Efford United in the Plymouth and District Combination League. One of the teams had arrived with only four players and feared a hefty fine if the match didn't take place so the teams agreed to fake the scoreline and persuaded Mr Arnold to support them. The ruse proved a costly exercise all round since both clubs ended up being fined.

Law Breaker

Forced to sit on the bench because of injury, Denis Law was an anxious spectator at Manchester United's 1968 European Cup semi-final with Real Madrid. But he got so excited when Bill Foulkes scored for United that he forgot where he was and punched the air in his familiar fashion, only for his fist to smash through the roof of the dug-out. Law was left nursing a broken bone in the hand . . . and a longer injury lay-off.

Seven years earlier, Law had suffered even greater misfortune when scoring all six goals for Manchester City in a fourth round FA Cup tie at Luton and then seeing them all expunged from the records when the referee abandoned the game in the sixty-ninth minute because of a waterlogged pitch. To rub it in, City, who were leading 6–2 at the time, lost the replayed match 3–1. Law scored their only goal and was left to mourn the ones that got away.

Lost Count

Spanish national coach Javier Clemente lost track of the number of substitutes he had used in a friendly against Norway in April 1996. So when a player limped off fifteen minutes from time, the only substitute available to Clemente was goalkeeper Jose Molina who was promptly sent on to play on the left wing.

A Spate of Burst Balls

On the eve of the 1946 FA Cup final between Charlton Athletic and Derby County, the match referee, Mr E. D. Smith of Cumberland, was asked by the BBC what the chances were of the ball bursting during the final. Since such a thing had never happened before, Mr Smith confidently stated that the chances were about a million to one. A bet could have set someone up for life as the following day the ball did indeed burst just as Derby centre-forward Jackie Stamps shot for goal. Five days later, the same two teams met in a League match and again the ball burst. The following year Charlton were back at Wembley for the Cup final, this time against Burnley. And yet again the ball burst.

Referee Distracted by Fan's Shirt

Midway through the second half of the Second Division match between Leyton Orient and Blackpool in August 1992, referee Kelvin Morton stopped the game, went to the touchline and asked a spectator in the West Stand at Brisbane Road to move because his shirt was distracting him. The bright yellow shirt being worn by an Orient season-ticket holder apparently clashed with the linesman's flag.

Captaining a Sheffield XI in the annual fixture against a Glasgow XI in the 1930–31 season, Sheffield's Jimmy Seed found himself continually passing to the referee who, like Seed's team-mates, was wearing a white shirt. He eventually solved the problem by persuading the referee to put on a dark top.

And in April 1996 Manchester United famously complained that their new grey away strip meant that they couldn't pick each other out against the crowd at Southampton. Trailing 3–0 at half-time, United switched from the grey to a blue strip for the second half. But by then the damage had been done.

In February 1954 the Second Division match between Luton Town and Stoke City was stopped while the referee asked a small boy in the crowd to hide a bottle of orange squash because the bright sunshine was reflecting from the bottle into the players' eyes.

Trainer Carried Off by Team

Arguably the finest individual performance at the inaugural World Cup in 1930 came from the trainer of the United States team during their semi-final with Argentina. He was still fuming at a disputed Argentinian goal when he was called upon to run on to the pitch to treat an injured player. In a visible display of temper, he threw down his medical bag, broke a bottle of chloroform and accidentally anaesthetised himself, as a result of which he had to be carried off by his own team. Taking their lead from this splendid man, the United States went on to lose 6–1.

The Ground Opened Up

Footballers often trot out the line about wishing the ground would open up beneath them after making a particularly horrendous blunder. Well, the prayers of Woking and Hayes were answered during their Vauxhall Conference game in March 1997. The match had to be abandoned after twenty minutes when Woking captain Kevan Brown almost fell into a three-foot-deep hole which suddenly appeared in the pitch at Woking's Kingsfield ground.

Injured by Ref

Swindon Town striker Iffy Onuora sustained a fractured cheekbone after referee Roger Furnandiz accidentally clattered into him during the First Division game with Charlton in April 1998.

Twenty years earlier in Peru referee Hugo Bustamante knocked out Atletico Chalaco defender Escobar when he tried to prevent a quick free-kick being taken against Nacional Iquitos.

Flag Day

The words 'sloppy' and 'Germans' are about as likely to be used in conjunction as 'penniless' and 'Manchester United' or 'promotion' and 'Rochdale'. But the renowned German efficiency let them down on one occasion – at the 1974 World Cup finals. Having laid on a spectacular opening ceremony planned to the last detail, the Germans settled back for the opening game between Brazil and Yugoslavia. It was then that the referee at the stadium in Frankfurt realised that something wasn't quite right – there were no corner and centre-line flags. The rest of the world was therefore able to enjoy a quiet chuckle while embarrassed German officials scurried off in search of the missing flags.

Goal Wreckers

The first leg of the European Champions League semi-final between Real Madrid and Borussia Dortmund at the Bernabeu Stadium on 1 April 1998 was delayed for over an hour after Real fans broke the goal. The fans had been hanging on the back of the net before the kick-off and eventually the entire apparatus gave way. The start was put back while a replacement set of posts was ferried over from Real's training ground.

On a smaller scale, livewire Bournemouth left-winger Reg Cutler ran into the Molineux goalposts during his side's 1957 FA Cup giant-killing of Wolves and brought the lot crashing to the ground. There was a delay of seven minutes while emergency repairs were carried out. Cutler recovered to score the winning goal.

Cash Crisis

Hard-up Cardiff City were delighted when their third round FA Cup tie with Queen's Park Rangers in 1990 brought them record gate receipts of £50,000. But they weren't as happy on the Monday when they discovered that thieves had raided the club safe over the weekend.

Stuck on the M6

Carlisle United fan Geoff Tomlinson was justifiably proud of his attendance record. He hadn't missed a Carlisle game for thirty-eight years (spanning a total of 1,815 home and away matches) until fate caught up with him on the way to Walsall in October 1994. He was forced to miss the action after being caught up in a twenty-seven-mile traffic jam on the M6 in Cheshire. 'Words cannot explain how I felt,' he said. 'To make things worse, we came from behind to win 2–1.'

Shipwrecked

In 1930 Raith Rovers decided to embark on an overseas tour to the Canary Islands. It might have looked good in the brochures but on the way there Raith's boat capsized and the team were shipwrecked. Happily everyone was rescued but from then on Raith decided to stay a little closer to Kirkcaldy.

Sprake's Special

We all have our favourite own goals. Those with long memories might recall a classic moment from 1960 when, playing against Liverpool, Charlton winger Sam Lawrie suddenly elected to pass back to his own keeper Frank Reed from the half-way line. Alas Reed was looking the other way at the time and the ball rolled gently into the net. In the 1970s, Leicester City's Keith Weller, standing out on the touchline at Luton, some forty yards from goal, curled an exquisite back-pass over and round his own keeper. In 1990, Liverpool's Ronnie Whelan sent a cultured thirty-yard chip past his own keeper Bruce Grobbelaar against, of all people, Manchester United, and the following year that doyen of own-goal scorers, Arsenal's Lee Dixon, brilliantly lobbed his own keeper from way out on the touchline after just fifty-four seconds of the game with Coventry. The rule forbidding goalkeepers to pick up back-passes has led to a stream of bizarre mishaps. Hardly a month goes by without a seemingly harmless back-pass bobbling gently into the net after the keeper has swung a boot at thin air. But none of these clangers can compare to Gary Sprake's moment of madness in December 1967.

For those too young to remember him, Sprake was a talented, but occasionally erratic, Welsh international goalkeeper who plied his trade for Leeds United. His tendency to be brilliant one minute, hopeless the next put him out of step with the rest of the Leeds team who were a mean, well-organised machine not given to displays of human fallibility. It was like putting a nutty professor in a team of robots.

His finest hour came in a tense title clash against Liverpool at

Anfield. A minute before half-time Leeds were already trailing when an innocuous ball rolled through to Sprake. 'I was going to throw the ball wide to Terry Cooper,' he recalled many years later, 'when he screamed, "No, no" because Ian Callaghan was closing him down. So I went to pull the ball back to my chest, as I often did, and it just flew over my left shoulder into the net.' The rest of the Leeds team had moved away upfield in readiness for a counter-attack. Billy Bremner remembered: 'As I approached the centre-circle, the ground erupted with a great roar. I turned back to see Sprake standing on the edge of the 18-yard box with his hands covering his face. I looked in panic for the ball and there it was lying in the back of our net. Jack Charlton asked referee Jim Finney what had happened and Jim said in a matter-of-fact way: "Your goalkeeper has just thrown the ball into his own net." – Shortly after awarding the goal, Jim Finney blew for half-time. And as Sprake trooped off, the disc jockey put on 'Careless Hands' by Des O'Connor.

Barmy Army

The annual New Year's Day match between the Salvation Army and a church at Sheringham, Norfolk, in 1994 erupted into violence with five players injured. Baptist minister Mike McGill broke an ankle and two others suffered broken noses. McGill admitted: 'It was a very rough game and it turned into a bit of a bloodbath.' The Salvation Army won 4–3.

Police Dog Attacked Its Handler

At the height of crowd disturbances during the 1991 European Cup tie in Sofia between Red Star Belgrade and Italian club Sampdoria, a Bulgarian police dog-handler accidentally kicked over a smoke-bomb canister. Immediately concluding that this made the man a football hooligan and therefore its mortal enemy, the dog on the other end of the lead began to savage the hapless officer who had to be rescued from further injury by his fellow policemen.

Feuding Team-Mates

The strange notion of team-mates fighting each other in the course of a game manifested itself in January 1979 when the Charlton strike force of Derek Hales and Mike Flanagan slugged it out to such good effect in an FA Cup tie with Maidstone United that they were both sent off. More recently, Hearts' Graeme Hogg and Craig Levein were each banned for ten matches in September 1994 for brawling with each other in a pre-season *friendly* against Raith. And a year later, Blackburn Rovers' European dream turned sour when David Batty and Graeme Le Saux traded punches during the Champions' League match with Spartak Moscow.

Goalkeeping Gaffes

Gary Sprake certainly didn't have the monopoly on goalkeeping howlers. Back in 1954, after being injured while collecting a cross at Plymouth, Fulham's Frank Elliott tried to throw the ball out of play but merely succeeded in lobbing it into his own net.

Earlier still, the 1927 FA Cup final was decided by a shot from Cardiff's Hugh Ferguson which slithered tamely through the arms of Arsenal's Welsh international keeper Dan Lewis. The Arsenal hierarchy blamed the mishap on the fact that Lewis was wearing a new jersey, the sheen of which had prevented him from holding on to the ball. From then on, Arsenal made sure that every new goalkeeper's jersey was softened up in the wash before being worn on the field of play.

In March 1990, Manchester City goalkeeper Andy Dibble was balancing the ball on the palm of his hand ready to kick clear when Nottingham Forest's Gary Crosby nipped in behind him, headed the ball off Dibble's hand and turned it into the net. The goal stood.

Another embarrassed custodian was Brentford's Kevin Dearden who, as he gathered a through ball at Bristol Rovers on 29 October 1996, thought he heard the referee's whistle for offside. Dearden put the ball down to take a free-kick but before he could do so, Rovers' Marcus Browning ran over and rolled the ball into the empty net. The referee hadn't blown at all and so the goal was given, helping Rovers to a 2–1 win. Dearden said afterwards: 'I got a lot of stick off my team-mates but was amazed when I made *News at Ten.*'

Fans' Fury

Italian Serie A club Salernitana decided to sack coach Delio Rossi in January 1999 and called a press conference to announce his successor. But the conference was stormed by protesting Salernitana fans who wanted the popular Rossi to be reinstated. The club had little choice but to bow to their demands.

Lean Spell

After losing their first fourteen games at the start of 1993, Thetford Town players were hypnotised in an effort to improve their luck. They lost their next match 9–0.

Referees in Brawl

In September 1995 referee Dave Lucas was banned from football for five years for knocking fellow referee Pete Wall unconscious in front of two schoolboy teams. Owing to a mix-up, both men had turned up to referee the under-11s match between Birmingham teams Springfield Lions A and Oldwinsford. In a row over which of the two should take charge of the game, Mr Wall was laid out. He was eventually able to referee the game after treatment. A spokesman for the Birmingham County FA said: 'There are regular cases of players or managers assaulting referees but as far as I'm aware it is unprecedented for a ref to hit another ref.'

Neate Solution

Reading were forced to cancel pre-season friendlies at their Elm Park ground in 1986 after groundsman Gordon Neate accidentally sprayed the pitch with concentrated weedkiller instead of a selective solution. Seventy-five per cent of the playing surface was ruined.

Send in the Clowns

Yugoslav teams Kotor and Bokeljan turned up to play a Third Division match in 1990, only to find that the pitch had been double-booked and that a circus was taking place on it instead. If nothing else, the players were given free admission to the Big Top.

Goalkeeper Locked Out of Ground

After twenty minutes of their Third Division (South) game at Walsall on 13 November 1948, Millwall were leading 1–0 when their goalkeeper Malcolm Finlayson was carried off with a head injury. Accompanied by a Millwall director, Finlayson was taken to a nearby hospital but, following treatment, was ruled fit enough to resume his place between the posts. So Finlayson and the director hurried back to the ground where the match was already into the second half. But the ground was locked and nobody could be found to let them in. Left with no alternative, the resourceful director (and somehow it's hard to imagine Ken Bates doing this) climbed the perimeter wall and alerted the stewards to their plight. Finlayson was re-admitted to Fellows Park to find Millwall 3–1 down but, although he was still decidedly groggy, his presence must have had a galvanising effect on his team-mates for they ended up winning an eleven-goal thriller 6–5.

Captain Swallowed Coin

At the start of a French club match in 1950 one of the captains inadvertently swallowed the 5-franc piece which the referee was tossing for choice of ends.

Lincoln Relegated by Police Dog

The issue of relegation to the Vauxhall Conference went to the final day of the 1986–87 season and was decided in the most unlikely fashion, by canine rather than human means. It was the first year that demotion to the Conference had been in force and hot favourites for the dreaded drop were Torquay United who had finished bottom of the Fourth Division of the Football League for the previous two seasons. With United 2–0 down at half-time at home to Crewe, their cause looked hopeless. Their fans certainly thought so and during the interval the 50p matchday programme was fetching upwards of £5 in the near-certainty that it would be Torquay's last game in the League for some time. Early in the second half, defender Jim McNichol pulled one back for Torquay, and then came the incident which turned the course of events. With just eight minutes to go, a police dog called Bryn slipped the attentions of his handler, ran on to the pitch and proceeded to sink his teeth into the same Jim McNichol. The player needed lengthy treatment for the wound and in the five minutes that the referee added on for the injury at the end of the ninety minutes, Paul Dobson was able to snatch a last-gasp equaliser. The point for Torquay was enough to send Lincoln City down instead. Bryn certainly left his mark on the season, as well as on Jim McNichol, prompting Torquay chairman Lew Pope to promise: 'I'm going to buy Bryn the biggest steak in Torquay.'

Injured in Bath

Everton and England centre-half Brian Labone needed stitches over one eye before the European Championship encounter with Scotland

---

at Hampden Park in 1968 after colliding with team-mate Martin Peters in the bath.

Oh, Unhappy Day!

As virtuoso performances go, Norman Wood's for Stockport against Fulham in 1913 takes a lot of beating. The hapless Wood scored an own goal, gave away a penalty for hands from which the visitors scored and then missed a penalty himself. Fulham won 3–1.

Leo Dunne's début for the Republic of Ireland, against Switzerland, in 1935, was marred when, thinking that a Swiss player was offside, he picked the ball up inside the penalty area. The converted spot-kick turned out to be the only goal of the game. Dunne won only one more cap.

Over a period of four days in 1972, Everton defender Tommy Wright twice managed to score own goals in the first minute. On 4 March he put through his own net in the Merseyside derby with Liverpool at Anfield and then repeated the feat against Manchester United at Old Trafford.

Goalkeeper Steve Milton let in thirteen on his début for Halifax at Stockport in 1934; Crewe's Dennis Murray conceded eleven on his début against Lincoln in 1951; and Nicky Rust saw nine go past him in his first match in goal for Barnet, against visiting Peterborough in 1998. Another Barnet keeper, Maik Taylor, also suffered when, making his League début on 12 August 1995, he was beaten by a long kick from his opposite number, Hereford United's Chris Mackenzie.

And Leyton Orient defender Terry Howard was deemed to have given such a poor first-half performance against Blackpool in February 1995 that he was sacked at half-time. It was his 397th appearance for the club.

The Team That Finished with Minus One Point

The Wheatsheaf pub team from St Helen's Auckland in County

Durham made some sort of history by finishing the 1994–95 season with fewer points than they had started with. The Wheatsheaf drew one and lost the other twenty-nine of their thirty League games, conceding 208 goals in the process, but were also docked two points for failing to field a team on one occasion. Thus they ended up with a points total of minus one. Team secretary and centre-half Gordon Heseltine said: 'This has to be the worst season in history. I can't remember anyone ever ending up in the red before. It's pretty embarrassing but at least we know we can't get any worse.'

Fingered

A friendly at Salta, Argentina, in 1956 between inmates of the local prison and a team of outsiders ended in a mass punch-up after two of the prisoners recognised one of the visiting team as a police officer.

Meaningless Shoot-Out

Rangers won the European Cup Winners' Cup in 1972 despite losing a penalty shoot-out against Sporting Lisbon in the second round. The Scots had actually won the tie on away goals but the referee seemed oblivious to the rules of the competition and ordered a penalty shoot-out which Sporting Lisbon won. The decision was subsequently revoked, allowing Rangers to progress to the next round.

Twin Confusion

When Paul Pullen of Diadora Leaguers Bognor Regis Town became involved in a skirmish with opponents Dulwich Hamlet in 1992–93, the referee ended up sending off Paul's identical twin brother Mick by mistake. Mick, Bognor's player/manager, protested his innocence but the referee wouldn't be swayed. 'Paul thought it was hilarious,' said Mick afterwards, 'but I'll make sure he serves the three-match suspension!'

French club Union Sportive of Metz practised a spot of twin deception during their 1967 Lorraine League match with Bataville. Shortly before half-time, Union Sportive were reduced to ten men when Charlie Wetzel was carried off with a bad knee injury. But rather than play on a man short, at half-time they secretly replaced Charlie with his identical twin brother Claude who went on to score a fine solo equaliser. However, the switch was uncovered at the end and the game was awarded to Bataville. While Charlie recovered in hospital, Claude received a three-month suspension.

Spectator Landed on Linesman's Foot

Bournemouth's fine FA Cup run of 1956–57 provoked scenes of wild enthusiasm not usually associated with the South Coast resort. As the local team defeated mighty Spurs in the fifth round, one fan got so excited when Bournemouth went 2–1 up that he jumped into the air from his seat on a bench beneath the main stand and landed on the foot of linesman Mr C. Staite. The game was held up while the unlucky official received treatment.

A Corner with a Difference

Taking a corner-kick at Leyton Orient, Fulham's charismatic winger of the 1960s 'Tosh' Chamberlain was intent on an accurate delivery. As he ran up, he focused on the goalmouth, missed the ball completely and uprooted the corner flag instead.

The Fastest Goal?

A claim for the fastest goal ever was launched by Kevin Curry of Midlands Regional Alliance outfit D&R Motors who scored straight from the kick-off against Melbourne Dynamo in February 1999. According to observers, Curry's wind-assisted effort sailed into the back of the net in just 1.5 seconds. It was particularly hard luck on

Melbourne Dynamo player/manager Mark Bryant for whom it was definitely a case of being in the wrong place at the wrong time. Bryant was only in goal for a few minutes at the start of the match, and that because the regular keeper had been delayed. When the number one did turn up, Bryant happily handed over the goalkeeper's jersey.

Goal Went in Off Referee

After travelling all the way up to Barrow for a Third Division game in 1968, Plymouth were beaten by a goal that was deflected in off the referee. A Barrow shot was flying harmlessly wide until it struck referee Ivan Robinson and rebounded into the net for the only goal of the game.

A 1932 match between Nacional and Peñarol in Uruguay featured an equally unlucky rebound. A shot from a Nacional player was drifting wide of the goal but it hit a photographer's briefcase, which had been left close to the by-line, and bounced back into play straight to the feet of another Nacional player, who scored.

Pitch Battles

Arbroath had little opportunity to celebrate their 4–3 victory over visiting Rangers in 1884 because the Glasgow club immediately lodged an objection to the size of the pitch. They complained that it wasn't wide enough and indeed when it was measured, it was discovered to be 35 inches short. A replay was ordered and this time, on a full-size pitch, Arbroath lost 8–0.

Switzerland were none too thrilled about losing to a penalty in a 1983 friendly in the Ivory Coast, particularly when it emerged that the groundsman had painted the penalty spots two yards too near to the goals.

When Derby County were awarded a penalty against Manchester City at the Baseball Ground in April 1977, the referee realised that the penalty spot was completely obscured by mud. So he paced out the distance and had the spot repainted by groundsman Bob Smith who trotted on to the pitch with his bucket of whitewash. Gerry Daly scored from the new visible spot for the fourth goal in Derby's 4–0 win.

Playing Kit Burned

At the start of the 1979–80 season the kit of Derbyshire team West Hallam was mistakenly collected by the local dustmen and incinerated. After a game the kit had been left in a black plastic bag near a dustbin at the home of the woman who did the club's washing.

Over-Age

Doncaster Rovers' goalkeeper Ken Hardwick was selected to play in an England Under-23 trial in 1955 . . . until the FA discovered that he was thirty.

Referee Sent Off Linesman

When the officially appointed referee became unavailable for a crucial 1998 Andover and District Sunday League game between The Lardicake pub and Over Wallop Reserves, Over Wallop manager Terry Gilligan, himself a fully qualified referee, agreed to take charge. Running the line was Lardicake landlord Phil Cooper, who became frustrated when referee Gilligan ignored his flag for a foul and waved play on. The referee did eventually stop play but only to order the linesman off. But Cooper refused to hand over his flag and so Gilligan picked up the ball and abandoned the match with his side – Over Wallop – winning 1–0. Linesman Cooper was subsequently fined £60 by the Hampshire FA and banned from the game for ninety-one days.

The Wembley Hoodoo

Between 1952 and 1965, no fewer than nine players suffered serious injuries in FA Cup finals which, those being the days before substitutes, left their teams in a depleted state. The spate of injuries became known as the 'Wembley Hoodoo' and has usually been attributed to the lushness of the turf.

The first victim was Arsenal's Wally Barnes who tore the ligaments behind his left knee after half an hour against Newcastle. Barnes limped on for a few minutes but was in too much agony and had to leave the field. Arsenal soldiered on with ten men but could not prevent Newcastle winning 1–0.

In 1953 Bolton Wanderers' Eric Bell injured a leg after just fifteen minutes. He hobbled around on the wing and actually scored with a header (leaping off his good leg) but Bolton eventually succumbed 4–3 to a Stanley Matthews-inspired Blackpool.

Two years later Manchester City right-back Jimmy Meadows suffered an almost identical injury to Wally Barnes', and in virtually the identical spot on the pitch. The injury forced Meadows, who had just won his first England cap, to quit playing at the age of twenty-four. Injury-hit City lost the final 3–1 to Newcastle.

In 1956 it was the turn of another Manchester City player – goalkeeper Bert Trautmann. Fifteen minutes from time, with City leading 3–1, Trautmann dived at the feet of Birmingham City forward Peter Murphy and suffered a broken neck. Amazingly Trautmann played on and kept Birmingham at bay although he could stay on his feet only by holding on to the goalposts.

The following year Manchester United goalkeeper Ray Wood sustained a fractured cheekbone after being barged by Aston Villa's Peter McParland just six minutes into the game. Jackie Blanchflower took over in goal, wearing a cap borrowed from a photographer, while Wood was consigned to the wing. United, who had already won the First Division title and were strong favourites to complete the first League and Cup double of the century, could not overcome the handicap and were beaten 2–1.

In 1959 Nottingham Forest's Roy Dwight (uncle of Elton John) broke his leg after thirty minutes of the final against Luton Town.

Dwight, who had earlier opened the scoring, listened to the rest of the match on radio in hospital as Forest held on to win 2–1. The injury effectively ended Dwight's career.

In 1960 Blackburn's Dave Whelan broke his right leg in a tackle just before half-time in the final with Wolves. Whelan never played for Blackburn again.

After nineteen minutes of the 1961 final against Spurs, Leicester City full-back Len Chalmers injured a leg in a tackle and played the rest of the match as a passenger on the left wing. Leicester lost 2–0.

And in 1965 Liverpool defender Gerry Byrne broke a collarbone after only three minutes of the game with Leeds following a collision with United's Bobby Collins. Byrne gallantly played on – extra-time and all – and helped Liverpool to a 2–1 triumph.

Exposed at the Back

In the 1921 Scottish Cup final, Rangers' left-back Jimmy Bowie had to leave the field briefly to replace his torn shorts. His absence left Partick Thistle right-winger John Blair unmarked to score the only goal of the game.

Butt of Jokes

In the middle of August 1979, eleven thirsty footballers had to be treated in hospital after drinking water from a pitch-side container at the end of a Sunday morning game between Winthorpe Wanderers and British Seedhouses at Newark, Nottinghamshire. Unbeknown to the players, who were ribbed about their misfortune for weeks afterwards, the container also held paraquat and a corrosive acid used for burning holes in the pitch.

Chairman Sent Off

Owing to an injury crisis, thirty-seven-year-old David Lane, chairman of Tring Town, was named as substitute for the local derby against Berkhamsted in the 1990–91 season. Called off the bench, Lane was sent off before he'd even touched the ball.

Accused of Witchcraft

A match between Nairobi teams Abaluhya and Hakati in 1973 was abandoned amid allegations of witchcraft. The trouble started when the Hakati goalkeeper tossed his cap into the back of the net, prompting Abaluhya to claim that their opponents had used witchcraft to cast a spell on their goal and prevent them scoring. Midway through the game, one of the Abaluhya players decided to take matters into his own hands by dashing into the Hakati goal, snatching the cap and running to the touchline, a journey which saw him chased by the entire Hakati team. In the ensuing chaos the match was called off and both teams were fined 200 shillings (about £11.50). Informed sources revealed that the alleged spell consisted of a needle, an old coin and a mixture of crushed herbs, roots, leaves and animal skin, all sewn into the band of the cap.

Big Mouth

Manchester United goalkeeper Alex Stepney spent so much time shouting at his team-mates during a game at Birmingham City in August 1975 that he was taken to hospital with a dislocated jaw.

Referee Ordered Off by Wife

During an Endsleigh Cheltenham League Division One match in April 1997, referee Phil Pawsey was ordered to leave the field by his wife Trish. Mrs Pawsey strode on to the pitch to inform her husband that she had locked herself out of the house and that she wanted him to fetch his keys from the dressing room. He did as she requested but when he returned to the pitch to resume the game, he discovered that all the players had gone.

In February 1972 Mansfield referee Richard Massey walked off and went home in the middle of an East Midlands League game between Eastwood Town Reserves and Breadsall, telling the players, 'I am fed up. I am resigning.'

In 1995 referee Roy Meadows abandoned the match between Fleur-de-Lys and Abertillery Town after seventy minutes because of general foul language. Mr Meadows and linesman Bill Edwards said they just couldn't take any more.

And in 1981 the referee abandoned a match between two Cheshire police teams five minutes before half-time because of persistent foul play. Officers from Runcorn and Ellesmere Port were battling it out for the Chief Constable's Cup but the referee called a halt because he was 'concerned for the safety of the players'. One player described the match as 'forty minutes of aggravated assault'.

Italian Cheek

As he scored the semi-final penalty against Brazil that earned Italy a place in the 1938 World Cup final, Peppino Meazza felt his shorts, already torn earlier in the game, slip down around his ankles. Fortunately his celebrating team-mates hid his blushes until a new pair were brought out.

Easy to Spot

In 1993 the Cardiff-based *Western Mail* carried what must be the world's easiest spot-the-ball competition. For instead of the current poser, the newspaper mistakenly printed the previous week's solution which meant that, instead of the ball being blanked out, it loomed large in the sky. And in case readers couldn't believe their eyes, a huge white arrow helpfully pin-pointed its precise location. The own goal was spotted after 1,000 copies of the paper had been run off and all but a handful were hastily withdrawn. The contest certainly lived up to its slogan: 'It's so easy to be a winner.'

In a Fix

Legia Warsaw and LKS Łódź went into the final round of matches in the 1992–93 Polish season on the same number of points with both looking for a big win to clinch the championship. And both got them – Legia won 6–0 away while LKS triumphed 7–1. However, the authorities were suspicious about the ease with which the matches had been won, and investigations revealed that both games had been fixed. So Legia and LKS were each docked two points, thus handing the title to third-placed Lech Poznan.

Sentimental Journey

The problems of trying to combine careers in cricket and football were well and truly brought home to Mickey Stewart in 1956. Although on tour with the England cricket team in the West Indies, Stewart was desperate to play soccer for his beloved Corinthian Casuals in the FA Amateur Cup final. So he embarked on a marathon 4,500-mile, two-and-a-half-day journey from the Caribbean, eagerly anticipating the thrill of running out at Wembley. Alas he arrived at the Twin Towers three minutes after kick-off and was thus unable to play. To add to his woes, Casuals lost 4–1.

Early Baths

On 13 March 1994 Crewe goalkeeper Mark Smith went into the record books as the fastest sending-off in British history when he was dismissed after just nineteen seconds of the Third Division match at Darlington for hauling down Darlington striker Robbie Painter. The resultant penalty proved to be the only goal of the game.

Smith's departure took the record away from Wrexham's Ambrose Brown who had shown a distinct lack of festive spirit by being sent off after twenty seconds of the Third Division (North) match with Hull City on Christmas Day 1936. Perhaps he was in a hurry to get home to stuff the turkey.

Both Smith and Brown were slouches compared to Bologna's Giuseppe Lorenzo who was ordered off after only ten seconds of the Italian League match with Parma on 9 December 1990 for striking an opponent.

Vinnie Jones managed to get himself booked after five seconds for Sheffield United at Manchester City on 19 January 1991, a prelude to being sent off in the fifty-fourth minute. But he broke his personal best on 15 February the following year when, playing for Chelsea in an FA Cup fifth round tie against his old club Sheffield United, he was shown the yellow card after just three seconds. Indeed the ball hadn't even left the centre circle!

Jones would surely have been envious of St Mirren captain Billy Abercrombie who was sent off three times in the same match, against Motherwell in 1986. Shown the red card by referee Louis Thow for the original offence, he was then red-carded again for talking back and a third time for dissent. Abercrombie was banned for twelve matches.

Hereford United had four players sent off in their Third Division fixture at Northampton on 6 September 1992 but still held out for a 1–1 draw. However, Brazilian club America Tres Rios went one better by having five players sent off in the first ten minutes of a Cup tie with Itaperuna in Rio on 23 November 1991 following a disputed goal. The match was abandoned and the tie awarded to Itaperuna.

Colchester United had two goalkeepers sent off in the same match at Hereford on 16 October 1993. John Keeley and Nathan Munson were both dismissed for professional fouls. Colchester lost 5–0.

On 24 November 1989 managers John Bird of York City and Ray McHale of Scarborough were sent off for squaring up to each other and trying to trade punches following a foul on Scarborough midfielder Paul Dobson. Both were banned from the touchline for three months.

In 1996 referee Gerry Cullen showed red cards to every member of the Crowmarsh under-13s team for chanting obscenities at him in the dressing room after the match. Mr Cullen had angered the boys by sending off their goalkeeper in the Beeline Oxfordshire Boys Sunday League fixture with Littlemore and after blowing the final whistle he returned to the changing rooms to be greeted by a barrage of abuse. So marching up to the players, he reached for his top pocket and brandished first the yellow, then the red card, to indicate that each had been officially sent off. One parent said: 'It was like a scene out of a comedy – a man in his forties walking among a bunch of twelve-year-olds brandishing a yellow then a red card. He was acting like it was the Premier League. It was totally over the top. He should have told them to shut up.'

On 4 January 1977 Uruguayan referee Hector Rodriguez, in charge of his first international, raised doubts about his impartiality by sending off the entire Ecuador team in the second half of the game against . . . Uruguay. He sent them off one by one after they had protested about one of their colleagues being ordered off for a foul. Mr Rodriguez had earlier sent off the Ecuador goalkeeper for time-wasting.

But surely no player has ever made a longer walk than Chiswick and District Sunday League footballer Dragan Kovacevic who was sent back to his native Yugoslavia following an unsavoury incident in a 1978 match against Shoreditch College Old Boys. Playing for Sloga, Kovacevic was sent off for violent conduct, behaviour which so incensed the Shoreditch players that they chased him on to the next pitch. When the Yugoslav Embassy in London (where he worked) heard about the sending-off, they sent Kovacevic back to his homeland.

The Last Post

In the summer of 1986 bailiffs removed the goalposts from the ground of cash-strapped Hartlepool United to help pay off debts.

Portsmouth were so hard-up in 1967 that when Wolves' Peter Knowles celebrated a goal at Fratton Park by kicking the ball out of the ground, the club sent him a bill for a replacement.

Beaten by an Escaped Prisoner

Southampton St Mary's had the misfortune to be knocked out of the

1893–94 FA Cup by a goal scored by an escaped prisoner. Opponents Reading desperately wanted to field a player by the name of Jimmy Stewart who served as a private in the King's Own Regiment at Aldershot. The problem was that Stewart was being held in detention in the guardroom for a breach of discipline and was thus seemingly unavailable for the third qualifying round tie. However, Reading secretary Horace Walker wasn't one to give up without a fight. Taking a couple of bottles of scotch to the barracks and getting the officer watching Stewart totally drunk, he managed to secure the prisoner's release for the afternoon. After scoring the winning goal in Reading's 2–1 victory, Stewart was smuggled back to the barracks that night under cover of darkness. When the story leaked out, Southampton protested to the FA and demanded a replay but the Association decreed that because none of its rules had been broken, the result should stand.

A One-Off

Italy's equaliser in their 2–1 victory over Czechoslovakia in the 1934 World Cup final came from their little Argentinian winger Raimundo Orsi. It was an amazing effort, his shot dipping and swerving at the last minute to deceive the Czech keeper Planicka. With typical Latin bravado, Orsi insisted that it was no fluke and demanded the right to prove the point before the world's press the following day. And so the day after the final, Orsi returned to the Rome stadium to demonstrate his skills in front of a battery of photographers and journalists. Time and time again he tried to repeat the famous shot . . . without success. After twenty dismal failures – he couldn't even hit the ball into the empty net, let alone make it swerve and dip – he finally gave up in disgust.

Rescued from the Crowd

If the referee who took charge of the Palermo–Napoli game in March 1969 was expecting a nice quiet afternoon, he was sorely mistaken.

For after Palermo had lost 3–2, the referee and his linesmen had to be rescued by a police helicopter which landed on the pitch to save them from the clutches of 5,000 bottle-throwing fans.

In Germany in 1965 the referee had to be smuggled out of the Karlsruhe ground in a policeman's uniform following angry crowd scenes at the end of the game with Nuremberg. Some 2,000 spectators besieged the referee's changing room, angry at a controversial Nuremberg winner. Even the introduction of a helicopter to swoop low and stir up dust had failed to disperse them and so the police launched their undercover operation to ensure the referee's safety.

And in Britain in 1992 Shrewsbury Town manager John Bond was forced to watch his team's match at Burnley in disguise. Bond, who had previously enjoyed a less than successful spell in charge at Turf Moor, had received threats from Burnley fans and it was felt that it would be safer for him to watch the game from the back of the stand, dressed as a steward. To round off a miserable day, Bond saw his side lose 2–1 to two goals in the last four minutes.

I Wanna Kiss the Ref

When struggling Arbroath sealed a 5–2 victory over high-flying East Stirlingshire in 1995, it was all too much for one Arbroath fan. As his team's fifth goal went in, thirty-year-old Sye Webster was so ecstatic that he ran on to the pitch and kissed the referee. But the club took a dim view of his behaviour and banned him from Gayfield for a year.

The Goal the Fans Missed

The most important moment in the history of Morecambe Football Club was missed by all but a handful of its supporters. On 25 November 1961, little Morecambe, then in the Lancashire Combination, defeated Fourth Division Chester 1–0 in the second round of the FA Cup thanks to a first-minute goal. But none of the

700 Morecambe fans who travelled to Chester by train arrived in time for the goal. Their train was thirteen minutes late anyway arriving at Chester station and then the buses hired to ferry them to the ground were held up in heavy traffic. So they had to read the papers the next day to find out what they had missed.

A Supreme Penalty

The Americans don't do anything by half. So when it came to the opening ceremony for the 1994 World Cup finals, they wanted a big star to introduce the American public to the game of soccer. Stars don't come much bigger than Diana Ross and, even though she wasn't exactly built like Maradona, the organisers reckoned that if they put the ball near enough to the goal, she would be able to put away a symbolic penalty kick. So it was that the ball was placed no more than a few yards from the goal and Miss Ross was invited to step forward to bury the spot-kick. No doubt in rehearsals she'd repeatedly sent the keeper the wrong way with a swivel of the hips or lashed it into the roof of the net *à la* Geoff Hurst. Whether it was big-match nerves, high heels or simply sheer incompetence we'll never know but when it came to the ceremony itself she tottered forward and somehow managed to drag the ball feebly wide at an angle of forty-five degrees. It was an almost impossible feat but one which ensured that the name of Diana Ross will go down in World Cup history.

Sheep Dip

If mascots are supposed to be endowed with good luck, nobody told Toby, the sheep who was meant to bring fame and fortune to Greenock Morton in the years leading up to the First World War. For after one match, while the team celebrated their victory in a local hostelry, Toby was left in the changing room and drowned in the players' bath.

Plans Scrapped

City authorities in Verona who planned to name a new stadium after Italy's 1938 World Cup winning goalkeeper Aldo Olivieri cancelled the idea in 1996 after discovering that he was still alive.

The Bill Gassed

Trying to break up a fracas at the end of Gor Mahia's 1–0 victory over AFC Leopards in September 1987, African police were overcome by their own tear gas. As a result they were unable to arrest anyone.

2 Cricket

Wife Struck by Six

While wheeling their baby around the boundary during a club match in 1994, Sharon Scott of Kington, Herefordshire, was hit on the head by a six struck by her husband Clive. There was a sad sequel to the blow. 'She probably cost me a century,' moaned Clive. 'I went into my shell after that.'

Lost on the Northern Line

After being 1 not out overnight against Surrey at the Oval in 1921, Leicestershire wicket-keeper Thomas Sidwell was unable to resume his innings the following morning because he got lost on the London Underground. When he eventually reached the ground, he was too late to bat and went down in the scorebook as 'absent, lost on Tube'.

Completely Guttered

Patrolling the deep for Victoria against Queensland at Brisbane in the 1976–77 season, Jeff Moss made a desperate attempt to cut off a shot from Greg Chappell. But in the act of preventing the boundary, he managed to jam his right foot in an adjacent gutter so that the batsmen were still able to run four with the ball tantalisingly out of Moss's reach.

Driven to Long Leg

Bunny Tattersall kept wicket for I Zingari with an artificial leg. On the first evening of a two-day game in Hampshire in 1926, he was alarmed to find that the limb had broken, as a result of which he was forced to get in his car and make a 180-mile round trip to fetch a spare leg from home in order to be ready for the following day's play.

Spot of Bother

Batting for Oxford University against Cambridge in the 1912 Varsity match, the unfortunate G. E. V. Crutchley had to retire with measles on 99 not out.

Wrong Team, Wrong Ground

When Buckinghamshire club Winslow Town arrived in Kempston, Bedfordshire, to play a match in June 1996, they ended up playing the wrong team at the wrong ground. Their opponents were supposed to be Kempston Ramblers but, aided by a singular lack of communication, they found themselves playing against Kempston Meltis whose own opponents had failed to turn up. It appears that nobody realised the mistake until one of the Ramblers players, in search of the missing Winslow boys, tracked them down and dragged them off to the right game. When asked how such a monumental mishap could have occurred, Winslow batsman Ron Phillips pleaded by way of defence: 'I have played against Ramblers a number of times over the years and I thought all their batsmen must have retired or died off!'

Of Doubtful Benefit

Somerset all-rounder Bertie Buse was anticipating a bumper crowd for the three days of his benefit match against Lancashire in 1953. Having prayed for clear blue skies for weeks in advance, he was at least rewarded with a dry day although the pitch looked decidedly lively. So lively in fact that, after Somerset had been skittled for 55, Buse quickly ripped the heart out of the Lancashire innings, taking six wickets as the visitors were bowled out for 158. But Somerset's second attempt was only marginally better than their first and they were routed for 79 to leave Lancashire the winners by an innings and 24 runs, the game being over in the first day partly as a result of Buse's own bowling. Thus with two days idle, a terrible result for Somerset proved equally disastrous for Buse's bank account.

Entire Career Rained Off

Gloucestershire batsman Sidney Wells was selected for just one first-class game – against Kent at Bristol in 1927. Alas the heavens opened and the match was abandoned without a ball being bowled.

Double Booked

The bitter rivalry between the Melbourne Cricket Club and the New South Wales Cricket Association in the formative years of Australian cricket brought about a situation where the country ended up playing host to two England teams in the same summer. Supporting one tour financially was difficult enough but breaking even with two was well nigh impossible. It was in 1886 that Melbourne CC invited Middlesex's George Vernon to bring a team to Australia under the captaincy of Lord Hawke, but the tour was postponed for a year. Then in the autumn of 1887 New South Wales, believing the Vernon tour to have been cancelled altogether, announced that they had invited a professional England team, led by James Lillywhite and captained by C. Aubrey Smith, to visit as part of the centenary celebrations to mark the first settlement in Australia back in 1787. Because they had heard nothing more about the Vernon tour New South Wales had simply assumed that it was not happening; for their part, Melbourne had failed to keep them abreast of developments. And so it was that two teams set forth from England on the steamer *Iberia* bound for Adelaide. The South Australians prepared a civic reception for the grand arrival on 25 October 1887 but, as befits the general planning surrounding the tours, they had no idea that the two England teams were travelling on the same ship. Thus when Lillywhite's professionals disembarked first, the welcoming committee were thrown into a state of confusion as they were only expecting Vernon's team. Inevitably the rival tours ended up cutting each other's throats and the matches created little more than lukewarm interest from the Australian public. Both nations suffered heavy losses, Lillywhite's team alone losing some £2,400 on the venture . . . all because of a lack of liaison.

Camels Stopped Play

Play in the match between Launceston and Old Suttonians in August 1984 had to be halted on no fewer than four separate occasions after a herd of camels strayed on to the pitch from a nearby circus.

Colour Blind

During the Wills Triangular Series contest between Pakistan and South Africa in Karachi in 1995, third umpire Atiq Khan was asked to rule on whether or not South Africa's Dave Richardson had been run out. After studying the replay, Khan was satisfied that Richardson had made his ground and pressed what he thought was the green button to signify 'not out'. Instead, to Khan's surprise, the red light came up and Richardson was judged run out for 7.

Bird Before Wicket

On 22 November 1969 John Inverarity of Western Australia was bowled by a delivery from South Australia's Greg Chappell which hit a swallow in mid-air and was deflected on to the stumps. The umpire signalled a no-ball and Inverarity, who had yet to score, went on to make 89.

An identical incident took place at Trimdon, County Durham, in August 1994 when a ball bowled by Chris Thomas hit a swallow in flight and was deflected on to batsman Joe Hall's stumps. After some deliberation, the umpires ruled that because the delivery was missing the stumps, both ball – and swallow – were dead.

A sparrow was the unfortunate victim of a ball bowled by Jehangir Khan of Cambridge University to T. N. Pearce who was playing for MCC in July 1936. The dead bird ended up as a stuffed exhibit in the museum at Lord's.

Overslept After Eight-Year Wait

In July 1997 left-arm spinner Philip North, captain of the Wales Minor Counties team, was called up by Glamorgan for the first time in eight years. He was picked to face Nottinghamshire in the County Championship fixture at Colwyn Bay but his dream soured when he turned up late and was promptly dropped again. In mitigation, he said that his early morning wake-up call hadn't come through.

The Galloping Gover

Touring in the Indian subcontinent can be a hazardous affair, particularly where matters of the bowels are concerned. On an MCC tour of India under Lionel Tennyson, half of the team were laid low with dysentery, so Alf Gover, who had also been struck down, was forced to leave his sick-bed to make up the numbers. Gover put a brave face on it but as he came in to bowl his third over, it all proved too much for him. On his run-up, he suddenly felt the urge to visit

---

the toilet as quickly as possible and, without delivering the ball, carried on running past the umpire, the startled batsman and the wicket-keeper and straight up the steps of the pavilion.

No Ball

Just as Derbyshire and Shropshire were about to take the field for their NatWest Trophy encounter at Chesterfield on 27 June 1990, red-faced officials suddenly realised that a vital ingredient of the game was missing – the ball. In the wake of the unfortunate oversight, the start of play was delayed for 45 minutes while a complement of balls (or whatever the collective noun is for balls) was hastily despatched up the M1 from county headquarters at Derby.

Such slip-ups can happen even at the highest level as Pakistan and New Zealand discovered before the Second Test at Rawalpindi in November 1996. Here, the opening day's play was delayed for twenty minutes because the Pakistan Cricket Board had omitted to supply any balls. The solution was found in a local sports shop.

Costly Collision

A decisive innings during the 1975–76 series between the West Indies and visitors India was Clive Lloyd's 70 in the Second Test which enabled the West Indies to hang on for a draw and ultimately defeat India 2–1. But he would have been back in the pavilion much earlier had two Indian fielders not made a hash of a clear chance. As Lloyd lofted the ball towards mid-off, Eknath Solkar and Brijesh Patel both went for the catch, each seemingly unaware of the presence of the other. In the inevitable ignominious collision, both bodies and the ball fell to earth and Lloyd breathed again.

Divine Intervention

A bishop who saw a clergyman collapse at the crease while

attempting a risky second run jumped into his car and drove across the outfield to help. Batting in a village game in September 1992, the Very Rev. Brandon Jackson, Dean of Lincoln, pulled a hamstring when turning sharply, prompting the Bishop of Grantham, the Rt Rev. William Ind, to leap into action. Play was stopped as the bishop drove up to the wicket and eased the stricken dean into the car. Reduced to ten men, the dean's team were left praying for a miracle.

A Close Call

Former Pakistan Test player Parvez Mir was banned by the Carrow club of Norfolk in 1995 for interrupting his bowling to take a call on his mobile phone. Parvez was in the middle of an over when his phone went off. Taking the contraption from the umpire, Parvez concluded the conversation with his fiancée before continuing with the business of bowling out opponents Downham Market.

Premature Celebration

Fielding on the boundary for England against Victoria on the 1962–63 tour of Australia, the Rev. David Sheppard, whose hands had been known to let him down on occasions, excelled himself to hold a catch from Bill Lawry. However, unknown to Sheppard, it was a no-ball and while he was throwing the ball up in the air in celebration, the batsmen went through for an extra run.

Head Cases

There was bad luck all round when Bishop Auckland's West Indian professional Ricky Waldren launched into a straight drive in a match in July 1995. The ball ricocheted off the head of the umpire at the bowler's end, George Simpson, and was caught by an opposing fielder on the boundary. While a disbelieving Waldren made his way back to the pavilion, Simpson was taken to hospital for ten stitches in his head wound.

Waldren's dismissal was reminiscent of that of Martin Young playing for Gloucestershire against Yorkshire at Bristol on 25 July 1962. Young had made 12 when he pulled a delivery from Ray Illingworth hard to short leg where the fearless Brian Close was fielding. The ball struck Close in the temple and bounced to Phil Sharpe who caught it at first slip. When a concerned team-mate asked Close what would have happened if the ball had hit him between the eyes, Close replied in a matter-of-fact sort of way: 'He'd have been caught at cover.'

A Fly in the Ointment

Faced with a first innings deficit of 304 after Australia had posted a massive 729 for 6 declared, England looked like making a fight of the Second Test at Lord's in 1930. Percy Chapman was going along nicely and had reached 121 when a bluebottle suddenly flew into his mouth. He was still choking on the insect when he was caught behind without adding to his score. Australia went on to win by seven wickets.

A Late Cut

During the summer of 1825, a woman by the name of Stapley ran a gingerbread stall at the cricket ground at Ticehurst, East Sussex. One day a shot from Thomas Cooper flashed to the boundary with such force that the ball embedded itself on a knife which, at that precise moment, Ms Stapley was using to cut her slices of gingerbread. While fielders struggled to remove the ball from the blade of the knife, the poor woman received medical treatment for cuts to her hand.

A Cruel Blow

Former Warwickshire and England captain M. J. K. Smith was facing up to a ball against Hampshire at Edgbaston in 1962 when a sudden gust of wind whipped his cap from his head. Sadly for Smith, the cap fell on to his stumps and he was given out 'hit wicket'.

A similar fate befell India's Dilip Vengsarkar during the First Test of the 1977–78 series in Australia. Unbeaten on 48 in the first innings, Vengsarkar ducked out of the way of a ferocious bouncer from Jeff Thomson but, in doing so, his cap fell on to the wicket and he was given out. The incident was to prove crucial since India went on to lose the match by just 16 runs and the series 3–2.

Scorer's Error

When Lancashire's Harry Makepeace reached his maiden century – just before lunch against Sussex at Eastbourne in 1907 – his captain Archie MacLaren wasted no time in declaring the innings closed. But during the luncheon interval it became apparent that the scoreboard was inaccurate and that Makepeace had really only made 99. He had to wait another four seasons for that elusive hundred.

Twelfth Man

The Hampshire League match between Southampton Travellers and Hamble Aerostructures in July 1997 was declared void after it was discovered that the Travellers had been fielding with twelve men. The mistake came to light at the drinks interval when one of the fielders complained that he hadn't got a drink.

The previous year Derbyshire took the field for an AXA Equity and Law League game against Worcestershire at Chesterfield with twelve men. When the error came to light, urgent discussions were held, at the conclusion of which Colin Wells was withdrawn to sympathetic applause from the spectators. The confusion had arisen because captain Dean Jones was injured.

Fielding in the Deep

Whenever noted big-hitter Charles Inglis Thornton came in to bat, fielders were scattered far and wide. However, one poor man took things to extremes and ended up in a pond. The occasion was Scarborough's 1922 visit to Yorkshire neighbours Malton, a ground which, in one corner, boasted a pond just beyond the boundary rope. With Thornton at the crease, the fielders retreated further and further into the distance but still he managed to bisect them with alarming regularity. Finally he lofted a ball dangerously close to one of the men on the boundary. Sensing that the ball might clear his head, the unnamed fielder ran backwards in a desperate attempt to make the catch, forgot all about the pond and finished up getting a thorough soaking.

Irate Driver Parked Lorry on Pitch

A report in *Wisden* recounted how in June 1993 a lorry-driver was so angry after his windscreen had been shattered by a six from the adjoining cricket ground at Wansford, near Peterborough, that he drove off the A1 and parked his lorry on the pitch in protest. He refused to move the vehicle until insurance details had been exchanged.

Short-Handed

At the end of the first day's play in the match between Tasmania and Victoria at Hobart in 1890, the home team had made 30 for 2 in reply to Victoria's total of 338. On what appeared a decent batting surface, two of the lower-order Tasmanian batsmen – Charles McAllen, the captain, and George Vautin – reckoned that their services would not be required until much later in the day and so they ambled to the ground shortly after noon. However in the forty minutes since the start of play at 11.20, wickets had fallen with alarming regularity to the extent that Tasmania had slumped to 39 for 7 by midday. With

William Sidebottom unable to bat because of injury and McAllen and Vautin having failed to arrive, Tasmania had to close their innings on 39 and follow on. Not surprisingly, they ended up losing by an innings and 147 runs.

At Leyton in 1925, only two of the Surrey team arrived in time for the start of the day's play against Essex. The sporting Essex openers did not attempt to score off the two emergency bowlers until the other nine Surrey players turned up ten minutes later.

Middlesex weren't as lucky on the second day of their County Championship fixture with Kent at Tunbridge Wells on 17 June 1963. Kent were all set to take the field when it emerged that only three of the Middlesex team were present, the rest having been delayed in Monday morning traffic. Of the three, one had already been out, another was twelfth man, leaving only Bob White, who was unbeaten on 43, able to continue the Middlesex innings. White got padded up and waited patiently out in the middle in the hope that a partner might soon arrive but when none was forthcoming, the umpires declared the innings closed. Ten minutes later Kent came out to bat, by which time two more Middlesex men had arrived. To make up the numbers, the twelfth man was allowed to keep wicket and Kent loaned the visitors six substitute fielders, one of whom, John Prodger, caught his own team-mate Brian Luckhurst at second slip. The rest of the Middlesex team eventually arrived three overs later and after all the fun and games, a heavy downpour meant that the match petered out as a draw.

The game between Darlington and Synthonia in June 1990 ended in farce after a breakdown in travel communications meant that only two of the Synthonia side turned up for the start of play. The Synthonia innings ended after just four balls when Steven Eland was bowled for 0. The redoubtable Eland then opened the bowling to a field containing nine substitutes borrowed from Darlington. Alas, his fourth ball was a wide, gifting the game to Darlington.

The following year, heavy traffic prevented eight of the Cleethorpes team from arriving in time for the start of the Yorkshire League match at Harrogate. The home side showed little sympathy for Cleethorpes' plight and insisted that play start as scheduled. Cleethorpes batted first but were forced to declare on 11 for 2, allowing Harrogate to knock off the dozen runs needed. However the League took a dim view of Harrogate's performance and deducted 12 points for 'not playing in the proper spirit of the game'. Harrogate skipper Austin Jeffs refuted the charge, maintaining that if he had really wanted to be unsporting he would have batted first.

Tour Abandoned

The first overseas cricket tour was to have been undertaken in August 1789 by an England team to Paris. It had been arranged by the Duke of Dorset, a prime mover in cricketing circles, and who was the country's ambassador in Paris at the start of the French Revolution. Acting on assurances from the Duke that they would be guaranteed a safe passage in such troubled times, the team made their way to Dover in readiness for the Channel crossing. However, on reaching Dover they were confronted by the sight of the Duke fleeing from the French capital. In the circumstances, it was decided that it would be wise to call the tour off.

Nothing Personal

A woman spectator hoping for a nice quiet day watching Sussex play Gloucestershire at Hove in June 1995 instead endured a torrid experience. As Gloucestershire's Andrew Symonds began to cut loose on his way to a first innings 83, the woman was hit in the face by a powerfully struck four. Then no sooner had she returned from treatment than a mighty six from Symonds hit her on the leg. To add insult to injury, the woman was a Gloucestershire supporter.

Sex Discrimination

Escaping from Horsham market one day in 1934, a bull wandered on to the nearby cricket field where the local team were entertaining South Hampstead. The square leg umpire took one look at the beast and bolted for the sanctuary of the pavilion but his colleague remained behind the stumps in the misguided belief that the intruder was a female of the species.

The Fatal Fifth Run

Australia appeared to be in a healthy position when they reached 75 for 0 in reply to England's 145 in the final Test at the Oval in 1896. But then Frank Iredale was run out going for a fifth run and Australia collapsed to 119 all out. They ended up losing a low-scoring match by 66 runs and the series 2–1.

Bee-ware

A Cornwall League First Division match between Helston and Falmouth in May 1997 was held up for ninety minutes after thousands of bees swarmed on to the ground. Two players were stung and play was only resumed after bee experts had been called in.

On his way out to bat for Middlesex at Lord's, Patsy Hendren was half-way to the wicket when he flung his bat in the air, emitted a cry of anguish and hobbled back to the pavilion. There was a wasp in his box!

Two Bad Attacks of Nerves

Playing for Oxford University against Cambridge at Lord's in 1882, W. D. Hamilton was said to have been so nervous at the crease that at one stage he ran in the wrong direction. His discomfort was reflected in his scores of 9 and 0.

In 1930 Somerset's Cecil Case was given out 'hit wicket' in the match with Nottinghamshire at Taunton after falling on to the stumps while trying to get out of the way of a hostile ball from Bill Voce. Case was so unnerved by the experience that he left for the pavilion carrying a stump under his arm instead of his bat.

Hot-Air Balloon Stopped Play

The 1982 fixture between Hampshire rivals Curdridge and Medstead was temporarily halted when a hot-air balloon promoting a new burger bar ran out of fuel sooner than anticipated and came to earth between the stumps.

The same ground witnessed another bizarre incident in 1997 when an out-of-control Vauxhall Astra sent fielders running for cover during Curdridge's match with Denmead. The car was driven by eighty-year-old Grace Cummins whose foot got jammed between the brake and the accelerator. Three other cars and a player's wife suffered minor damage to their bodywork before Ms Cummins was able to free the offending foot.

Chopper Shambles

Kenya were beginning to scent the possibility of a first victory against a Test-playing country when they reduced Zimbabwe to 45 for 3 in a 1996 World Cup group match at Lahore before rain stopped play. There was still a chance if the pitch could be dried out and, to this end, Pakistan officials enlisted the services of a helicopter. However, it merely succeeded in blowing the covers away and spilling water on to the wicket, thus causing the match to be abandoned. When the match was replayed the following day, Kenya lost by five wickets.

An Early Streaker

Those who think streaking at cricket matches is a relatively modern phenomenon will be surprised to know that an incident of nudity on the field of play occurred as far back as May 1869. The occasion was a match at Casino, New South Wales, between two teams of single men and married men. Contemporary reports stated that the combination of a hot day and cold beer caused play to be held up by a male member.

More recently, eight male streakers, believed to have been attending a nearby stag party, brought play to a halt during the Pembrokeshire League match between Neyland and Lawrenny in 1996.

Unusual Injuries

Injury is part and parcel of the game of cricket but sometimes it can occur in the most innocuous situations. England's Derek Pringle once had to miss a Test match after injuring his back while writing a letter, and in 1989 another Essex player, Don Topley, missed the pre-season matches after getting his hand trapped in a letter-box. But pride of place goes to Leicestershire captain Nigel Briers who, fielding against Lancashire in 1993, succeeded in spraining a thumb when he caught it in his trouser pocket.

Ran Out Three Partners

When the England team led by George Vernon toured Australia in 1887, they owed their victory against South Australia to the efforts of one man – George Giffen. Nothing unusual in that, except that Giffen played for South Australia. One of the finest batsmen of his day, Giffen's running between wickets was sometimes so erratic that there have been suggestions that the likes of Denis Compton (who ran out his brother Leslie during Leslie's benefit match in 1957) and Geoffrey Boycott later used him as a role model. On this particularly memorable occasion, he managed to run out no fewer than three of his partners in quick-fire time. From the last ball of the first day, a careless call from Giffen resulted in his partner 'Affie' Jarvis being run out for 45. The following morning, Giffen ran out Jack Lyons to make the score 116 for 2 and he completed his hat-trick five runs later by running out his own brother, Walter! At first the umpire gave George out instead of Walter and, following a heated dispute, both batsmen stormed from the field. However a short while later George returned to the crease and batted on without inflicting any further damage on his own side.

Giffen's performance was actually surpassed by Jim McNichol of Scottish club Luncarty who livened up a Haig National Village tie with Manderston by running out three of his partners, including his captain, without facing a ball.

LBW – Lizard Before Wicket

The First Test between Young Sri Lanka and Young England in 1987 was stopped when a large iguana crept ominously across the square at the Colombo Cricket Club ground.

Crossed Wires

In 1994 one Chinmay Gupte travelled to Blackheath in Greater London to play for MCC, only to find that the match was taking place at Blackheath, Surrey. Anxious not to make the same mistake again the following year he went to Blackheath in Surrey, but this time the match was being played at Blackheath, London.

Umpire Downed Tools

Umpire J. Hodges refused to continue officiating after tea on the third day of the Australia–England Test at Melbourne in 1885 because he was fed up with the England players disputing his decisions. His place was taken by an Australian player, Tom Garrett.

Salad Tossed Out

During the England–Australia Test at Headingley in July 1997, university lecturer Brian Cheesman, who had gone to the match dressed as a carrot, was ejected from the ground for alleged 'drunken and abusive behaviour'. At the same match, officials rugby-tackled a pantomime cow at close of play. The man playing the back half of the cow, Branco Risek, had to be taken to hospital for treatment.

Protesters Wrecked Pitch

Most people remember the 'George Davis Is Innocent' campaign where protesters sabotaged the Headingley pitch before the final day of the Test with Australia in 1975, causing the match to be abandoned, but back in 1907 there was an instance of unintentional sabotage to the pitch. Middlesex were entertaining Lancashire at Lord's but rain on the first day delayed the start of play until the middle of the afternoon. And then after little more than an hour's action, the rains came again and washed out play for the day. By the following morning, further overnight rain had left the pitch under water and the umpires decided that they had no option but to announce that play was abandoned for the day. But the decision angered some of the spectators who felt they had been charged admission money under false pretences. They chose to voice their feelings in front of the pavilion, on the way passing close to, or actually across, the wicket. They were duly placated by an assurance that they would be allowed in free on the final day, but ironically in making their protest they had ensured that there would be no final day's play. For the trampling of the hallowed turf had, in the opinion of Lancashire captain Archie MacLaren, rendered the surface unplayable. In a harsh statement he declared: 'Owing to the pitch having been deliberately torn up by the public, I, as captain of the Lancashire eleven, cannot see my way to continue the game, the groundsman bearing me out that the wicket could not be again put right.' So the match was abandoned with Lancashire not even bothering to turn up for the third day although some observers thought that the pitch was playable by then. MacLaren's high-handed attitude seemed to have an adverse effect on Middlesex who, unbeaten at the time of the abandoned match, saw their form slump badly in the second half of the season.

Another instance of spectators inadvertently damaging the pitch occurred at Sabina Park, Kingston, Jamaica, in March 1958. When the West Indies declared at a colossal 790 for 3 against Pakistan, the 20,000 crowd swarmed on to the pitch to chair Gary Sobers (who had made a Test record score of 365 not out) all the way to the pavilion. But they did so much harm to the pitch that the umpires ordered it to be repaired and abandoned play for the day fifty-five minutes early. The lost time did not affect the result, however, the West Indies triumphing by an innings and 174 runs.

Dead Dogs and Englishmen

Wisden reported that a match at Boddington, Gloucestershire, in 1995 had to be abandoned because the pitch was engulfed by smoke emanating from the Companion's Rest animal crematorium at nearby Elmstone Hardwicke.

Thou Shalt Not Pass

To mark his country's first appearance in England for twenty-nine years, Archbishop Desmond Tutu, the leading Anglican cleric in South Africa, decided to pop into the South African dressing room at tea on the first day of the First Test at Lord's in July 1994. However the archbishop had reckoned without the Lord's stewards who stopped him from entering the pavilion because he was not wearing a jacket.

Snakes Alive

During school cricket practice at Cowell, South Australia, in the 1967–68 season, batsman Tony Wiseman spotted a 3ft 6in poisonous snake slithering up the pitch towards him just as the bowler delivered the ball. Allowing the ball to pass, he left his crease and killed the snake with his bat. Surprised not to hear an appeal for a stumping, he turned round to see that the wicket-keeper had vanished.

A snake also prompted evasive action when it slithered on to the wicket just as batsman Pieter Marrish played a delivery at Johannesburg in 1972. Marrish didn't hang around long enough to discover whether or not the serpent was poisonous, allowing the wicket-keeper, who was obviously made of sterner stuff, to remove the bails and stump him.

Easily Distracted

In the course of the 1870 Varsity match at Lord's, J. W. Dale of Cambridge University put down a straightforward catch because, on his own admission, he had one eye on a pretty lady stepping out of a carriage. Despite Dale's momentary lapse of concentration, Cambridge still won.

Pointless Exercise

Fielding for New Zealand in the First Test of the 1973–74 series in Australia, David O'Sullivan embarked on a long chase, at the end of which he launched himself into a full-length dive and managed to stop the ball just short of the boundary. He may have saved the four but in the time it took him to dive, pick up and throw, the batsmen ran five.

Absent Without Leave

Young Surrey batsman Frederick Buckle struggled to make an impact in the match with Middlesex at Lord's in July 1869. In the first innings he went down in the scorebook as 'absent, not sent for in time . . . 0' and in the second innings he was listed as 'absent unwell . . . 0'. Without him, Surrey lost by 43 runs.

Kent's C. J. M. Fox saw himself as something of a gourmet. So rather than sample the standard lunchtime fare on offer at the Brighton ground during the match with Sussex in 1891, Fox chose to dine out. The meal obviously met with his approval as by the time he returned to the ground the Kent innings had ended and he had been put down as 'absent'.

Sussex batsman H. J. Heygate was given out in the match against Somerset at Taunton on 22 May 1919 because he failed to reach the crease within two minutes of the fall of the previous wicket. Poor Heygate was crippled with rheumatism and couldn't make it to the middle in time when the ninth Sussex wicket fell in their second innings. He was shown on the scorecard as 'absent'.

A less enigmatic scorecard was used in the final of the 1958–59 Qaid-I-Azam Trophy in Karachi. Abdul Aziz was injured in the first innings and the scorecard thus read: 'Abdul Aziz retired hurt . . . 0'. The injury proved to be fatal and the scorer, not wishing to leave any room for doubt, wrote for the second innings: 'Abdul Aziz did not bat, dead . . . 0'.

Playing for Whiteleas against East Rainton in the North East Durham League in August 1995, Robin Wightman was so annoyed when his captain wouldn't let him bowl the final over even though he had already taken seven wickets that he stormed off the pitch and refused to return. When Whiteleas batted, Wightman was recorded in the scorebook as 'absent, huffed'.

And in a match between Kent villages Cliffe and Yalding in June 1996, a batsman by the name of Cordingly was listed as 'absent, babysitting'.

Snowed Off

The England Cricket Board decided to bring forward the start of the 1999 County Championship season by two weeks to 13 April. They were rewarded when the traditional first-day washout was supplemented by two inches of snow covering the pitch at Chester-le-Street where Durham were due to play Worcestershire.

Turning a Deaf Ear

Australia's Charlie McLeod suffered an unfortunate dismissal in the

First Test against England at Sydney on 16 December 1897. Seeing his stumps shatter, he assumed he was out and began walking. In fact it was a no-ball but McLeod, being deaf, hadn't heard the umpire's call. In his absence from the crease, McLeod was run out.

The same thing happened to Dean Jones while batting for Australia against the West Indies in the Second Test at Georgetown, Guyana, on 27 March 1991. Hearing the stumps break but not the no-ball call, Jones set off for the pavilion in the belief that he had been bowled by Courtney Walsh. Realising what had happened, Carl Hooper swooped in from the slips, picked up the ball and ran Jones out.

Arguing the Toss

The whole of the first morning's play in the 1996 Ranji Trophy semi-final in Madras between Tamil Nadu and Delhi was lost after both captains claimed to have won the toss. The dispute concerned which face of a newly introduced coin constituted 'heads'. As the arguments continued, the umpires ordered a second toss but Delhi's Ajoy Sharma refused. Two hours later he finally agreed and, to his delight, won the toss. Choosing to bat first, he then saw his team lose by eight wickets.

Alderman's Arrest

Australian bowler Terry Alderman suffered a dislocated shoulder after tackling a pitch invader during the First Test against England in Perth in November 1982. A bevy of England supporters ambled on to the pitch waving Union Jacks to celebrate their team reaching the 400 mark. A few appeared reluctant to leave and Alderman became involved in an angry exchange with one. Trying to hand the trespasser over to the police, Alderman brought him down with a rugby tackle but came off considerably worse and had to be stretchered from the field.

Self-Destruction

Playing at Chandler's Ford, Hampshire, in August 1996, Rob Owens hit a six which smashed the rear window of his own car. Craig Scully repeated the feat the following month when his match-winning blow for Chipping Sodbury broke the windscreen of *his* car. These accidents were self-inflicted, but spare a thought for Walsden bowler Peter Green playing against Rochdale in the Central Lancashire League. He saw one of his deliveries hit for a mighty six by Rochdale's Wilson Hartley. The ball sailed out of the ground and smashed through the window of a house in an adjoining street. It was Peter Green's house.

Handled the Ball

Dismissals for handling the ball are pretty rare in first-class cricket. Most are for deliberately knocking the ball away from the stumps – as happened to Graham Gooch against Australia at Old Trafford in 1993– but occasionally there is a more unusual variation on the theme. Batting for Northern Transvaal against Orange Free State at Bloemfontein in the 1973–74 season, Christopher Dey was backing up when he collided with a fielder. The impact caused Dey to fall and he hit the ground with the ball wedged beneath his body. While lying on the ground, he calmly tossed the ball aside and was promptly given out for handling the ball.

An equally unlucky exit was that of George Linton while batting for Barbados against the Windward Islands at the Kensington Oval, Bridgetown, on 17 January 1986. After dropping a dead bat on a lifting delivery from Desmond Collymore, Linton innocently picked up the ball to return it to the bowler, only to be given out for handling the ball.

Too Many Cooks

On England's 1862 tour to Australia, the tourists played the country 22 of the Ovens Valley in Victoria. All 22 of the home side chose to field at the same time with the result that fielders repeatedly collided with each other when trying to catch high balls. England profited from the situation to win inside two days by an innings and 191 runs.

Head Bye

In 1997 France beat Germany by one run to win the European Nations Cup at Zuoz in Switzerland. Batting first in the 50-over final, France ultimately owed their success to their last man, David Bordes, who, off the last ball of the innings, was hit on the forehead but still managed to stagger through for a single before collapsing with a fractured skull. In the end that run was to prove the difference between the two sides.

Animal Interlopers

Back in December 1876 when James Lillywhite's touring England professionals challenged a 22 of Goulburn in Australia, play was disrupted when six hares and two young kangaroos invaded the pitch. Then in 1890 it was reported that play in a match between Royston and Cambridge Victoria was stopped while a stoat ran across the pitch. Two years later a runaway horse and cart halted proceedings during the MCC–Yorkshire fixture at Scarborough. And on 4 August 1948, the Glamorgan v Gloucestershire match at Ebbw Vale was disrupted by the arrival on the pitch of a flock of sheep. But these seem positively commonplace compared to a game at Bristol in 1986 when play was stopped by a dead mackerel. Old Cliftonians were taking on Stowe Templars in the first round of the Cricketer Cup when the dead fish plummeted from the heavens, narrowly missing the head of Cliftonians' batsman Simon Hazlitt. Local wisdom suggested that the mackerel had been stolen by a seagull from the sealion enclosure at Bristol Zoo and that the seagull had been flying over the ground when it had inadvertently dropped its booty. Undeterred by the experience, Hazlitt went on to make 45 although some of his colleagues floundered.

The Bald Truth

For the 1993–94 tour of the West Indies, England's injury-prone all-rounder Chris Lewis decided to go for a new image and shaved his head. On the opening match of the tour, he left his hat off and got sunstroke.

Grace to the Rescue

Fielding at Old Trafford in 1887, A. C. M. Croome of Gloucestershire impaled himself on the spiked railings around the boundary while trying to cut off a four. He sustained a badly gashed throat and owed his life to the swift intervention of his illustrious team-mate, Dr W. G. Grace.

The Batsman Who Set the Game Alight

A batsman by the name of Stan Dawson goes down as possibly the only batsman in the history of cricket to lose his wicket while attempting to put out a fire. Dawson was batting at Kalgoorlie, Australia, in the 1970s when he was hit by a quick delivery that immediately ignited a box of matches which he kept in his hip pocket. As the poor man was hopping around trying to beat down the flames with his bare hands, his unsympathetic opponents ran him out.

An Inside Job

Wisden reported that a match between the South African Under-19 team and the Northern Transvaal Colts at the Correctional Services ground in Pretoria in 1994 was reduced from 55 overs a side to 50 after the start had been delayed because the stumps had been stolen.

Two years later the start of the Sri Lanka–Zimbabwe tie in the Singer World Series at Colombo was delayed for eight minutes while the umpires desperately searched for the missing bails. They were eventually found in the groundsman's pocket.

The Day England Walked Off

In the days when under-arm or round-arm bowling was the norm, Edgar Willsher, playing for England against Surrey at the Oval in August 1862, fell foul of umpire John Lillywhite for bowling over-arm. After being no-balled six times by Lillywhite, Willsher was so angry that he walked off and was followed by the rest of the England team, thereby causing play to be abandoned for the day. When proceedings resumed the following morning, Lillywhite had been replaced and Willsher took six wickets forcing Surrey to follow on.

In 1994 a North Herts League game between Codicote and Luton College was abandoned after a Luton bowler kicked one of the umpires for turning down a run-out appeal. The Codicote players were so enraged by this behaviour that they decided they wanted no further part in the game and walked off.

When club cricketer Cliff Spinks elected to walk off during a match in June 1996, it had nothing to do with the umpire's decisions – it was simply because he was fed up. Batting for Langleybury against Northwood, Spinks was unbeaten on 31 when he inexplicably hurled his bat at the stumps. The bemused fielders immediately appealed – although they weren't quite sure what they were appealing for – but their pleas were rejected on the grounds that the batsman had neither been playing the ball nor attempting a run. Spinks himself then appealed and when this too was turned down, he stomped off to the pavilion. He said afterwards that he had been playing too much cricket lately.

The Secret Policeman's Ball

The origins of cricket in Latvia date back to a game in the capital, Riga. However, the authorities were worried about the dangers involved in the new sport and, possibly fearing a case of 'Rigamortis', dispatched a policeman to observe the proceedings in secrecy. For some reason this noble upholder of the law concluded that the best way to study the game was to hide himself among the close-to-the-wicket fielders. It is not known whether his efforts to remain inconspicuous were hampered by having to remain in uniform. After making copious mental notes for a few minutes, he was just beginning to fear that his investigation would prove inconclusive when he was hit on the head by the ball. This was just the answer he was looking for and from his hospital bed he was able to declare the game of cricket to be thoroughly dangerous. Thereafter cricket was banned in Latvia.

Fund-Raising Flop

In 1989 Twyford CC near Bristol staged a special fund-raising match in the hope of obtaining much-needed cash for ground maintenance. In one respect, the fixture was a success since it brought in an invaluable £44. On the other hand, in the course of the match a window was broken by a six and the club had to cough up £45 to have it repaired!

Chance in a Million

During the County Championship game between Leicestershire and Lancashire in 1975, Leicester's substitute wicket-keeper Barry Dudleston stumped Lancashire batsman David Lloyd, only to see the bails jump up and miraculously land back in their sockets. Buoyed by his reprieve, Lloyd went on to make a century.

Hard to Stomach

Most people choose to deliver a pizza to the door but Warwickshire and England's Neil Smith preferred to deliver his pizza all over the wicket. Playing against United Arab Emirates in the 1996 World

Cup in Peshawar, Pakistan, Smith followed up his 3 for 29 in the Emirates' total of 136 by making a confident-looking 27 not out. At that point a re-heated pizza from the night before returned to haunt him and caused him to throw up on the pitch. 'It's part of playing cricket out here,' said his rueful captain Mike Atherton. Smith was named man of the match for his pains.

Robbed of Century by Seagull

Batting for South Melbourne in the Downing Shield under-16 competition in 1995, young Australian Blair Sellers struck a lofted drive which looked a four all the way until it hit a passing seagull on the back of the head. While the stunned bird vowed to avoid cricket grounds in future, Sellers and his partner were only able to run two. The significance of those two lost runs became apparent later when Sellers was dismissed for 98 – two short of his century.

Boating Accident

When England toured Australia in 1883, the unluckiest player was Nottinghamshire bowler Fred Morley. Morley was injured on the journey out to Australia after the team boat had been in collision with a sailing vessel at Colombo. Although he did bowl on the tour, he was considerably handicapped and unable to do himself justice.

Fielder Caught Bus Back to the Ground

Perched on a steep hill, the Ilfracombe Rugby Club ground at Hele presents an unusual challenge for fielders, as Paul Crabb discovered to his cost when playing for the club's cricket section against Devon neighbours Woolacombe in July 1996. When a ball was hit out of the ground, Crabb gave chase as it ran down the incline of an adjoining road, finally catching up with it a quarter of a mile from the wicket. As chance would have it, just as he was about to contemplate the return climb, a bus approached and so he hopped on and caught the bus back to the game. The driver clearly took pity on him because he waived the 46p fare.

India Rubber Shock

The West Indies first visited India for a Test series in 1948–49 and after three draws and a West Indies victory at Madras, the host nation needed to win the Fifth and final Test at Bombay to square the rubber. Having bowled out the visitors for 286 and 267, India needed 361 at a run a minute to gain that historic first win over the West Indies. It went right to the wire. With two overs left, India required 11 to win with two wickets standing. They were on schedule with five off the first five balls when Indian umpire A. R. Joshi inexplicably ended the over a ball too soon with India on 355 for 8. He then proceeded to remove the bails, thus formally ending the match, even though the clock at the ground indicated that there was still 90 seconds to play and therefore ample time for the last over. His curious actions merely succeeded in depriving his own country of the seven balls which could have brought them a famous victory against the West Indies. Instead they had to wait until 1971 to record that particular milestone.

In a 1946 match between Barbados and British Guyana, the umpires struggled to come to terms with the eight-ball over which was in force at the time. One over from Guyana's D. F. Hill, which contained neither wides nor no-balls, was allowed to continue unchecked for fourteen deliveries. Indeed the umpire's miscalculation might have gone unnoticed had he not given Everton Weekes out lbw off the fourteenth ball.

New Zealand have also featured in two instances in which the umpire couldn't do his sums. Bowling against England at Auckland in 1963, Kiwi spinner John Sparling sent down eleven successive deliveries after umpire Dick Shortt had got in a right state with his hand counter. Following a great deal of head scratching, Shortt ordered Sparling to start the over again from scratch. And during New Zealand's 1994 series with Pakistan, umpire Steve Dunne became so confused that he permitted two five-ball overs, two seven-ball overs and one over containing eight balls.

However, nobody could have blamed the umpires if they had lost count of an over bowled by paceman Gladstone Small for Warwickshire against Middlesex in 1982. For Small's over lasted a seemingly interminable eighteen balls, thanks to ten no-balls (including nine in succession) and two wides.

Players Went Home

When rain stopped play with two hours left on the final day of the County Championship game between Hampshire and Glamorgan at Bournemouth on 17 June 1969, the Hampshire players left the ground and went to their respective homes, thinking that the match had been abandoned. And so when the rain cleared and play again became possible, the Hampshire boys were nowhere to be found. Glamorgan, on the other hand, had stayed on and, after turning out for the necessary two minutes, were awarded a win by the umpires. However, the MCC subsequently rescinded the decision, saying that Hampshire were the victims of a misunderstanding.

Penalised for His Enterprise

In a match between Warwickshire and Northamptonshire at Edgbaston in the 1970s, Warwickshire's West Indian star Rohan Kanhai glanced a delivery from leg-spinner Mushtaq Mohammad behind the wicket. Northants wicket-keeper George Sharp gave chase, throwing off his gloves as he did so, and quick-thinking team-mate David Steele promptly put them on to take John Dye's return. But Australian umpire Tom Brooks said that Steele's action in donning the gloves was illegal and awarded Kanhai five extra runs to add to the three he had already run for the stroke.

Denture Despair

In April 1997 groundsman Brian Lucas had his false teeth crushed by his roller while going about his duties at the Perkins Cricket Club in Shropshire. They had flown out of his mouth when he sneezed.

Victoria Whine

There was precious little love lost between New South Wales and Victoria in the 1860s, and an 1863 encounter was a typically hostile affair. Matters came to a head after New South Wales batsman Sydney Jones had been struck on the leg by a fast delivery, as a result of which he required the services of a runner. Jones continued to hobble around in pain and when he momentarily wandered out of his crease, George Marshall of Victoria whipped off the bails and appealed for a run out. Richard Driver, the New South Wales-appointed umpire, rejected the appeal, insisting that he had already called 'over' when the unsporting incident occurred but, predictably enough, the Victoria umpire, J. A. Smith, disagreed and gave Jones out. As tempers became frayed, the Victoria players left the field and returned to their hotel. The discussions continued through the night and it soon became apparent that Marshall, another Victoria player, William Greaves, and umpire Smith had been disowned by the rest of the team. Accordingly, the following day while those three caught a ship back to Melbourne, nine Victoria men resumed the match and immediately withdrew the appeal against the wounded Jones. A degree of dignity was therefore restored although the dispute did little for Victoria's prospects, the nine men going down by 84 runs.

Prior Engagement

In December 1993 Lulma Masikazana should have been keeping wicket for Eastern Province against England 'A' on the latter's tour of South Africa. However, he had to pull out at the last minute because, in accordance with local custom, he was being circumcised.

A Prizegiving With a Difference

The final of a six-a-side festival at Beaconsfield CC, in Buckinghamshire, in July 1992 was abandoned after a car careered across the pitch, injuring four spectators. The car was driven by the club president, eighty-six-year-old Tom Orford, who had come to present the prizes . . .

Greig's Gremlins

After injuring a finger while batting against Pakistan in 1987, Surrey's Ian Greig went to hospital for an X-ray, which confirmed that the finger was fractured. But Greig's problems weren't over yet. As he got up to leave, he cracked his head on the X-ray machine and needed two stitches in the wound.

Run Out After Bat Broke in Half

Sometimes batsmen don't hear a no-ball call until the last split second, giving them precious little time to improvise. But judging by the way he charged down the wicket with reckless abandon, Surrey opening bat Laurie Fishlock must have had plenty of warning when facing Kent at the Oval in 1938. However, he launched himself into a drive of such ferocity that as he swung at the ball, his bat broke in two. As a result he got nothing more than a faint touch which carried through to the wicket-keeper. All too aware that a batsman cannot be out caught or stumped from a no-ball, the quick-thinking keeper broke the stumps and the hapless Fishlock, with no bat to ground, was adjudged run out.

Musical Interlude

Play was twice held up during the Lancashire–Sussex match at Lytham St Anne's in 1995 when excerpts from Holy Communion at nearby St Cuthbert's Church mysteriously came over on the ground's public address system.

Hot-Headed

The image of cricket as a genteel game was well and truly blown away by events during the final of the Inter Zone tournament for India's Duleep Trophy at Jamshedpur in January 1991. In a match where the short-pitched delivery had been all too prevalent, tempers finally boiled over when West Zone bowler Rashid Patel appeared to deliver a fearsome bouncer to North Zone batsman Raman Lamba from way beyond the popping crease. Lamba immediately remonstrated with Patel who responded by running to the batsman's end, grabbing a stump and attacking both Lamba and his North Zone colleague Ajay Jadeja. The fracas in the middle inspired the crowd to start hurling stones and the match was abandoned with North Zone being declared the winners by virtue of their first innings lead. Patel was banned for thirteen months for his part in the incident and Lamba for ten.

North Wales staged a scaled-down version of the Jamshedpur bout in 1996. The setting was a fixture between Buckley and Shotton which passed peacefully enough until wicket-keeper Marcel Carrino dropped a relatively straightforward catch. Words were exchanged with batsman Andy Cummings and soon the verbal assault became physical. The umpires sent both men off.

Incorrect Diagnosis

Captaining Northants on a wet wicket in the early 1960s, South African Jon Fellows-Smith chose to lead by example when his pace men seemed reluctant to open the bowling. Assuring them that there was nothing treacherous about the surface, he promptly slipped on his run-up, broke his ankle and was stretchered off to hospital.

Out Before the Ball Was Bowled

Batting for Sussex against Kent at Gravesend in 1866, G. Wells was given out after hitting his wicket while the bowler was running in. He thus had the distinction of being out to a ball which wasn't even delivered.

Futile Journey

Some people will go miles for a game of cricket . . . often for minimal results. One Gerald Pedder travelled all the way from Nicaragua to Ditchling, Sussex, to play in a game in 1948, only to be dismissed for a duck. In 1960 film star Trevor Howard agreed to appear in a match at Buxton. To do so, he got up at five o'clock in the morning, journeyed 180 miles to Derbyshire . . . and was caught behind first ball!

Blinded by the Light

Tea in the Fourth Test between England and the West Indies at Old Trafford in 1995 was taken 15 minutes early because the light reflecting from a nearby glass roof was dazzling the batsmen.

Double Dislocation

In 1996 twins Chris and James Sell both dislocated a shoulder playing in the same match for Brighton College against Old Brightonians.

Unsighted

An umpire was the victim of a tragic accident during a game in which Wanstead played Essex Club and Ground in 1909. Usually

Wanstead's groundsman, Mr Hockenheimer found himself on umpiring duties on this particular occasion – a job which brought him into contact with a leg-spinner by the name of Dr Holton who had a tendency to run across the wicket after delivery, thus obscuring the umpire's view of the batsman. One of the doctor's offerings was met with a hearty straight drive by the batsman. Seeing the ball flying towards him, Dr Holton ducked out of the way but the unsighted Hockenheimer took the blow full in the face and died in hospital a few days later.

Tactical Error

With Transvaal needing one run from the final ball to win their match against Natal in the 1967–68 season, Natal captain Barry Versfeld, standing in for regular captain Jackie McGlew, came up with a tactical masterplan. To counteract the threat of a leg-bye, he cunningly posted an additional fielder on the leg side. Mike Procter bounded in to bowl and rearranged batsman Eddie Barlow's stumps but Natal's hopes of having secured a tie were rudely shattered. For Versfeld's move in adding an extra man behind the wicket on the leg side had contravened the rules of the competition. The ensuing no-ball cost Natal the match.

Lost in the Long Grass

The Macleod fielders endured a torrid time against Banyale in a Victoria country fixture at Windsor Reserve in 1990. For when Banyale batsman Garry Chapman hit a ball to mid wicket, it disappeared into ten-inch high grass. While the fielders desperately searched for it, the batsmen ran seventeen!

The incident was reminiscent of an even more profitable stroke in Australia over a century earlier. On that occasion Bunbury of Western Australia were entertaining a touring team from Victoria. Off the very first delivery of the match, the Victoria opener smashed the ball into a tall tree where it stuck fast. While the batsmen ran . . .

and ran . . . and ran, the fielders tried every means possible to dislodge it. After searching in vain for an axe to fell the tree, someone produced a rifle and the ball was shot down from its perch. By the time it was returned to the middle, the batsmen had run 286 . . .

Batless Botham

Going out to bat against Western Australia on the 1986–87 tour, England's Ian Botham was half-way to the wicket when he felt a tap on his shoulder. It was the twelfth man proffering a bat with the suggestion that such an implement might come in useful. In his eagerness to join the action and flay the ball to all parts of the ground, Botham had forgotten to pick up anything to hit it with.

Diary Blip

West Indian Test star Viv Richards forgot to attend his OBE investiture at Buckingham Palace on 1 December 1994.

Injured by His Team-Mates

So delighted were his Darfield team-mates when wicket-keeper Gavin Roebuck performed a crucial stumping in a 1996 Barnsley Sunday League match that they all rushed to congratulate him. Unfortunately, in their enthusiasm they succeeded in breaking his elbow.

Test Flops

Tucked away beneath the greats of Test cricket – such as Trumper, Bradman, Hobbs and Hammond – are numerous long-forgotten names of players who haven't exactly distinguished themselves at the highest level. Top of the list is probably Dr R. L. Park, picked to play for Australia against England at Melbourne in 1920. He was out first ball in his only innings and bowled a solitary over which cost nine runs.

One who performed only marginally more successfully was Ken Burn, chosen to tour England with the Australian team of 1890. But at least he had mitigating circumstances. For having been selected as reserve wicket-keeper, it wasn't until the team were half-way to England that it emerged that Burn had never actually kept wicket before. So instead they played him as a batsman although the fact that he batted at numbers 10 and 11 in the First Test rather belied that status. He played in two Tests on that tour but performed with such mediocrity that he was not selected for the national team again.

Frog Chorus

When England toured South Africa in 1922–23, the Final Test at Durban was interrupted by a peculiar natural phenomenon. After a ball had pitched and almost stopped dead, the batsmen went to prod the wicket to see what had prompted the irregularity. Instead of a crack or a bump, they found the cause to be a pile of little green frogs. Play was duly halted while the frogs were loaded into two buckets and removed to safer pastures.

Ball Split in Two

During the semi-final of the 1996 NatWest Trophy between Lancashire and Yorkshire at Old Trafford, a ball struck by Yorkshire's Michael Bevan split in two. The leather cover had come adrift as it made contact with Bevan's bat. Neither piece of ball was caught.

Indoor Game Rained Off

Plans to stage an indoor game at Basingstoke in 1993 were wrecked when the game was rained off. The pitch was flooded after water had poured through a hole in the sports hall roof.

Adding Injury to Insult

One of the most notorious runners between wickets was England wicket-keeper Godfrey Evans and he truly excelled himself during the Third Test with Australia at Sydney in the 1950–51 Ashes series. He managed to get Doug Wright run out after sending him back and then changing his mind. To make matters worse, as the thoroughly confused Wright tried to respond to Evans' stop–go technique, he pulled a groin muscle and was unable to bowl for the rest of the match. Their attack depleted, England lost by an innings and 13 runs.

An equally unfortunate run out was experienced by South African captain Jackie McGlew in the Third Test with England at Trent Bridge in July 1960. McGlew had made 45 when he set off for a run and accidentally collided with England bowler Alan Moss. As a result McGlew failed to beat a direct hit from Brian Statham and was run out. England skipper Colin Cowdrey felt sorry for McGlew and urged the umpires to have him reinstated but there was no way back for the South African. England went on to win by eight wickets.

Tea in the Middle

Colin Wells of Derbyshire was so crippled in the County Championship match with Surrey at the Oval in 1996 that he couldn't even manage to hobble back to the pavilion for tea on the final afternoon. The considerate ground staff rose to the occasion by taking a deckchair and a cup of tea out to the middle for him and team-mate Dominic Cork stayed to keep him company. Wells' heroics were not in vain since his painstaking 28 enabled Derbyshire to hold on for a draw.

Painful Start

Lancashire and England's Ernest Tyldesley endured a traumatic Test début against Australia at Trent Bridge in 1921. In the first innings he was out first ball, playing on. In the second innings he had batted half an hour for 7 runs when he tried to hook a bouncer, missed and was hit on the jaw. He was knocked out cold and it took several minutes to bring him round. When he finally came to, Tyldesley was helped to the pavilion by sympathetic Australians where, to complete his anguish, he discovered that he was out, the ball having dropped from his jaw on to his wicket.

Duty Calls

Proof that Britain's fire services are never really off-duty occurred during a Winchester Evening League game in 1995 between the brigade and the local rugby club. Play was held up when the firemen formed a human chain to rescue an eleven-year-old boy who had fallen out of a tree at the ground and had become trapped in the lower branches. But there was no happy ending to the rescue – the firemen lost the match.

Parliament Gassed

Among the worst scenes ever witnessed in first-class cricket was the riot which took place during the Second Test between the West Indies and England at Sabina Park, Kingston, Jamaica, on 12 February 1968. The spectators had seen red over the dismissal of West Indian batsman Basil Butcher and began hurling bottles on to the pitch, one of which struck England captain Colin Cowdrey on the foot. After Cowdrey had appealed unsuccessfully for calm, the police responded by spraying the crowd with tear gas. Unfortunately the wind direction meant that the gas drifted into the pavilion and even as far as the parliament building, forcing the Jamaican Cabinet to suspend its sitting.

The West Indian police were also out in force during a game at Queen's Park Savannah, Trinidad, which featured Test star Phil Simmons. Play was stopped for several minutes when it was discovered that the over-enthusiastic law enforcers had slapped parking tickets on the cars of the players and match officials.

Bowling Machine Ran Amok

Over the winter of 1985–86 Martyn Goulding of Torquay took the opportunity to sharpen his batting against a bowling machine. The fact that the machine wasn't programmed for 'sledging' and didn't appeal for lbw every other ball made a pleasant change and the pair got along famously until Goulding was felled by a 75mph delivery which broke a bone in his foot. As he lay on the ground, writhing in agony, the merciless machine hurled down its next delivery which hit him again, this time breaking two ribs.

Reflex Catch

Dismissals don't come much unluckier than that of R. N. Exton playing for the Combined Services against Surrey at the 1946 Kingston-on-Thames Festival. Poor Exton was out caught at short leg by Alf Gover off the bowling of Jim Laker (incidentally, this was Laker's first wicket in first-class cricket) yet Gover couldn't even see what was going on. At the time he had been in the process of pulling his sweater over his head and had instinctively closed his legs on the ball, catching it between his thighs.

Australian tail-ender Craig McDermott also had a hard-luck story to tell after his country lost a thrilling Fourth Test to the West Indies at Adelaide in 1993 by the margin of 1 run. Not normally renowned for his expertise with the bat, McDermott had put on 40 for the last wicket with Tim May to take Australia to the brink of victory. Then, with his own score on 18, McDermott tried to sway out of the path of a rising ball from Courtney Walsh, only for the ball to strike the peak of his helmet, deflect on to his glove and carry through to jubilant wicket-keeper Junior Murray.

And what about the unnamed batsman at Valparaiso Cricket Club, Chile, in 1922 who was given out after his lofted drive landed in the pocket of a white tennis cardigan being worn by one of the fielders?

An Untimely Call of Nature

In 1995 Wayne Radcliffe of Yorkshire club Newmillerdam was banned for five years by the Wakefield and District Cricket Union for urinating on the pitch while fielding in the covers. In mitigation, Radcliffe explained that he was absolutely desperate and that he had turned towards some trees so that none of the spectators could see.

Lancastrians' Lament

With visitors Surrey needing just 2 runs to beat Lancashire in July 1922, Lancashire's Vic Norbury bowled to Miles Howell. Norbury was ecstatic when Howell was caught but his joy was short-lived as the umpire called 'no-ball'. This brought the scores level. Off the very next ball, Norbury had Howell caught again, only for the umpire to signal another 'no-ball' to hand Surrey victory.

Caught in the Act

Batting for the Jesters CC against Totteridge in 1975, Richard Johnson launched a mighty six which landed on a spectator's car. On hearing the thud, the car owner, who had been otherwise engaged with a young lady on the grass, leapt to his feet in anger, at which point his trousers fell down.

The Most Expensive Miss

Dropped catches are so commonplace in cricket that they are

scarcely worth mentioning in a book dedicated to mishaps. However, one case of butterfingers from recent years proved so costly that it merits retelling. It was at Edgbaston in June 1994 that Warwickshire's Brian Lara, having made 18, edged a simple catch to Durham wicket-keeper Chris Scott. It was such a routine offering that Lara had even started to walk, yet somehow Scott spilled it. Realising that he had blown the chance of getting rid of the Warwickshire danger man, the dejected Scott turned to his slips and said: 'I suppose he'll go on and get a century now.' Scott was only partly correct – Lara went on to make 501 not out. If nothing else, Chris Scott assured himself of a place in cricket trivia.

Late Result

South Australia left the field at the end of their 1996 Mercantile Mutual Insurance Cup tie with New South Wales in Sydney in the belief that they had lost the 50-over contest by 1 run. However, after the game was over South Australia's total was increased by 2 when it was discovered that the scorers had overlooked a no-ball in the forty-eighth over. The additional 2 runs transformed the defeat into an improbable three-wicket win.

A Long Hit

In 1997 it was reported that a ball hit out of the ground during the match between King's School, Macclesfield and Bangor Grammar bounced on to a passing lorry and was last seen heading towards Alderley Edge.

Made Up for Lost Time

Lancashire left-arm fast bowler Harry Dean missed play before lunch on the second day of the Roses match at Liverpool in July 1913 because he didn't think the proceedings were due to start until two o'clock. He had gone to the ground in the morning but had left under the impression that, because of overnight rain, no play would be possible until after lunch. When he did arrive, Dean made amends for his earlier absence by taking 9 for 62 and 8 for 29 as Lancashire got home by three wickets.

Cyclist Hit by Six

Wisden recounted how in May 1993 an elderly lady pushing her bicycle past the ground at Burghill, Herefordshire, while the match with Hay-on-Wye was in progress had to be taken to hospital after being struck by a huge six. 'It was certainly very unlucky,' sympathised Burghill chairman Len Sparrow, 'especially as the lad who hit it normally can't play leg-side.'

Wrong Size Bails

The start of the Fifth Test between South Africa and England at Durban in the 1930–31 series was held up for an hour because the bails were the wrong size. The delay was particularly frustrating for England who, after losing the First Test and drawing the next three, needed a win to square the rubber. But the lost time meant that once again the best they could manage was a draw, thus allowing South Africa to take the series 1–0.

The England 'A' team enjoyed better fortune against Transvaal in December 1993. Once again the odds appeared to be stacked against the tourists when the third morning's play was abandoned because they couldn't field eleven players, no fewer than seven men having been laid low by gastro-enteritis. They managed to resume the match after lunch, with five substitute fielders including coach Phil Neale and physio Wayne Morton, a player of club cricket standard. Yet remarkably three hours later England had triumphed by nine wickets. The only healthy batsmen knocked off the winning runs.

In and Out

In the match between Surrey and Cambridge University on 20 June 1868, the students' Charles Absolom was given out for 38 for the unusual offence of obstructing the field. A leg-weary Absolom had been attempting to complete a seventh run when his bat was adjudged to have prevented a fielder's throw from hitting the stumps. On reaching the pavilion, Absolom was told that he wasn't out after all so he made his way back to the middle. But when he got there, he was informed that he definitely was out. This time he stayed in the pavilion and could only look on helplessly as Cambridge went down by 14 runs.

Athers Away

Thirty cardboard cut-out Mike Athertons, which had been produced for a pub promotion, went missing from a Leeds warehouse in June 1995.

Super Sub

Coming on as a substitute fielder for Leicestershire in 1919, Yorkshire twelfth man Bill Williams took four catches against his own team.

A Fishy Problem

Cricket balls have landed in some unusual places over the years but they rarely end up in a meal. Yet that's what happened when South African teams Border and Boland met in February 1995. Border's Daryll Cullinan hit a six which landed in a frying pan containing hot calamari. Fearing that the ball would add little to the flavour of the squid, officials managed to remove it from the pan but it was another ten minutes or so before the ball had cooled down sufficiently for the coating of grease to be removed. Even then it remained so slippery that the bowlers couldn't grip it properly and it had to be replaced.

Slipped His Mind

Captaining Australia in a country match in South Africa, Bobby Simpson forgot to tell the opposing skipper that, with a lead of nearly 450, he wished to enforce the follow-on. As a result of this breakdown in communications, when the tea interval was over both teams came out to field.

Bad Flight Stopped Play

That was the headline a Lincolnshire newspaper gave to a bizarre story from April 1997 in which a fielder was hit by a hang-glider. John Hague was minding his own business patrolling the boundary for Horncastle in their friendly with Bardney when a hang-glider suddenly swooped from the skies and caught him a glancing blow on the head. While the players helped to drag away the shattered glider so that play could continue, the pilot meekly explained how he had been trying to avoid a field of crops. As for Hague, he was left nursing a distinctly sore head. He said: 'I nearly didn't play because I'd woken up with a migraine. Being biffed on the head by a hang-glider was all I needed.'

Aimless Steele

Making his way out to bat in his Test début, against Australia at Lord's in 1975, Northants and England's David Steele descended one flight of steps too many and finished up in the pavilion toilets.

3 Boxing

For Whom the Bell Tolls

The concept of dividing a sports hall in half to stage two separate contests simultaneously has always worked perfectly satisfactorily for the World Snooker Championships. However, as the organisers of the 1988 Seoul Olympics discovered, boxing presents more of a challenge. For whoever had the bright idea of advocating that two rings be in use in the boxing hall at the same time had overlooked one thing – the bell. In the general commotion surrounding the fights, it became impossible for the boxers to determine whether the bell they were hearing was for their fight or for the one in the next ring. The most dramatic result of this flawed thinking occurred towards the end of the first round of a light-welterweight contest between Todd Foster of the United States and Chun Jin Chul from South Korea. Hearing a bell, Chun immediately thought that it referred to his bout, little knowing that it was in fact from the other ring and that there were still another seventeen seconds remaining of his round. The referee looked puzzled but did nothing to dissuade Chun from walking back to his corner. However, Foster realised what was going on and caught the unprepared Chun with a left hook which sent the Korean reeling to the canvas. The referee started the count but then changed his mind. As confusion reigned supreme, the judges ordered a rematch to take place the following day which Foster won fair and square.

The Boxer Who Knocked Himself Out

Irishman Jack Doyle was hot favourite to win his heavyweight bout with Eddie Phillips at Harringay, London, in September 1938 but a rush of blood brought about an ignominious defeat. In the second round Doyle, going for a spectacular kill, suddenly flew at his opponent, missed him completely and sailed through the ropes out of the ring. Failing to get back before the count of ten, he was counted out and Phillips was declared the surprised winner.

Punch-up Before the Fight

In 1994 WBO champion Michael Bentt and challenger Herbie Hide from Norwich were each fined £10,000 by the British Boxing Board of Control after their pre-fight press conference at a Knightsbridge hotel had degenerated into an unseemly brawl. Prior to their bout at Millwall Football Club's New Den in March of that year, the two boxers attended a photo call at the Sheraton Park Towers Hotel on 10 January. The trouble started when a woman placed a Millwall baseball cap on Bentt's head and Hide knocked it off saying, 'I want a Norwich cap.' At this, Bentt swung round and landed a right on Hide's head, dropping the challenger to his knees. Within seconds, the pair were rolling around trading punches while their handlers tried to prise them apart. Imposing the fine, John Morris, secretary of the Board of Control, said that both men were equally to blame. Bentt said of the altercation with Hide: 'You don't get anything for fighting outside the ring, but he compromised my manhood.'

Many a Slip

The bare-knuckle bout between 'Gentleman' John Jackson and George Inglestone which took place in Surrey on 12 May 1789 was marred by torrential rain which turned the ring into an ice rink. As both men slithered around, it seemed only a matter of time before there was a serious accident and, sure enough, Jackson slipped once too often and ended up breaking a leg and dislocating an ankle. Even the gutsiest of fighters would have conceded defeat at that point but Jackson was determined to carry on and offered to be strapped into a chair from where he was prepared to slug it out with Inglestone. The latter declined however.

A more recent reminder of the strain boxing puts on ankles came during the 1989 WBC super-welterweight decider between France's René Jacquot and John Mugabi of Uganda. Defending champion Jacquot was forced to relinquish his title in the very first round, having to retire after twisting an ankle.

Fed Up

South African lightweight Thomas Hamilton-Brown was suitably distraught at losing a split decision to Carlos Lillo of Chile in a first-round contest at the 1936 Berlin Olympics and to try and overcome his disappointment he decided to embark on a massive eating binge. However a couple of hours after the fight had finished, it became apparent that one of the judges had mistakenly reversed the scores and that Hamilton-Brown, not Lillo, was the winner. The South African's manager urgently set off to find his man to tell him the good news but sadly by the time he tracked down Hamilton-Brown, the boxer had drowned his sorrows to such an extent that he had put on 5lb in weight. As a result he was over the limit and disqualified.

Ref Trod on Fighter's Foot

When Sheffield's Johnny Cuthbert defended his British feather-weight title against Liverpool's Nel Tarleton at Anfield in October 1931, the fight got off to a sensational start. For in the first round the referee, in trying to break the two men up, succeeded in treading heavily on Tarleton's foot, leaving him in considerable pain. For the next five rounds Tarleton hobbled around in front of his home crowd while Cuthbert threw everything at him, mixing legal punches with sneaky attempts to stand on his opponent's bad foot. Yet remarkably

Tarleton, who also had only one lung, held firm and eventually won a points decision. 'Losing the title was bad enough,' moaned Cuthbert afterwards, 'but it didn't half rub it in when I realised I'd been beaten by a bloke with one lung and only one foot!'

The Battle of the Long Count

On 22 September 1927 in Chicago Gene Tunney retained his world heavyweight title at the expense of Jack Dempsey, but only after one of the most controversial incidents in the history of boxing. It was in the seventh round that Dempsey launched a furious all-out attack on the champion which ended with Tunney lying flat out on the canvas. As Dempsey stood over the prone Tunney, referee Dave Barry refused to begin the count until Dempsey retreated to a neutral corner. It was some five seconds before Barry ushered Dempsey across the ring and started to count – time which allowed Tunney to regain his senses and stagger to his feet. By the time the count had reached nine, it was a full fourteen seconds since the blow had been landed and Tunney was able to continue. Tunney recovered sufficiently to win on points but Dempsey complained afterwards: 'I was robbed of the championship.' The fight has been known ever since as 'The Battle of the Long Count'.

There was actually a fight in 1948 which made 'The Long Count' look like the blink of an eye. It took place at Madison Square Garden, New York, on 12 March between French Moroccan Marcel Cerdan and Lawrence Roach of Texas. The fun started when Cerdan floored Roach with a right-hander but as Roach toppled, he pulled his opponent down with him. Cerdan quickly got to his feet but the referee, Arthur Donovan, and the timekeeper, Jack Watson, then began arguing furiously among themselves. Donovan reckoned it was a knockdown and wanted to start a count but Watson maintained that Roach had slipped and therefore refused to count. As the war of words over their differing interpretations of the incident continued, the two officials seemed oblivious to the plight of Roach who was still lying on the canvas though slowly coming to his senses. When the count finally began, he had been there for twenty-four seconds.

Since he got up at eight, that meant he had enjoyed a break of thirty-two seconds since being decked. Not that the rest did Roach much good – he was stopped in the eighth round.

Referee Overcome by Heat

Obviously there's nothing unusual about boxers having to retire during a fight but it's not very often that the referee has to. Yet that is precisely what happened to Ruby Goldstein who was in charge of the world light-heavyweight title bout between Ray Robinson and Joey Maxim in New York on 25 June 1952. The bout took place in the middle of a heatwave and the oppressive conditions sapped the energy of boxers and referee alike. Time after time, Goldstein had to separate the two men and the sheer physical exertion required to pull apart such mountains of flesh in the tropical heat took its toll at the end of the tenth round when Goldstein announced that it was all too much for him. With Goldstein receiving medical treatment, Ray Miller took over as referee and two rounds later, Robinson too retired as a result of the heat.

Ring Destroyed by Crowd

Rules were few and far between in the days of bare-knuckle fighting and the contests were invariably unruly affairs with no prisoners taken. But few matched the mayhem of a clash between London's Caleb Baldwin, a former England champion, and Irish Bill Ryan which took place on Blackheath on 6 August 1805. In the twenty-sixth round, Baldwin, reeling from exhaustion, slumped to the ground and was hit by his opponent while he was on his knees. Baldwin's supporters instantly cried 'foul' and fights broke out among the crowd, requiring the Dragoon Guards to be summoned to restore some semblance of order. But by the time they had arrived, the ring had been destroyed and the referee was forced to declare the contest a draw. It was Baldwin's last fight.

Under-Age

At the 1968 Mexico Olympics, Puerto Rican flyweight Heriberto Cintron was standing in the ring before his first-round bout when he was suddenly disqualified for being under the minimum age of seventeen. It turned out that he was just sixteen years and one month.

Frankham Freaks Out

It is fair to say that Newmarket light-heavyweight Bobby Frankham didn't entirely agree with referee Richie Davies's decision to stop his fight with Hackney's Billy Sims in the first round. Frankham, who had already been floored twice by Sims in the opening moments of the bout at Wembley on 2 December 1987, flatly refused to accept the verdict. He showed his anger first by throwing punches at referee Davies – hitting him twice in the face – and then by launching himself at Sims' corner men. While Frankham's own corner men struggled in vain to restrain him, he even attempted to start an unofficial second round with Sims. The fracas led to a punch-up between rival fans with the referee needing a police escort from the ring. John Morris, secretary of the British Boxing Board of Control, said: 'It was utterly disgraceful. I have never seen a referee attacked like that in a British ring before.' Although remaining adamant that the fight should not have been stopped, Frankham did concede: 'I just had a brainstorm . . . it was a bad way to get famous.'

Frankham was following in the none-too-noble footsteps of German middleweight Pete Muller, who felled referee Max Pippow in 1952. Muller lashed out at the official during the eighth round of his bout with Berlin's Hans Stretz in Cologne on 7 June – a gesture which saw him banned for life by the German Boxing Association.

Thumping the referee has not always been confined to the professional ranks, however. At the 1964 Olympics in Tokyo, Spanish featherweight Valentin Loren saw red after being disqualified for repeated holding and open-glove hitting. He took out his frustration on Hungarian referee Gyorgy Sermer and punched him in the face.

Loren was subsequently banned for life from international amateur boxing.

The Boxer Who Fled from the Ring

One of the most bizarre moments in British boxing occurred in April 1933 when Tommy Farr, the future British heavyweight champion, was still a nineteen-year-old hopeful. Farr was called up as a late replacement to fight Eddie Steele of Norwood at Crystal Palace and acquitted himself admirably until the seventh round when Steele caught him with a jab to the throat. At that, Farr ran from the ring and bolted straight to his dressing room, to the astonishment of opponent and spectators alike. And even in later years, he never offered any explanation for his uncharacteristic behaviour.

A French bare-knuckle fighter by the name of M. Pettit fled for his life back in July 1751. He had been engaged in a gruelling slog with Jack Slack, a Norwich butcher, at Harlston in Norfolk. Although Pettit spectacularly failed to live up to his name and actually dwarfed the Englishman, Slack was a mean fighter. After twenty-five minutes, Pettit decided he had been through enough, leapt from the ring and ran away, leaving the referee with little option but to declare Slack the winner.

Holding Back the Tears

After winning the flyweight gold medal at the 1990 Commonwealth Games in Auckland, Northern Ireland's Wayne McCullough stood proudly on the victory podium in anticipation of the national anthem. However, the tape machine which was meant to churn out the music inexplicably jammed and no amount of tinkering by Games official Bob Gibson could induce it to play. So Gibson took matters into his own hands by grabbing the microphone and launching into a rendition of 'Danny Boy'. The crowd joined in and McCullough was so moved that he could be seen fighting back tears.

Unsuitable Settings

It must have sounded like a promoter's dream to stage a world title fight on the seafront. And so it was that Johnny Reagan and Jack 'Nonpareil' Dempsey came face to face for the middleweight championship of the world on the waterfront at Huntington, Long Island, on 13 December 1887. But the fight was doomed. It had already been postponed because of fog and unfortunately when opting for this dramatic setting, the organisers had omitted to take into consideration the rhythms of the tide. So it was that in the eighth round the tide came in and flooded the ring. With Reagan refusing to fight on sand, the bout was abandoned and the twenty-five spectators, led by Reagan and Dempsey, boarded a tug and moved to another spot some miles away. The contest was resumed later that same day and Dempsey was eventually home and dry.

Almost as inadequate a venue was the barge in Miami's Marine Stadium chosen to stage the WBC bantamweight title fight between Miguel Lora of Colombia and Antonio Avelar of Mexico on 25 July 1987. Despite being anchored to the ocean bed, the ring still bobbed up and down during the fight with the result that both men were more likely to be sea-sick than punch-drunk.

Short Cut to Success

At the weigh-in for his first bout at the 1948 London Olympics, Argentine bantamweight Arnoldo Pares was found to be marginally overweight. There was no time for intensive training so team officials decided to cut his hair instead, hoping that the lost locks would tip the scales. When he was still over the limit even after being scalped, the officials launched a protest and it turned out that the scales had been wrong all along. Pares had been shorn for nothing and took to the ring with the severest of haircuts.

At the same chaotic Games, another Argentine boxer – flyweight Pascual Perez – was also disqualified before the competition for being overweight. Olympic officials then realised that they had confused him with his bantamweight team-mate Arnoldo Pares (he of the haircut) and reinstated him. After this early scare, Perez went on to win gold.

Faked Injury

We have all become accustomed to seeing footballers feigning injury but you don't usually expect it from boxers. However, Cyril Minnus of the Bahamas proved the exception to the rule when, on 26 April 1989, he was disqualified by referee Larry O'Connell for feigning injury in a cruiserweight contest with Londoner Lou Gent at Battersea Town Hall. By round three, Gent was very much on top but he was then warned for a left that was slightly below the belt. Perhaps seeing his chance, Minnus immediately fell to the canvas, clutching his groin in apparent agony. But the referee was not impressed by Minnus's injury. He gave the fighter every chance to get up but when Minnus refused, he was disqualified.

A Lucky Escape

Just occasionally a mishap can work in a sportsman's favour, as was certainly the case with former world light-heavyweight champion Bobby Czyz. Selected for the United States amateur squad to fight Poland in 1980, Czyz had to withdraw at the last minute after damaging his nose in a car smash. While Czyz stayed at home licking his wounds, the rest of the US team and the officials flew to Poland . . . and tragically all were killed when their plane crashed outside Warsaw.

The Winner Fainted

The outcome of the light-welterweight final at the 1962 Common-wealth Games in Perth seemed a foregone conclusion. Everyone in the arena was convinced that Scotland's Dick McTaggart had out-pointed Clement Quartey of Ghana. But the judges thought differently and awarded the decision to Quartey who was so stunned that he promptly fainted. He lay face down and unconscious on the canvas for a good five minutes after the announcement and eventually had to be revived by medics.

Beaten by His Opponent's Wife

Everything was going according to plan for James J. Corbett of the United States in his world heavyweight title defence against Cornwall's Bob Fitzsimmons at Carson City, Nevada, in 1897. By the fourteenth round, Corbett was well on top but although he had seemingly mastered Fitzsimmons, Mrs Fitzsimmons was a different prospect altogether. From her private box at the ringside, she started telling her husband to change his tactics and urged him to go for the body. No sooner had the instructions left her lips than Fitzsimmons smashed a left into the champion's solar plexus and knocked him out.

Lost Title Fight in Dressing Room

On 11 April 1988 IBF lightweight champion Greg Haugen of the United States was defending his title against Puerto Rican Miguel Santana. In the eleventh round there was a sickening clash of heads which left Haugen with a gash over his right eye and the doctor with little choice but to stop the contest. Santana was duly declared the winner even though Haugen was ahead on two of the three score-cards. Armed with this information, Haugen's camp protested but it was not until the fighters were back in their dressing rooms that the result was reversed and poor Santana was informed that Haugen had retained his title after all.

Haugen was involved in another controversial contest with a Puerto Rican in February 1991 by which time he had moved up to be WBO light-welterweight champion. He defended his crown against Hector Camacho in Las Vegas in a bout where ill-feeling constantly simmered just below the surface. At the start of the twelfth and final round, referee Carlos Padilla attempted to bring the two men together for the traditional gentlemanly touching of gloves which marks the start of the last three minutes. But Haugen didn't want to know and refused when the conciliatory Camacho held out his hand. When the referee tried again and Haugen still played hard to get, Camacho lost his temper and aimed three punches at his opponent over the referee's shoulder. None of them connected but referee Padilla docked Camacho a point. That point was to cost Camacho the fight – his first defeat in twelve years and thirty-nine bouts.

Hands Were Too Big

Just about the unluckiest disqualification in boxing history was that of Sierra Leone lightweight John Coker before the 1966 Empire and Commonwealth Games in Kingston, Jamaica. His only crime was that his hands were too big to find any gloves to fit. He shopped high and low in Kingston but couldn't find a pair to accommodate his exceptionally long thumbs and so was disqualified before the competition for failing to be properly equipped.

The Confused Official

The first-round featherweight contest between Jamie Pagendam of Canada and Mongolia's Tserendorj Awarjargal at the 1988 Seoul Olympics provided a perfect little cameo of incompetence allied to sheer bad luck. In the second round of the fight, Pagendam felled his opponent three times which, under amateur rules, should have made him the automatic winner. However, referee Marius Guiramo Lougbo of the Ivory Coast lost count of the knockdowns and allowed the fight to continue. Then in the third round it was Pagendam's turn to hit the canvas whereupon referee Lougbo stopped the fight and declared Awarjargal the winner. The Canadian delegation launched an immediate protest and eventually the decision was overturned, making Pagendam the victor by virtue of his three second-round knockdowns. But Pagendam's luck really was out. Since the punch that felled him (which, remember, happened after the contest should have been stopped) was a blow to the head, the Canadian received a mandatory thirty-day medical suspension and wasn't allowed to compete again in the Games. Less surprisingly, referee Lougbo was also banned from further participation.

Iron Jaw

Nicknamed 'the Pride of Paris', French heavyweight Georges Carpentier was by no means an unfancied challenger when he took on Jack Dempsey for the world crown in Jersey City in July 1921. But Carpentier broke his thumb on the champion's iron jaw and, his punching power greatly reduced, was battered into submission in round four.

Knocked Out While Adjusting His Gum Shield

It was hardly worth Ralph Walton stepping into the ring to fight Al Couture at Lewiston, Maine, on 23 September 1946. For Walton was still adjusting his gum shield when Couture knocked him out cold. The fight officially ended after ten and a half seconds – and that included the ten-second count!

Pat Brownson didn't last much longer when he took on Mike Collins in a Golden Gloves bout for amateurs at Minneapolis on 4 November 1947. Collins floored Brownson with his very first punch, a blow struck with such force that the referee straight away realised there was no point in bothering to count. Instead he stopped the bout there and then which meant that it officially ended after just four seconds.

Counted Out by Cramp

Fighting Winfield Braithwaite of Guyana in the light-welterweight final at the 1978 Commonwealth Games, Scotland's Jimmy Douglas was holding his own until he was suddenly forced to his knees by an attack of cramp. Puzzled by the fact that his opponent had gone down without being hit, Braithwaite looked to the referee for guidance but he too appeared to be at a loss as to what to do. After a moment's hesitation, he started to count. As the count reached ten, Douglas's cramp went and he sprang to his feet, ready to continue. But he was fractionally too late. He had been counted out and had to settle for the silver medal.

Tricked Out of Title

There was no shortage of subterfuge in bare-knuckle bouts but rarely was it as calculated as in the Oscar-winning performance given by Arthur Chambers against another English-born fighter, Billy Edwards, back in 1872. The pair were contesting the world light-weight title at Squirrel Island, Canada, but it soon became apparent that Chambers had more than met his match. He was receiving the mother of all beatings until he managed to con the referee into awarding him the fight on a foul. Coming out for the start of the twenty-sixth round, Chambers began screaming that he had been bitten by Edwards. Referee Bill Tracy saw teeth marks on Chambers' face and duly declared him the winner. It was only afterwards that it emerged that the biting had been done deliberately by Chambers' second, Tom Allen, between the rounds in the knowledge that there was no way Chambers was going to win by legal means.

Referee Knocked Out

Refereeing a boxing match can be a hazardous occupation, as Joey Walker found out when officiating at a welterweight contest between Mike De Cosmo of the United States and Watford's Laurie Buxton at Newark, New Jersey, on 18 May 1948. Aiming a punch at De Cosmo's head, Buxton missed his intended target and instead landed a knockout blow squarely on the jaw of referee Walker. As officials rushed to his aid, Walker eventually got to his feet but was too dazed to continue. A substitute referee took over for the remainder of the ten-round contest and just to show there were no hard feelings, declared Buxton the winner on points. Reflecting on his experience, Walker lamented: 'I guess I can't take a punch like I used to.'

Winds of Change

The 1988 European bantamweight title fight between Billy Hardy of Britain and the reigning champion, Vincenzo Belcastro of Italy was scheduled to take place in a huge marquee erected in Belcastro's home town of Fuscaldo in Southern Italy. But gales wrecked the marquee, forcing the contest to be moved along the road to a sports hall in Paola. Instead of being able to house all of the spectators who wanted to cheer on the local boy, in the sports hall there was barely room to swing a decent length of spaghetti. It was so cramped that one writer observed: 'The only people seated comfortably were the fighters!' The claustrophobic conditions obviously suited Belcastro, who retained his title, albeit by a slender margin.

No Comeback for Lazarus

At the 1924 Paris Olympics, US bantamweight Joe Lazarus knocked out his opponent yet still lost. While Oscar Andren of Sweden was being revived, the referee announced that Lazarus had been disqualified for hitting during a clinch a few seconds before delivering the knockout punch. Swedish team officials were so embarrassed by the ruling that they even offered a rematch but the presiding Olympic committee wouldn't hear of it. Andren was the winner whether he liked it or not.

The Amazing Case of the Vanishing Referee

The bare-knuckle contest between Tom Sayers of London and

John C. Heenan of the United States which took place at Farnborough, Kent, on 17 April 1860 was a typically robust affair. After thirty-seven rounds of hard slog, Sayers was staring defeat in the face when one of his supporters tried to have the fight abandoned by cutting the ropes. After spectators and police officers had spilled into the ring, some form of order was restored. The only trouble was nobody could find the referee who was lost somewhere in the mêlée. Undeterred, the two men fought on for another five rounds without a referee, and when he was eventually found, he immediately declared the contest a draw. So basically Sayers and Heenan had spent 2hr 20min slugging it out for nothing.

Another disappearing referee was a Mr J. Jenn who was loosely in charge of the world heavyweight title fight between John Knifton and Tom Scrutton in London on 29 August 1877. When the spectators started brawling in the ninth round, the owner of the venue, fearing for his property, decided to turn out the gas lights and plunged the place into darkness. This action had the desired effect and peace eventually broke out among the crowd. The lighting returned with the intention that the fight should be resumed, only for it to become apparent that referee Jenn had gone home in the confusion.

Fighting a Losing Battle

If ever a boxer had reason to feel that the gods weren't on his side, it was South African heavyweight Gerrie Coetzee when he defended his WBA title against American Greg Page in Sun City in December 1984. Coetzee's troubles began at the start of the second round – all because his seconds were slow leaving the ring. The bell had just rung but Coetzee had turned to chat casually to his handlers and was only half standing as they removed the stool. While Coetzee's back was still turned, Page shot across the ring and landed a fierce blow to the head. Coetzee was knocked out of his stride by the unexpected attack. He was caught out again – this time illegally – at the end of the sixth. As the bell rang, Coetzee dropped his hands but Page went through with a punch and floored him. The referee warned the

American but took no further action. Coetzee managed to pull himself together but was finally undone by an eighth round which lasted way over the stipulated period owing to a malfunction of the electronic clock which timed the rounds. As the end of the three minutes approached, Coetzee was clearly in need of a rest but the bell didn't sound. Sensing that his opponent was faltering, Page launched a furious assault and felled Coetzee who was counted out at 3min 50sec. His team protested but to no avail. It just wasn't Gerrie Coetzee's night.

Desperate Dan Eats Humble Pie

Preparing for his bout in the New York Golden Gloves Championships in January 1992, Daniel Caruso was psyching himself up by pounding his gloves into his face prior to the introductions. Unfortunately he overdid it and scored a direct hit with one punch, breaking and bloodying his own nose. On examining him, doctors ruled that he was unfit to box.

Who's That Sleeping in My Corner?

The world middleweight title fight between the challenger, George Bernard of France, and Billy Papke in Paris on 4 December 1912 had an ending that can only be termed unusual. The climax wasn't a knockout, a stoppage or even a disqualification . . . but more of a nap. For between the sixth and seventh rounds, Bernard fell asleep in his corner and couldn't be roused in time to answer the bell. Thus Papke was declared the winner. Bernard was officially recorded as having retired but there were widespread claims that the fight had been fixed and Bernard himself stated that he had been drugged.

Stubborn Dong-kih

To put it mildly, Korean flyweight Choh Dong-kih was a mite

peeved at being disqualified for holding his head too low after 1min 6sec of the first round of his quarter-final bout against Stanislaw Sorokin of the Soviet Union at the 1964 Tokyo Olympics. Indeed the Korean flatly refused to accept the verdict and staged a sit-down protest in the middle of the ring. He stayed there for fifty-one minutes until officials finally persuaded him to move.

Miserable Début

There was a great deal of apprehension in the air when Harvey Gartley and Dennis Outlette squared up to each other for a regional heat of the Saginaw Golden Gloves Championships in Michigan in 1977. For both men, it was their first fight in public and they had been instructed to size each other up for a while and not on any account to throw caution to the wind. So it was that forty-seven seconds of the fight had passed and neither boxer had yet managed to land a punch. With the crowd growing restless, Gartley forgot all about the pre-fight orders and panicked. Suddenly without warning he launched a wild swing in the vague direction of his opponent, missed by a considerable distance, collapsed in a heap on the canvas and was counted out.

Dislocated Shoulder

Colin McMillan's first defence of his WBO featherweight title – against Colombia's Ruben Palacio in London in 1992 – ended in disappointment and controversy. McMillan was ahead on all three cards when the fight was stopped in round eight after he dislocated his shoulder. Although McMillan's corner argued that the dis-location had been caused by a foul and that the decision should have rested with the judges' scorecards, the referee gave the fight to Palacio.

Seoul Representative

For Eduard Paululum it should have been the ultimate honour. The bantamweight went to Seoul in 1988 as the first-ever Olympic competitor from the tiny Pacific island nation of Vanuatu. But so captivated was he by life in a foreign land that he tucked into a hearty breakfast before his first-round weigh-in and was disqualified for being 1lb overweight. He thus had to return home without having fought.

KO'd by a TV Cameraman

On 26 February 1993 Virgil Hill retained his WBA light-heavy-weight title when he won a bizarre technical decision against Adolpho Washington in Fargo, North Dakota. Washington had been troubled by a cut eye and in his corner before the twelfth and final round, he had it examined by the ringside physician. With Washington's corner man and manager also hovering anxiously, a TV cameraman tried to get a close-up of the action but as he moved in he merely succeeded in banging Washington's eye with the camera. As a result of the collision, the eye began bleeding profusely and poor Washington was unable to continue. It is not known whether he sued the TV company.

4 Motor Sport

Crashed at Same Spot Two Years Running

The treacherous Italian road race the Mille Miglia had a hazard at every turn but Giacomi Ragnoli seemed to have an aversion to one corner in particular. In the 1932 race he and his co-driver were heading south from Bologna on the road to Florence when their Fiat shot off the road on a difficult bend. It so happened that an ambulance was parked nearby but the services of the medical crew were superfluous on this occasion since Ragnoli and his colleague were unhurt. Instead they walked to the bar on the corner and downed several brandies to steady their nerves. The following year, mindful of what had happened before, Ragnoli approached the bend with extreme caution but out of the corner of his eye he caught a glimpse of the same ambulance. In that split second his concentration wavered sufficiently for him to crash again . . . in the identical spot. Once more unhurt, he and his co-driver walked back solemnly to the same bar where the owner was nonchalantly polishing the glasses. When he looked up, he exclaimed: 'What, you two again! Did you notice we moved the ambulance nearer the scene of the accident this year so that you would have less distance to walk if you had been injured?'

Brabham's Long Push

Jack Brabham was coasting to the 1959 Formula One World Drivers' Championship. He was leading the last race of the season – the United States Grand Prix at Sebring – with barely a mile to go when the usually reliable Cooper Climax suddenly started to run on only two cylinders. Then the engine went dead and the awful truth dawned on the Australian – he had run out of fuel. As Brabham coasted towards the second last corner, team-mate Bruce McLaren, who had been lying in second place, caught up. Seeing the stricken car, he slowed down to find out what the problem was, only to be waved away by Brabham who knew full well that any outside assistance would have resulted in his disqualification. The car finally came to a standstill about 500 yards from the finish and Brabham knew there was nothing for it but to get out and push. So he took off his helmet and goggles, clambered out of the cockpit and began easing the car slowly towards the line. To make matters worse, it was a sweltering day and the finish straight was uphill. Up at the finish, the spectators were puzzled by Brabham's non-appearance until in the distance someone spotted a figure in blue overalls hunched over the car, pushing it. As Brabham inched nearer, the crowd went wild. While motorcycle police tried to keep the spectators back, the man with the chequered flag waved it to encourage him. After five minutes that must have seemed like five hours, Brabham pushed the car across the line in fourth place and promptly slumped to the ground with exhaustion. But he had the satisfaction of knowing that the points he had earned had been sufficient to clinch the title.

Curiously, almost the same thing happened eleven years later. In his final year in Grand Prix racing, Brabham was leading the British Grand Prix at Brands Hatch when he again ran out of fuel on the last lap. His misfortune allowed Jochen Rindt to snatch an unexpected triumph.

An Off-the-Road Vehicle

Taking part in the Monte Carlo Rally in the late 1920s, French driver

Louis Chiron skidded into a ditch. After hours of hard work, he managed to get the car back on the road but was immediately shunted back into the same ditch by another competitor.

Went Home, Missed Race

Austrian driver Otto Stuppacher never quite managed to qualify for the starting grid of a Formula One Grand Prix despite some valiant attempts. He missed his best chance at Monza in 1976 when, having apparently failed to qualify in his Tyrrell, he left the circuit. However, James Hunt, Jochen Mass and John Watson had their times disallowed due to fuel irregularities, a development which would have allowed Stuppacher into the race. But by that time he was back home in Vienna . . .

More Haste, Less Speed

Driving a Sunbeam in the 1923 French Grand Prix, Albert Divo was in the lead when he came in for refuelling on lap 30. But in his haste to effect a fast pit-stop, he jammed the quick-release filler cap. He and his mechanic Moriceau wrestled furiously with the stubborn cap. At one point Moriceau took a hammer to it while Divo stood on the cap in an effort to hold the spring down. Then they tried a wrench, then a hacksaw, then a chisel . . . but still the cap refused to budge. This performance went on for eighteen minutes until Divo came up with the idea of using a small reserve tank which, although it meant having to stop each lap to take on more fuel, at least got him back in the race. However, the episode with the cap cost Divo any chance of victory and he had to settle for second place behind Henry Segrave.

Disqualified for Giving Wife a Lift

A few yards from the Lisbon finish of the 1969 Portuguese TAP Rally, British driver Tony Fall stopped his Lancia to wait for the correct time at the final control. As Fall was greeted by his wife, the crowd surged forward and the police asked him to drive on towards the control. He told his wife to 'hop in' while he moved the car the required ten metres, only to be disqualified for carrying an unauthorised passenger when crossing the finish line . . .

The Absent Pit Crew

Leading the 1998 Australian Grand Prix at Melbourne on lap 36, Mika Hakkinen was called in to the pits by his McLaren team for refuelling. However, as he drove along the pit lane, he discovered to his horror that they weren't ready for him and were waving him through. He had been called in too soon! So he carried on and rejoined the race, cursing the fact that the detour had cost him the lead. Hakkinen said afterwards: 'I had just come up behind Eddie Irvine when I heard some noises over the radio. I thought I had to come in and refuel. As I was level with the pit-lane entry, I dived in without having time to check with the radio. And when I drove past my pit there was no one there!' Hakkinen went in again four laps later for a proper refuelling stop and was able to win despite the pit-lane fiasco after his McLaren team-mate David Coulthard let him pass near the end in a prearranged move.

Victims of Sabotage

Swedish driver Bjorn Waldegaard was denied victory on the last night of the 1979 Monte Carlo Rally when he found the Villars stage blocked by rocks which had been put there by spectators. His co-driver got out of the car and managed to lever them away but the delay cost the Escort seventy-five seconds and the rally. Instead victory went to the Lancia Stratos of Frenchman Bernard Darniche by a mere six seconds.

Then on stage three of the 1994 Monte, event leader Armin Schwarz and second-placed Colin McRae both left the road after skidding on snow thrown by spectators. Schwarz ended up in seventh place overall with McRae tenth.

That was not the first time a human-assisted snowfall had played havoc with the result of the rally. On the final night of the 1968 event, Gerard Larrousse was vying for the lead in a works Renault Alpine until, when negotiating a tricky mountain section, he crashed into a huge pile of fresh snow shovelled into the road by drunken spectators.

Drunken US servicemen were held responsible for an accident at the 1968 German Grand Prix at the Nürburgring. They threw empty bottles on to the track, one of which punctured a tyre on Dan Gurney's Eagle car.

A Weighty Problem

In March 1995, less than two months after signing for McLaren, Nigel Mansell withdrew from the opening two races of that year's Formula One World Championship because the cockpit in the McLaren–Mercedes was too small to accommodate him. He was replaced by Mark Blundell who did fit.

Crashed into Dog

The 1912 French Grand Prix was run over two days at Dieppe and, by the second day, American driver David Bruce-Brown held a commanding eleven-second advantage over his rivals. However, his victory hopes were shattered when he collided with a stray dog and damaged the car's fuel tank. Dog and driver were in a similar position – both had lost their lead. Unable to make it round to the pits, Bruce-Brown was forced to resort to illicit wayside refuelling which resulted in his ultimate disqualification.

A dog also ruined the chances of Ferdinando Minova in the 1929 Mille Miglia. The collision damaged the front axle of Minova's Alfa Romeo and it had to be changed at one of the service areas. The lost time caused him to drop from a promising third to a distant sixth.

In 1964 a loose dog on the circuit during practice for the Mexican

Grand Prix caused Mike Spence to spin his Lotus. Indeed dogs became an unwelcome feature of the Mexican Grand Prix and in 1970 Jackie Stewart's Tyrrell was forced out of the race when his steering went following a collision with an errant hound.

But Swedish rally ace Erik Carlsson went one better than a dog during the 1963 East African Safari Rally. He was leading the event in his little Saab until he hit an anteater.

Post-Race Shunt

Having safely negotiated the whole of the 1962 French Grand Prix at Rouen, Trevor Taylor, driving a team Lotus, contrived to run into the back of a fellow competitor after the cars had crossed the finish line. Having finished seventh, one place ahead of Taylor, Maurice Trintignant's privately entered Lotus was stationary when Taylor smashed into it at 80mph, a collision which left the Yorkshireman covered in bruises from head to toe. Two races later, Taylor ploughed through a hedge at the German Grand Prix.

The Rally With Three Winners

The 1974 Austrian Alpine Rally ended in total confusion with no fewer than three drivers claiming outright victory. On the face of it, Achim Warmbold's BMW had the lowest number of penalty points – that is until the organisers disqualified him for having approached a control from the wrong direction. Warmbold argued that the control was in the wrong place and that anyway the Renault team manager had deliberately blocked the route at one point. With Warmbold's elimination, Bernard Darniche in a Renault Alpine was declared the winner, just one second ahead of Per Eklund in a Saab. However, Saab pointed out that the regulations stated that timing was to be to the whole second but that throughout the rally the organisers had announced the stage times to one-tenth of a second. If all of these tenths were ignored, said Saab, then Eklund would win by a second. These protests continued for over a month until everybody was so bewildered that the results were expunged and the rally was dropped from the calendar.

Crossed Finish Line Backwards

The 1919 Targa Florio road race in Sicily was won by André Boillot in a Peugeot despite going off the road on at least seven separate occasions. The last was when he contrived to crash into a grandstand just ten yards from the finish, spun violently and crossed the finish line backwards. Since this would have meant instant disqualification, the spluttering car was hauled round so that it faced the right way and was driven across the line again.

Robbed of Title by a Cheap Washer

The 1962 Formula One World Championship boiled down to the South African Grand Prix at East London where Jim Clark needed to beat Graham Hill to snatch the title. Clark looked set fair for victory as he built up a thirty-second lead by lap 50 but then he saw smoke billowing out from the rear end of the Lotus. All too aware that something was woefully amiss, he went into the pits and discovered that the problem was an oil leak resulting from the fact that a small bolt in the distributor shaft hadn't been held securely in place by a washer. The bolt had fallen out during the race. The offending washer cost no more than a few pence but it cost Clark the title as Hill swept past him to win.

Time Trial

Nearing the finish of the 1925 sidecar Tourist Trophy on the Isle of Man, George Grinton thought he had the race in the bag, particularly when a pit signal bearing the figure '3' convinced him that he was three minutes in front. Not wishing to take any unnecessary risks on the last lap, he slowed right down, only to discover that he was really only three seconds ahead. By the time he had regained full power, it was too late. Two rivals had flashed past him and he ended up a dejected third.

Schumacher's Despair

Even the world's greatest drivers are not immune from mechanical problems. In two successive races – the crucial Japanese Grand Prix at the end of 1998 and the first race of the 1999 season, the Australian Grand Prix – Michael Schumacher had to start from the back of the grid after stalling at the start of the formation lap.

Lap of Luxury

The 1951 RAC Rally was scheduled to finish at Silverstone where each driver would complete a given number of laps of the circuit according to the class of car. The trouble was that the entrance and exit to the track were only yards apart and, rather than leave the circuit at the 'exit' sign which came first, many drivers not unreasonably felt that they ought to press on and complete their final lap by crossing the line at the point where they had started. So many ended up doing an unnecessary extra lap. But the organisers had failed to take this confusion into account and consequently all those who drove on found themselves rewarded with much slower times.

Lost His Rag

Rudolf Caracciola in one of the all-conquering Mercedes slowed dramatically towards the end of the 1937 British Grand Prix at Donington and could finish only a disappointing third. After the race it was discovered that one of his mechanics had left an oily rag inside the supercharger.

Lead Kept Changing Hands

Few Grands Prix have seen such hectic climaxes as the 1982 Monaco race where, over the last two laps, the lead changed hands with bewildering regularity. Coming into that final phase, Alain Prost was leading in a Renault but then he crashed. Riccardo Patrese briefly took command in his Brabham before spinning on the damp track. This handed the lead to Didier Pironi's Ferrari but he too came to grief when an electrical fault saw the car drift to a standstill. Andrea de Cesaris now seemed the certain winner, only for his Alfa Romeo to run out of fuel. By now Patrese's Brabham had been pushed off the track by a marshal and that got it into a position from where it was able to roll downhill and coast across the line for an eventful victory.

The 1950 Monaco Grand Prix was equally dramatic. Giuseppe Farina in an Alfa Romeo spun on a pool of water which had broken over the sea wall and the car rebounded broadside across the track where it was rammed by Froilan Gonzalez's Maserati. This accident triggered off a multi-car pile-up which eliminated half the cars in the race.

Deprived at the Death

As the trend for long-distance rallies grew in the 1960s, one of the most spectacular tests of endurance was the London to Sydney marathon of 1968. With a lead of eleven minutes over his pursuers and only 100 miles to go, victory seemed certain for the Belgian Lucien Bianchi driving a Citroën. After his trans-continental ordeal, Bianchi was taking the opportunity to catch up with his sleep in the back of the car, allowing co-driver Jean-Claude Ogier to progress towards Sydney. But it all went horribly wrong when Ogier was involved in an accident with a non-competing car. The result was that Bianchi ended up on a hospital bed instead of the winners' rostrum as the honours went to a Hillman Hunter driven by Andrew Cowan, Brian Coyle and Colin Malkin.

Italian driver Giancarlo Baghetti departed the same rally in less dramatic circumstances. He was forced to retire when his passport and all of his other documents were stolen in Bombay.

Hit Safety Car

The McLaren driven by Spain's Emilio de Villota was forced to retire from the 1977 Austrian Grand Prix after it collided with the course car.

Grim Determination

On the eve of the 1933 Mille Miglia, an Alfa Romeo went up in flames after an electric spark had ignited petrol vapour. For some strange reason nobody bothered to inform the driver, Franco Cortese, of this development and so when he arrived four hours before the event was due to start, he found that his sleek racing machine was little more than a burnt-out shell. Somehow keeping his Latin temperament under control, Cortese remained calm and went about overseeing the rebuilding of the car. All went amazingly well until, with just an hour to go to the start, one of the mechanics accidentally poured a can of water into the fuel tank, a blunder which meant that the tank had to be dismantled and cleaned. The delay made Cortese late for the start and the lost time proved crucial since he eventually finished in second place.

Trapped in the Pits

Austria's Niki Lauda was leading the 1974 British Grand Prix in the closing stages when one of his tyres began to deflate. He managed to keep going, hoping that he could reach the finish before the tyre gave up on him completely, but by the penultimate lap the tyre had totally disintegrated and he was obliged to pull into the pits. With a fresh tyre, he duly accelerated away down the pit lane to rejoin the race, only to be stopped by an official with a red flag. With the race all but over, the spectators at Brands Hatch had already started crossing the road to watch the finish and so a course car had been placed to block the exit from the pit lane. So Lauda was trapped and unable to rejoin the race. However, on appeal he was reinstated into fifth position which was where he would have finished had he been permitted to return to the track.

A Real Ducking

On the Portuguese Rally of 1990 Louise Aitken-Walker's Opel Kadett aquaplaned off the road in a thunderstorm and plunged into a lake. She and her co-driver, Christina Thorner, escaped by kicking out the car's rear window and swimming to safety.

Piquet Piqued

On lap 19 of the 1982 German Grand Prix at Hockenheim, Brazil's Nelson Piquet led by a comfortable twenty-seven seconds as he came up to lap Chilean back-marker Eliseo Salazar at the new chicane. As Piquet's Brabham drew alongside Salazar's ATS on the entry to the chicane, both drivers applied their brakes but Salazar, who was on the inside line, didn't slow down in time with the result that the right front of his car hit Piquet's left rear wheel. The collision sent the Brabham into the tyre wall from where it rebounded across the track, finally coming to a halt on the other side of the circuit. There Piquet stalled it. In fury, the Brazilian leapt out of his car and stormed over to Salazar who had already vacated the crumpled ATS. In front of a disbelieving world television audience, Piquet proceeded to punch and kick the hapless Salazar over a period of several seconds before stalking away and flinging his gloves to the ground in one last act of petulance. The two men are not thought to have exchanged Christmas cards that year.

Practice Makes Imperfect

Putting in a spot of last-minute practice before the 1957 Mille Miglia, French daredevil Jean Behra drove his Maserati into a lorry. The car was wrecked and Behra finished up in hospital.

Wrecked Hotel Room to Repair Car

The 1902 Paris–Vienna road race was one of those crazy pioneering events in which Dick Dastardly and Muttley would not have looked out of place. Among the competitors was Charles Jarrott in a Panhard but his race appeared to be over as early as the second day when the car's wooden chassis collapsed approaching the overnight stop at Bregenz. A lesser man would have called it a day there and then but Jarrott, supported by his devoted mechanic, George Du Cros, reckoned that if he could somehow manage to strengthen the frame, at least he would be able to complete the next stage to Salzburg. The pair succeeded in locating a drill and some bolts but were still unable to lay their hands on four lengths of wood. And so it was that with little hope of going anywhere in the morning, the pair retired to their hotel beds in Bregenz.

Yet it was in the unlikely setting of the hotel room that Jarrott found his salvation. He later recounted: 'I was just getting into bed and had turned to put out the light when my eye fell upon a stand used for carrying a tray, and in a second I perceived that the four legs of that stand were exactly what I wanted.' Concluding that it was too late at night to ask the hotel management whether they would consider selling them the table, Jarrott and Du Cros decided instead to steal it and worry about the consequences later.

Their task was to drill four holes in each length of wood to accommodate the bolts . . . but more importantly to do so without waking the entire hotel. Since the wood was hard, Du Cros suggested that it might be an idea to drill against the wall in order to obtain greater power. 'He was delightfully successful,' recalled Jarrott, 'but the trouble was that he drove it through too far and brought down half the plaster. And then, in endeavouring to show how easy it was on another portion of the wall, he succeeded in bringing that down also.' One catastrophe was quickly followed by another as Jarrott accidentally bored a hole through his arm instead of the wood and the next half-hour was spent ripping up the bed sheets to bandage the wound. 'There was nothing in the room we did not utilise for something or other,' said Jarrott. 'I hate to think what must have been the expression on the proprietor's face when he discovered what had taken place.'

By smuggling the strips of wood out of the hotel down the legs of their trousers, the duo succeeded in repairing the vehicle and getting it back on the road. They reached Salzburg and pressed on towards Vienna although their journey was not without further incident. At one point Du Cros had to lie on the bonnet with a towel wrapped around the pipe just to keep the water in the radiator. Then, less than four miles from Vienna, disaster struck again when the gearbox of the Panhard broke. The intrepid Jarrott 'borrowed' a bicycle and pedalled off to find help. In his absence, Du Cros had acquired the services of a horse-drawn cab and Jarrott returned to the action to see the Panhard being towed to the finish behind the cab. Appalled at the indignity, Jarrott promptly cut the tow-rope, jumped behind the wheel and guided the belching monster erratically across the finish line, at which point it finally expired.

Pride Before a Fall

Australian Kevin Magee was delighted to have finished fourth in the 500cc United States Motor Cycle Grand Prix at Laguna Seca, California, in April 1989. But while waving to the crowds on his lap of honour, he fell off his machine and broke a leg.

Pit Stop Perils

Most of the sensations at the 1935 German Grand Prix at the Nürburgring took place in the pits. Rudolf Caracciola was leading in a Mercedes until he called in for refuelling at the end of lap 10.

Hoping for a quick stop, he could only look on in anguish as the pumping device broke, forcing the crew to insert the carburant by hand. He eventually rejoined the race in sixth place, a position from which he never recovered.

Then on the following lap the new leader, Tazio Nuvolari, brought in his Ferrari Alfa Romeo for refuelling and a wheel change. But here too the gremlins struck when the handle of the fuel-pressure pump was broken by an over-enthusiastic mechanic so that the car had to be filled laboriously from a succession of churns. The excitable Nuvolari was hopping around impatiently as the seconds ticked by. Finally after a pit stop of 2min 14sec – a minute and a half slower than the norm at the time – he returned to the track back in fifth. But whereas Caracciola was unable to make up the lost ground, Nuvolari drove what many consider to be the race of his life to battle through and defeat the combined German might of the Mercedes and Auto Unions although it has to be said that he was assisted by the misfortune of Manfred von Brauchitsch whose Mercedes suffered a burst tyre on the final lap when thirty-five seconds ahead of Nuvolari.

Doctor Loses Patience

A total of 351 drivers entered the 1956 Monte Carlo Rally, seventy-three of whom started from Glasgow. But for one – Dr Alex Mitchell – it was to be a short journey as he had only gone 200 yards down the road before ploughing into a Glasgow Corporation bus. Six years later the unlucky doctor again failed to get out of Britain on the Monte when he crashed south of Scotch Corner.

Evasive Action

Shortly after the start of the 1954 Mille Miglia, Giuseppe Farina crashed his Ferrari into a tree while trying to avoid a spectator who had run on to the road. Farina suffered a broken arm and was out of racing for two months.

Uncomfortable Début

Nigel Mansell's Grand Prix début was at Austria in 1980 at the wheel of a Lotus but it was to prove a painful experience. While filling the car on the starting grid, mechanics accidentally spilt some fuel on to the seat. Although the crew poured water over the seat and over Mansell, the fuel began to burn through his overalls. He refused to back out of the race but by the time he had retired on lap 42, he had sustained third-degree burns and could barely walk.

Precarious Perch

On the 1000 Lakes Rally in Finland in 1990, throttle cable failure resulted in Juha Kankkunen having to get out and sit on the windscreen of his Lancia Delta with his legs and arm under the bonnet while Juha Pironen drove. Although the latter's view of the road ahead was severely restricted by his colleague's body, the pair only lost five minutes on a twenty-kilometre stage.

Visor Fell Apart

Having taken pole position in his Matra for the 1971 Italian Grand Prix at Monza, New Zealander Chris Amon carried on the good work in the race itself. He was in the lead on lap 48 until he tried to tear off one of the two visors on his helmet to improve his vision. However, instead of just one visor being removed, the whole lot came adrift. Within seconds, five cars had passed Amon who dropped back to finish sixth.

Fears Were Groundless

Among the entrants for the 1932 Mille Miglia were Tazio Nuvolari and his co-driver Gianbattista Guidotti in a Ferrari Alfa Romeo. When Nuvolari crashed into a tree outside Florence, Guidotti finished up lying unconscious in the road. On coming round, Guidotti could see no sign of Nuvolari but found himself on a stretcher flanked by four sinister figures wearing long flowing cloaks and hoods. Afraid that he was being kidnapped by a local branch of the Ku Klux Klan, Guidotti shut his eyes and pretended to be dead. Happily his stretcher-bearers turned out to be a local order of monks who traditionally helped the injured at the Mille Miglia and were taking him to the monastery hospital for treatment.

Expensive Exercise

Bobby Unser is a legend in IndyCar racing but his attempts to break into Formula One were markedly less successful. Unser, who won the Indianapolis 500 on three occasions –1968, 1975 and 1981– tried his luck at Formula One with BRM in 1968 but proved an expensive flop. First, he was due to race in the Italian Grand Prix at Monza but had to pull out because it clashed with a prior commitment in the United States. Then on home soil at Watkins Glen, he crashed the car in practice and also blew a couple of engines for good measure. Taking a different car for the race itself, he retired with engine failure. It was his only drive.

High Casualty Rates

New events invariably get off to tricky starts as drivers struggle to adjust to the requirements of the competition. For the inaugural London to Brighton run in 1896, it was also a case of getting used to the newfangled machinery, so it came as no surprise that only fourteen of the thirty entrants actually made it to the south coast by road. En route, a Bollée tricycle careered through a hedge and had to be towed out by a cart while another machine overturned and landed its occupants in a pond. Other vehicles which broke down were loaded on to the train at Brixton and reached Brighton courtesy of the railway.

It was a similar story for the first RAC Rally in 1932. One driver fell asleep at the wheel and smashed into a telegraph pole near Exeter while the car driven by a Miss R. H. Grimley collided with a horse and overturned just eight miles from her starting point at Leamington Spa.

Misleading Information

In the course of the final hour of the 1935 Le Mans 24-Hour Race, the Alfa Romeo driven by René-Louis Dreyfus gained relentlessly on the leading car, the Lagonda of John Hindmarsh and Louis Fontes. The Lagonda was in a pretty desperate state and had been forced to make several unscheduled stops owing to fading oil pressure so when Dreyfus was told by his pit team that he had finally passed the Lagonda, it came as no surprise. With the race seemingly in his pocket, Dreyfus decided to slow right down, safe in the knowledge that nothing could catch him. He treated the last few minutes leading up to the finish time of 4 p.m. on the Sunday like any other leisurely Sunday afternoon drive and crossed the line fully expecting to be proclaimed the winner. Therefore it came as something of a shock to learn that his pit crew had got it wrong. He hadn't overtaken the Lagonda at all and was still five minutes behind.

Careless Driving

Italian Formula One driver Andrea de Cesaris was fined £3,300 after he caused two accidents and knocked down a policeman on the way to practise for the 1983 German Grand Prix.

Hit Lions' Feeding Trough

When the organisers of the 1980 RAC Rally decided to include a stage at Longleat Safari Park, the drivers knew that at the speeds they would be travelling, even the most daredevil baboon wouldn't attempt to rip off their car aerials. But there were other hazards, not least of which were the lions' feeding troughs. To cope with wear and tear from the big cats, these troughs were made of stout metal and thus represented formidable adversaries to the front end of a speeding car. The first to discover this was rally favourite Tony Pond in a Triumph TR7. When he ploughed into one of the troughs, the impact smashed his windscreen and damaged the nose of the car. The three minutes which he lost on that stage put him out of contention for that year's rally.

Pond was again among the favourites for the 1984 event. The *Daily Mirror* recognised this and sponsored him in the hope that he would be able to provide the paper with a wealth of gripping stories over the ensuing five days. Unfortunately he was only able to file one story and that was somewhat sooner than the paper had anticipated. For, just two miles into the very first stage, at Knowsley Safari Park, he crashed into a tree, destroyed the front of his Rover and was out of the rally. In future Pond probably made a mental note to steer clear of safari parks.

Courageous Victory

The 1921 French Grand Prix at Le Mans got off to an inauspicious start for Irish-American driver Jimmy Murphy when he crashed his Duesenberg in practice and broke three ribs. Heavily bandaged, he insisted on taking part in the race and somehow won despite finishing with two flat tyres and a hole in the radiator. After taking the chequered flag, his physical state was such that he had to be lifted out of his seat. Murphy was certainly not the only driver to suffer during the race – Henry Segrave driving a Talbot-Darracq had no fewer than fourteen punctures.

Marshals Pushed Car Over Driver's Foot

Track marshals are supposed to be there to help the drivers but in the case of René Arnoux they ended up doing more harm than good.

Arnoux was in the middle of a qualifying session for the 1983 South African Grand Prix at Kyalami when his Ferrari stopped out on the circuit with an electrical fault. He persuaded the marshals to push the car to a safer place but in doing so, they pushed the car over his foot, leaving it badly swollen for the race.

Crew Member Was Left Behind

Every second counts in rallying and when he went off the road in his Rover 3-litre on the Chartreuse special stage of the 1963 Monte Carlo Rally, Raymond Joss was in no mood to hang about. Two of his crew of three jumped out to push him back on the road but such was the haste to make up for lost time that as soon as he was free he sped off . . . even before one of his crew had been able to get back in the car. As Joss roared off into the distance, the abandoned crew member consoled himself by spending the night drinking wine with the locals in a bakery and watching the other rally competitors flash by. And he had the satisfaction of enjoying the last laugh. For Joss's impetuousness backfired on him as, when the car reached Monte Carlo, he was disqualified for not having a full crew aboard.

Forgot to Check In

The name of Perry McCarthy doesn't figure too prominently in many histories of Formula One. This is perhaps hardly surprising since, although the British racing enthusiast entered eight Grands Prix in his Moda in 1992, he failed to qualify in seven and was excluded from the German Grand Prix at Hockenheim for missing the car weight check.

Swerved to Avoid Paper Boy

On the 1955 Mille Miglia just as Scottish driver Ron Flockhart was taking a tight corner in his Austin Healey so an Italian boy threw a ball of tightly rolled newspaper into the road. Flockhart instinctively swerved to avoid it and in doing so, smashed through the stone parapet of a bridge. The car came to rest on the river bed below and an angry Flockhart emerged covered from head to toe in thick black mud. The boy wisely made himself scarce.

Flockhart had another race he would rather forget in the 1959 French Grand Prix at Reims. After a stone from the circuit smashed his goggles, he drove on with the use of virtually only one eye and with a badly cut face. Nevertheless he still managed to guide the BRM to a highly creditable sixth.

Mansell Robbed by Exploding Tyre

Nigel Mansell went into the final race of the 1986 Formula One season – the Australian Grand Prix at Adelaide – needing only to finish in the first three to ensure that he could not be overhauled by his two chief rivals, his Williams team-mate Nelson Piquet and Alain Prost in a McLaren. With two-thirds of the race gone, everything was going according to plan. Mansell was lying in a comfortable third place behind race leader Keke Rosberg and was in sight of that first world title. But there was drama behind the scenes. Prost had suffered a puncture as early as lap 32, as a result of which worried Goodyear technicians had examined the Frenchman's remaining tyres. They came to the conclusion that the tyres would last the race. However on lap 63 leader Rosberg also had a puncture. Suddenly Goodyear realised that their tyres wouldn't last the distance after all and informed the Williams team so that they could bring in Mansell and Piquet. But for Mansell it was too late. Travelling at 200mph on the long straight, his left-hand rear tyre exploded, putting him out of the race. Prost went on to win and took the title by two points from Mansell who was left to reflect on a mishap in the previous race, the Mexican Grand Prix. On that occasion, Mansell had failed to put the car into gear on the grid with the result that he was last away and could only finish fifth. Those lost points cost him dear.

Bridge of Sighs

The 1907 Peking to Paris Race was the ultimate test of endurance with the drivers crossing some of the most inhospitable landscape on the globe. The event was won by Italian nobleman Prince Scipione Borghese and his co-driver Luigi Barzini in an Itala. Their winning time of two months was not achieved without incident. In Siberia the vehicle proved too heavy for a rickety wooden bridge and plunged into a ravine from where it was winched back on to the road by a gang of Siberian railway workers while the prince looked on anxiously. Then in Mongolia the car was sinking fast in a pool of deep slime until it was pulled clear by local tribesmen and their oxen. After surviving such ordeals, the winning car was naturally in great demand. It was paraded at the 1908 Olympia Motor Show but met an untimely end when, en route to being shipped to New York for another exhibition, it rolled into the harbour at Genoa. Although eventually salvaged, the car was damaged beyond repair. It thus went down in history as the only car to survive a 10,000-mile rally but not the subsequent exhibition.

Fangio's Fury

The legendary Juan Manuel Fangio lost any chance of success in the 1951 Belgian Grand Prix because his Alfa Romeo pit team were unable to remove one of the car's rear wheels. What should have been a routine tyre change turned into a nightmare as the crew struggled to lever off the wheel. As the minutes ebbed by, they eventually resorted to having to change the tyre on the rim. It was fourteen minutes before Fangio was able to rejoin the race and, despite doing the fastest lap, the best finish he could manage was a lowly ninth. Fangio later described the pit blunder as 'the most stupid of incidents'.

Crunch Corner

One particular corner in northern Greece claimed more than its fair share of victims during the 1963 Acropolis Rally. Erik Carlsson went off the road and suffered a broken front suspension; fellow Saab driver Olle Dahl overturned, and shortly afterwards the same thing happened to an Alfa Romeo; Bertil Soderström's Volvo hit a donkey and a Citröen plunged 100 feet off the side of the road, landing drivers Bob Neyret and Jacques Terramorsi in hospital. Even the eventual winner, Eugen Böhringer, went off at the same corner in his Mercedes but he managed to rejoin the road 100 yards further on.

Decision Reversed

Calling in to the pits during the 1983 German Grand Prix at Hockenheim, Niki Lauda overshot the McLaren pit and had to reverse to reach the crew. He went on to finish fifth but was subsequently disqualified for reversing in the pit lane, the rules stating that cars may only be pushed backwards in that area.

Gilles Villeneuve's Ferrari was disqualified from the 1981 United States Grand Prix in Las Vegas for starting from the wrong grid position. Villeneuve was third on the grid but lined up his Ferrari too far to the left of his starting box after completing the pace lap. Following lengthy consultation, the stewards told the Ferrari team part-way through the race that Villeneuve had been disqualified. Just as Ferrari were debating whether to call him in or lodge a post-race appeal, Villeneuve resolved the dilemma by pulling off the track with the car on fire.

Chain Reaction

When taking part in such incident-packed competitions as the Mille Miglia, the drivers tended to look out for colleagues in distress. But the exercise proved costly for Tazio Nuvolari in the 1932 race. After Pietro Ghersi and Giulio Ramponi had crashed in the mountain section, Nuvolari, who was following on behind, momentarily took his eyes off the road as he passed the stricken vehicle to check that Ghersi and Ramponi were all right. The brief lapse in concentration caused Nuvolari to crash too, sustaining a broken nose.

Digital Watch

Just about the most dangerous place to be at the old Brooklands circuit near Weybridge was in the trackside timing box which was situated perilously close to the infamous banking. In 1922 Count Louis Zborowski's Mercedes-based monster nicknamed Chitty I blew a tyre on the banking, hit the parapet, spun violently in circles and careered backwards through the timing box, removing several of the timekeeper's fingers as he dived for safety. The incident did not bring about any obvious safety improvements, however, and the timekeeper's reprieve proved a temporary one when he was tragically killed a few years later by a motorcycle that dived over the Brooklands banking.

Race Officials Booed

Before the 1953 French Grand Prix at Reims, the organisers staged a twelve-hour sports car race which ran through the hours of darkness. The leading contender was a 4½ litre V12 Ferrari driven by Umberto Maglioli and Piero Carini which had set up a new sports car lap record for the circuit. But as dawn approached, the car was spotted running without side-lights before the permitted time for switching off. Although Ferrari protested that other drivers had also switched off their lights, the organisers singled out that particular car for punishment and announced that no further times would be taken for it. The car did a few more laps before the team decided that it was pointless to continue and it was called in and withdrawn from the race. The decision was so unpopular that even the French crowd, not normally noted for their support of foreign teams, booed the race officials.

Crashed After Finish

Having won the Monte Carlo Rally in 1968, Britain's Vic Elford was quietly confident of a repeat performance the following year. However, his hopes were dashed when he crashed into a tree *after* crossing the finishing line at the end of a stage.

Diplomatic Disaster

With one race to go in the 1961 World Motorcycling 125cc Championship, German Ernst Degner held a two-point lead. The final race of the season was the Argentine Grand Prix but the luckless Degner was not allowed to take part. While out of his native country, Degner had seized the opportunity to seek political asylum in Argentina, thereby causing something of a diplomatic furore. As politicians and diplomats from Europe and South America continued to debate his defection, it was decided to suspend his racing licence. With Degner unable to race, the title went by default to Australian rider Tom Phillis.

Stuck in Tramlines

One of the most bizarre moments in Formula One took place during the 1960 Portuguese Grand Prix at Oporto, a street circuit more accustomed to the presence of trams than Coopers and Ferraris. On lap 2 Jack Brabham was lying in second place in his Cooper approaching a sharp left-hand hairpin. Moving up on the inside to overtake as he went into the corner, Brabham was horrified to find that his car was stuck on the tramlines and while he wanted to turn left, the tramlines went straight on. Unable to stop, all sorts of thoughts flashed through his mind, first and foremost that he would have to stay in the tramlines all the way to the depot . . . wherever that was. Fortunately it didn't come to that. Finally Brabham did manage to slow down and extricate the car from the tramlines before turning round and heading back for the circuit. The detour saw him drop from second to eighth but, in typically determined fashion, he recovered to win the race en route to a second successive world title.

Rat Droppings in Tank

Driving an old Bugatti in the 1945 Bois de Boulogne Race, France's Maurice Trintignant had to retire when the car succumbed to fuel starvation. Examining the car afterwards, he found the cause to be an accumulation of rat droppings at the bottom of the fuel tank. It seemed that while the Bugatti had sat idle during the war, the fuel tank had become home to several generations of rodents. Thereafter Trintignant was affectionately known as 'petoulet' meaning 'rat dropping'.

Size Is Everything

It is not uncommon for cars to be excluded from rallies because their exhausts are too large but Peter Harper's Sunbeam Tiger was disqualified from the Coupe des Alpes in 1966 for having an exhaust that was too small. Harper had good reason to feel hard done by since the small exhaust could not possibly have given him any advantage and he was actually leading the GT category at the time.

Missed the Pit-Board

At the Australian Grand Prix of 1997 Jean Alesi was lying in second place on lap 35 when he ran out of fuel. He hadn't seen the pit-board hung out by the Benetton team, telling him to come in and refuel. 'Once again, I'm going to be taken for an idiot,' he declared solemnly.

Checked in Too Early

On the 1985 Monte Carlo Rally Ari Vatanen's co-driver made the elementary mistake of checking in at a time control four minutes early, thus earning Vatanen a colossal eight-minute penalty. Remarkably Vatanen's Peugeot made up the lost ground and stormed to victory.

Cramped His Style

Of all the ailments or accidents that can cause the downfall of a Formula One driver, one of the most unusual is a sudden attack of cramp. Yet that is exactly what forced Italian driver Paolo Barilla to retire from the 1990 United States Grand Prix at Phoenix. The mishap, in only his second Grand Prix, did little to enhance his reputation and after a string of disappointing results he was replaced in the Minardi team by Gianni Morbidelli before the season was out.

Bedazzled

Alberto Ascari's adventure in the 1951 Mille Miglia lasted just fifteen minutes. In the early hours of the morning Ascari was hurtling along the roads of Italy when an enthusiastic spectator shone a light on his car in order to read the race number. Dazzled by the light, Ascari failed to spot a patch of oil on the road and crashed out of the race. He was so infuriated by the incident that he refused to enter the event the following year.

In common with many of his nationality, the Italian had a history of spectacular crashes, the best known being his plunge into the harbour at the 1955 Monaco Grand Prix after he had lost control of his Lancia. The car locked a brake on the approach to the chicane, burst through a line of straw bales and somersaulted into the harbour. Although he quickly bobbed to the surface and escaped from the ducking with minor facial injuries, Ascari was less fortunate four days later when he crashed again, at Monza – this time fatally.

A Freak Accident

Of all the tragic accidents which have blighted the history of motor racing, the one which ended the life of Tom Pryce was surely the most freakish. The young Welshman was driving a Shadow in the 1977 South African Grand Prix at Kyalami and was well down the field on lap 21 when his team-mate, Renzo Zorzi, stopped just beyond the pits with engine failure. Zorzi's fuel line had come adrift and the fuel had started to catch fire. It was nothing serious but two marshals thought otherwise and raced across the track just as four cars – headed by Hans-Joachim Stuck and Pryce – approached at 150mph. Pryce had no chance of avoiding one of the marshals and in the collision the marshal's fire extinguisher hit Pryce and sent his car careering out of control and into a fatal crash.

Scotland for the Brave

So bad was the weather in Scotland during the 1971 RAC Rally that only the hardiest competitors survived. Heavy snow caused chaos with cars having to turn back because roads were blocked and special stages having to be cancelled. The resultant tail-backs were more reminiscent of the M25 than Highland byways. When the traffic did move, it was in both directions, which created further problems. Cars turning back from a cancelled stage would meet cars on their way to the same stage because, even though it was obvious that the stage was not being run, competitors still had to obtain the relevant marshal's signature. So with cars travelling in opposite directions along narrow roads – all in a tearing hurry – collisions were inevitable and among the casualties was Billy Coleman's Alpine which was written off after being hit near Pitlochry by Seppo Utrainen's Saab coming the other way. Even those who made it to the finish of the rally couldn't quite free themselves of the legacy of the Scottish climate. Dave Thompson thought he had survived the worst until the rear axle on his Vauxhall Viva seized in the closing stages of the rally. Determined to complete it, he managed to locate the Vauxhall service crew who changed the entire axle, thereby allowing him to finish. But on reaching the finish, he was informed that he had been disqualified for being late in Scotland three days previously. He was not a happy bunny.

Ill Feeling

In the high-octane world of Formula One, team-mates aren't necessarily paid to like each other. There was certainly no love lost between Frenchman Erik Comas and his 1992 partner at Ligier, Belgian Thierry Boutsen. The two were barely on speaking terms for much of the season, their relationship not improved by two unfortunate comings-together. The pair first crashed in the Brazilian Grand Prix at Interlagos and in the process took out Johnny Herbert's Lotus. Later that year at the Hungarian Grand Prix, Comas and Boutsen collided again, this time on the very first lap. Another car was also forced to retire after spinning off while avoiding them – Johnny Herbert's Lotus.

Drove Wrong Way

Close behind leader Emilio Materassi's Bugatti with nine laps to go in the 1927 Spanish Grand Prix at San Sebastian, Robert Benoist in a Delage had to take swift evasive action when Materassi crashed into a wall. Going into a full-scale spin, Benoist missed Materassi's car by a matter of inches. Disorientated by the spin, Benoist was so confused when the car finally came to a halt that he restarted facing the wrong direction. Fortunately he quickly realised his error, turned round and went on to win.

Partial Visibility

Towards the end of the 1967 1000 Lakes Rally, Finnish driver Timo Makinen became worried when his Mini Cooper showed signs of overheating. So he decided to drive with the bonnet slightly open and secured in place by a leather strap. But along the bumpy roads of Finland the strap broke and the bonnet flew up obliterating all but a tiny section of windscreen vision. Makinen knew there was no time to stop and, by slackening his seat belt, he was able to crane his neck around the raised bonnet and keep the car going at full speed. It was a hair-raising end to the rally but it proved worthwhile as he emerged victorious by eight seconds. If he had stopped to close the bonnet, he would have lost.

Rammed a Sheep

The idea of motor racing at Silverstone was conceived by an enthusiast by the name of Maurice Geoghegan who lived in the Northamptonshire village and saw the possibilities of staging events at the nearby disused airfield. The first race there took place in September 1947 but Geoghegan's participation ended early on when his Frazer Nash car was in collision with a hefty, slow-moving sheep which chose an inadvisable moment to cross the circuit. From then on, the race became known as the Mutton Grand Prix.

Second Time Unlucky

In 1996, at the first corner on the opening lap of the first Australian Grand Prix to be held at Albert Park, Melbourne, Martin Brundle cartwheeled out of the race after being involved in a collision with two other cars. Unhurt, he took the spare car for the restart and promptly spun off at the same corner.

Time to Give Up

Veteran French driver Eugène Chaboud was repeatedly denied in his attempts to win a post-war Le Mans 24-Hour Race. He had triumphed in the race in 1938 and looked set for a repeat performance in 1949 but, when something like nine miles ahead of his nearest rival, he had to retire after his car caught fire. Three years later he was going well in sixth place with less than two hours to go when he crashed. While lying under the overturned Talbot waiting to be pulled out, he had ample opportunity to decide that it was time to give up motor racing.

Arrested as Spies

The crew of an Italian Züst car taking part in the epic 1908 New York to Paris Race had to overcome two major headaches to achieve their goal. First the vehicle's crankshaft bearing went and they were forced to improvise a new one from a cough-sweet tin, mud, wood and bullets. Potentially even more serious was the delay at Omsk in Russia where the crew were seized as spies because they had tried to send a cable in Italian. Against all the odds, the car eventually completed the course but, with echoes of the Itala which perished on its way to an exhibition after the previous year's Peking–Paris event, the Züst too suffered a fatal post-race mishap. For having arrived in Paris, it was transported to England, only to be destroyed by a fire in a railway station.

First-Lap Chaos

Coming out of Woodcote at the end of the first lap in the 1973 British Grand Prix at Silverstone, Jody Scheckter's McLaren slid wide on the grass and spun across the track to crash into the pit wall. The accident caused a multi-car pile-up which wiped out a good proportion of the field. There was a delay of an hour before the race could be restarted.

For sheer drama however, it was no match for the 1998 Belgian Grand Prix at Spa. Jacques Villeneuve had already experienced a hairy crash in Friday practice – which he described as 'the best accident of my F1 career' – but the real fireworks were saved for race day itself. The race didn't get much beyond the first corner – La Source hairpin – when David Coulthard and Eddie Irvine touched, causing the Scot to slew across the track and eliminate no fewer than thirteen of the field. The race was restarted but with only eighteen cars on the grid. At the second start, Coulthard's McLaren team-mate, championship leader Mika Hakkinen, clipped Michael Schumacher's Ferrari and slid along the track before being hit by Johnny Herbert's Sauber. Both Hakkinen and Herbert were eliminated. The safety car came out for one lap while Hakkinen's car was towed away. But there was more to come. On lap 25, Schumacher, holding a thirty-seven-second lead and looking certain to pick up the ten points which would enable him to overhaul Hakkinen, slammed into the back of Coulthard's McLaren as Coulthard slowed to let the German lap him. And on the following lap Giancarlo Fisichella failed to see Shinji Nakano's Minardi through the rain and spray and ran straight into the back of it. Once again the safety car came out while the remains of Fisichella's Benetton were cleared from the track. When the safety car finally went in, there were just twelve laps remaining and Damon Hill held on to give the Jordan team its first Grand Prix win in 126 attempts.

Hung Out of Window

Winner of the Mille Miglia in 1930 and 1933, Tazio Nuvolari had a truly uncomfortable drive in the 1947 race. At the wheel of a Cisitalia, Nuvolari was so badly affected by the car's exhaust fumes that he found himself constantly short of breath and coughing blood. In a bid to combat this, he drove with his head out of the window so that he could breathe in some fresh air. At one point the usually irrepressible Italian had been so distressed that he had dropped down to eleventh but the fresh-air remedy enabled him to recover to finish second.

Goggle-Hitch Hits Hill

Graham Hill went into the 1964 Mexican Grand Prix – the last race of the year – knowing that he needed to finish third or higher to have any chance of winning the world championship. Qualifying had been a disappointment and he could get the BRM no higher than sixth on the grid, but worse was to come in the seconds before the start. As Hill pulled his goggles down, the elastic gave way and they fell over his face. In desperation he tried to find a way of getting them to stay on. 'I began fiddling with the elastic,' he recalled, 'but as I had my gloves on it was a bit difficult to work the tiny adjustment catch. While I was doing all this the starter dropped the flag. I lost four places . . .' Hill managed to fight his way back up through the field but two unscheduled pit stops dropped him to eleventh at the finish and he lost out on the title to John Surtees by a solitary point. Who knows what the story might have been but for those wretched goggles?

Something of an Anti-Climax

The 1970 London to Mexico Rally was launched with a great deal of pomp and ceremony. It was to be a colossal sporting occasion to mark the start of the decade and to tie in with the England football team's defence of the World Cup in Mexico. The organisers even recruited the services of the usually publicity-shy England manager Sir Alf Ramsey to start the cars off from Wembley Stadium on their tortuous 16,000-mile endurance test which would see the survivors arrive in Mexico City in time for the World Cup finals. With the cars tuned to perfection by the nation's leading mechanics, Sir Alf duly waved the first starter away anticipating a mighty roar of the engine and for the vehicle to disappear into the distance in seconds amidst a cloud of dust and smoke as it embarked on its journey to the other side of the world. Instead it spluttered off in a series of kangaroo hops and finally broke down after just 100 yards.

Hit in Face by Bird

Reigning World Formula One champion Jim Clark had to miss the 1966 French Grand Prix at Reims after being hit in the left eye by a bird during practice. Clark lived to fight another day but five years earlier, another Lotus driver, Alan Stacey, had been less fortunate. A bird flew into Stacey's face while he was travelling at around 140mph during the Belgian Grand Prix at Spa. He lost control of the car and was killed.

More of a Hindrance Than a Help

Riding in his first Isle of Man TT, the 1922 junior race, Ireland's Stanley Woods called in to the pits for refuelling but decided to keep the engine running in a bid to save valuable seconds. As Woods roared in, an enthusiastic helper materialised with a two-gallon churn of petrol and a huge funnel. Alas the mystery assistant was a shade too enthusiastic and clearly knew little of the basics of motorcycling – or indeed physics – for he proceeded to try to pour in the whole two gallons in one go with the result that fuel spilt all over Woods and the machine. With the engine still running, Woods burst into flames and had to jump off the bike and roll around on the ground in an effort to douse the fire. He was eventually saved by a spectator who threw a coat over him. Remarkably Woods recovered from this drama and was able to continue and finish a respectable fifth. He went on to win ten TTs between 1923 and 1939 but only because he learned to be more choosy about his mechanics.

Mansell Misery

Comfortably ahead in the 1991 Portuguese Grand Prix at Estoril, Nigel Mansell brought the Williams in for what should have been a straightforward tyre change. Instead it ended his race. The problems were caused by one of the wheel nuts cross-threading. As the mechanics used the pneumatic gun to wrench it off and replace it, the signaller at the front of the car wrongly assumed that the gun was coming out and that the wheel was safely on. Accordingly, Mansell was waved away but as he drove off down the pit lane, the wheel came off completely, leaving Mansell beating his fists against the cockpit in frustration. The team rushed to re-fit the wheel and Mansell rejoined the race but he was subsequently black flagged and disqualified because his car had been worked on outside its pit area.

Police Misinformant

It is a widely acknowledged fact that if you want to know the time or the way, ask a policeman. So when Rauno Aaltonen and Tony Ambrose approached a junction near Bonneville on the 1965 Alpine Rally at which they had turned right on the pre-rally reconnaissance but where a helpful gendarme was now telling them to go left, they followed the advice of the man in uniform. It was their misfortune to have stumbled across a distant relative of Inspector Clouseau because, on following his directions, they became temporarily lost. Fortunately they realised his incompetence fairly swiftly and were soon able to regain the correct path, but the minute they lost in doing so was enough to deprive them of any chance of victory.

No Way to Treat the Boss

Mika Hakkinen drove from the McLaren garage out to the starting grid for the 1999 Australian Grand Prix at Melbourne, unaware that the air-line was still attached to the car. This had the effect of pulling down a gantry on to the head of team boss Ron Dennis.

5 Golf

Trial by Television

Playing in the 1987 San Diego Open at Torrey Pines, Craig Stadler hit a wayward shot which ended up underneath a bush. Such was the lie of the ball that the only way Stadler could contemplate playing it was to kneel down on the ground. Anxious not to get his trousers dirty, he therefore knelt on a towel which his caddie used to clean balls and thought nothing more of it. But viewers who had witnessed the incident on television knew something that Stadler didn't – that the use of the towel constituted building a stance, a deed contrary to the rules of golf. And the next day they phoned in and 'shopped' him with the result that Stadler was disqualified for not having included the penalty in the score which he had signed for the previous day. To compound his misery, he would have finished joint second . . . if he had been prepared to get his trousers dirty.

Tom Watson was another to be penalised following a complaint from a viewer after a TV microphone had picked up his conversation. Watson was playing in a tournament with Lee Trevino and the pair were chatting as they walked from the green to the next tee. Watson was telling Trevino how to cure a fault in his game. The presence of the microphone meant that this conversation was overheard and a zealous viewer – only the one, mind – phoned in to say that Watson was in breach of the rules because he had been dispensing advice. The complaint was duly upheld and Watson was penalised.

Injury Prone

Australia's Brett Ogle was just one shot off the lead in the final round of the 1990 Australian Open at Sydney as he stood on the 17th tee, but a wild drive sent his ball scurrying into the trees. Endeavouring to play out of the woodland and salvage the situation, he hit his second shot straight at a tree trunk from where it rebounded on to his knee. This was unlucky on three counts: it stopped him reaching the fairway and put him back in the trees; he incurred a two-stroke penalty for being hit by his own ball; and it hurt like hell. After receiving medical attention, Ogle bravely limped on but finished up taking nine for the hole – a score which wrecked his chances of victory.

Five years later – this time at the Hawaiian Open – Ogle was in the wars again. He should have known better than to court danger on the 13th hole on Friday 13 January but the lure of the trees proved too great. Playing a five-iron from a difficult stance, the shaft of his club struck a tree trunk on his follow-through and broke into three pieces, one of which flew into his face smashing his sunglasses and hitting him just below the left eye. Ogle was forced to withdraw from the event with double vision. By a strange coincidence, both the events in which Ogle suffered his injuries were won by the same golfer – a relatively obscure American named John Morse.

An Undulating Lie

Golfers always try to aim for the cup but Hale Irwin took things too literally during a 1973 United States tour event by landing his shot in a spectator's bra. In theory he could have personally retrieved the ball from its unusual lie but, being a gentleman, he allowed the lady to do it herself.

The Sad Case of Brigadier-General Critchley

The keen golfer will go to any lengths for a game and so it was that one Brigadier-General Critchley prepared to travel all the way from New York just to compete in the 1937 Amateur Championship at Sandwich, Kent. Being a military man, he had left nothing to chance and had organised the journey right down to the last detail . . . or so he thought. But he had reckoned without thick fog in the Atlantic which served to delay his crossing on the *Queen Mary* and made the ship late for docking at Southampton. This was where phase two came in. He had taken the precaution of hiring an aeroplane to take him from Southampton to Sandwich but, in spite of the pilot's best efforts, the Brigadier-General realised that he was cutting it desperately fine as the Kent coast came into view. In an attempt to let the championship officials know that he would be arriving at the course any minute, he even arranged for the pilot to circle over the clubhouse, but these aerial pleas fell on deaf ears. Rules could not be waived even if you had travelled over 3,000 miles. Thus when the Brigadier-General finally reached terra firma and rushed to the clubhouse, he was a full six minutes late. His teeing-off time had been and gone and his name had been irrevocably struck out from the tournament. Still, there was always the return journey to look forward to!

If it was of any consolation to Brigadier-General Critchley – and it probably wasn't – another would-be competitor was in the same boat, or rather the same ship. For an unnamed entrant from Burma, who had journeyed across the Pacific and the American continent, also had the misfortune to be on board the fog-delayed *Queen Mary*. But he lacked the vision of the Brigadier-General and had to settle for travelling from Southampton to Sandwich by car, eventually arriving four hours after his allocated starting time. For him too, there was to be no reprieve despite having trekked half-way round the world.

Hiss-trionics

On the final day of the 1994 Wild Coast Challenge at Wild Coast Country Club in South Africa, Ernie Els nearly stood on a three-foot-long highly venomous night adder. He was so shaken by the experience that he put his next shot into a pond and took a bogey six.

The jitters continued on to the next hole where he took a double bogey five. These two lapses cost Els the title as he finished in joint second place. Afterwards he reflected: 'It's no excuse. This is Africa and I've seen enough snakes before.'

Ball Hit Aircraft

Teeing off at the 9th hole at Lossiemouth, Scotland, in June 1971, golfer Martin Robertson saw his drive strike a Royal Navy aircraft which was coming in to land at a nearby airfield.

A Crying Shame

Australia's Jack Newton lost an 18-hole play-off for the 1975 Open at Carnoustie by one stroke to Tom Watson. A crucial moment came on the 3rd hole when Newton was disturbed by a child as he hit his drive. The wayward tee shot caused Newton to take a costly five and go two down.

Watson's embarrassment came at the presentation afterwards when R & A captain Sir John Carmichael warmly congratulated him on his triumph but referred to him in his speech as 'Tom Kite'.

Insect Aside

One of the unluckiest defeats in any of the four majors was that suffered by Lloyd Mangrum of the United States in the 1950 US Open. Spotting that an insect had landed on his ball, he instinctively picked the ball up and flicked away the offending creepy-crawly, only to be penalised two strokes for his misdemeanour. The penalty cost Mangrum the championship as at the end of 72 holes he was tied for first place with Ben Hogan but lost the resultant play-off.

An insect also spelled defeat for H. Dowie in a tournament final at Kirkfield, Ontario, in 1921. Dowie and his opponent P. McGregor were all-square coming to the final green where McGregor needed to sink a long putt to win the match. McGregor's putt came to rest on the very lip of the hole but then a large grasshopper landed on the ball with such force that the ball dropped into the hole. One would imagine that Dowie's golf shoe exacted a degree of revenge on the overweight grasshopper.

Knocked Out by His Backswing

Half-way through his backswing while driving off at the 17th at Lyme Regis, sixty-nine-year-old Derek Gatley received a nasty blow when the steel shaft of his club snapped, hit him on the back of the head and knocked him out. When he came round, Mr Gatley admitted: 'It was the first thing I had hit all day.'

Less fortunate was Edward M. Harrison who, playing alone at Inglewood Country Club, Seattle, in 1951, bled to death after the shaft of his driver broke in two. The split shaft pierced his groin and, although he tried to reach the clubhouse, Mr Harrison collapsed 100 yards from the 9th tee where the accident had occurred.

A broken club shaft also accounted for Rudolph Roy at Montreal in 1971. Playing out of woods, his club shaft snapped, rebounded off a tree and sank into his body.

Another golfing casualty was fifty-year-old Myrl G. Hanmore who died at Riviera County Club, Los Angeles, in 1956 when he lost control of a golf buggy on a steep slope.

And a golf cart played its part in the demise of Richard McCulough at the Ponoka Community Club, Alberta, Canada, in 1973. Frustrated after a poor shot, he banged his club angrily against the cart whereupon the club shaft broke, flew up and fatally severed his carotid artery.

A Race Against Time

On the evening before the start of the 1962 US Open, American club professional Charles Smith was suddenly informed that he was needed in the line-up as a replacement for another competitor who had withdrawn. Smith jumped into his car and hared down the Ohio Turnpike towards Pittsburgh but at three o'clock in the morning his speed brought him to the attention of a highway patrolman. Exasperated at the delay, Smith recounted the story in full – how he was a last-minute call-up for the Open – but the patrolman didn't believe him and detained him for the best part of an hour before finally letting him go with a $20 fine. Smith did just about make it to the 1st tee on time but his preparations were scarcely ideal and rounds of 83 and 84 meant that he failed to make the cut. If nothing else, his early exit gave him an extra two days in which to make the return journey.

Captain Under Par

In 1927, shortly before the Great Britain team set sail on the *Aquitania* for the United States and the first-ever Ryder Cup match, team captain Abe Mitchell was laid low with appendicitis. Consequently he had to miss out on the great adventure although he did manage to get to Waterloo station to wish the pioneers bon voyage. In his absence, Britain lost 9½–2½.

The United States' Billy Casper had to miss the singles matches in the 1971 Ryder Cup after breaking a toe while groping around in the dark trying to find his St Louis hotel bedroom.

Practice Blunder

Reaching the 8th green in the final round of the 1937 New Zealand Open Championship at Hamilton, A. Murray had to wait for his playing partner to putt. To pass the time, he casually dropped a ball on to the apron of the green and made a practice putt along the edge – the sort of thing any rabbit golfer would do on a Sunday morning. But this was a leading tournament and Murray found himself disqualified for taking an illegal practice putt. To underline the folly of his action, his score would have enabled him to recapture the title he had won two years previously.

Rescued from Bunker

Many a golfer has felt the need to be rescued from a bunker but with D. J. Bayly MacArthur it was the real thing. The 14-stone MacArthur was playing at Rose Bay, New South Wales, in 1931 when his ball landed in a bunker. However, because of heavy rain, the sand in the bunker had turned to quicksand so that when the burly MacArthur set foot in the trap he found himself sinking fast. The sand was up to his armpits before his cries for help brought a timely rescue. The experience made him even more determined to keep to the fairways in future.

Henry's Left Hook

The boxer Henry Cooper was famous for his left hook. Sadly, when he took up golf, it was sometimes much the same story. One person who could testify to that was a BBC continuity girl who was hit in the chest by one of Cooper's hooked drives during a pro-am tournament being filmed by the Corporation. Cooper was so upset that his game fell to pieces that day. On another occasion Cooper's trousers split in an embarrassing place as he bent down to line up a putt. 'I didn't have a clue what to do,' he said later, 'but about thirty women around the green rushed forward offering safety pins.'

Porky Gets the Chop

Ed Oliver, known to his friends as 'Porky', missed out on a play-off for the 1940 US Open because he teed off too early. Oliver was one of six players disqualified for starting their final round before the scheduled starting time – a decision the six had taken to combat deteriorating weather conditions. Despite being told that he had violated the rules, Oliver played on and his four-round total of 287 equalled that of Lawson Little and Gene Sarazen who tied for first place.

Fans Proved a Hindrance

There was no doubt whom the crowd were rooting for at the 1925 Open at Prestwick, Ayrshire – it was Scottish-born Macdonald Smith. Five shots clear after three rounds, the championship seemed his for the taking but the final day turned into a disaster, mainly because of those same spectators who were willing him to win. As early as the 3rd, Smith was subjected to a lengthy delay on the tee while stewards desperately tried to control the throng. The wait affected his concentration and, after hitting a poor drive, he took six. Out in a mediocre 42, he was again hustled by the crowd at the 11th where his wild tee shot landed among spectators who were running across the course, and rebounded into trouble. Dropping more shots there, he eventually struggled round in 82 – a score which pushed him back to fourth place, three strokes behind winner Jim Barnes. The fiasco led to the imposition of gate money for spectators the following year and also saw Prestwick lose its place on the Open Championship rota.

Signed for Wrong Score

Argentina's Roberto de Vicenzo lost out on a play-off for the 1968 US Masters because playing partner Tommy Aaron filled in his card incorrectly. In the final round, Aaron accidentally put de Vicenzo's score at the 17th down as a four instead of a birdie three. De Vicenzo left the last green convinced that his 65 had earned him a play-off against America's Bob Goalby but he didn't spot the mistake on the card and signed for a 66. Since the carded score has to stand – even if it is wrong – he finished one shot behind Goalby.

Kel Nagle went even further during one tournament, inadvertently putting his nine-hole total in the space allotted for the 9th-hole score. He signed it and was thus recorded as having taken 37 strokes at the 9th hole.

Lost Seven Balls in a Round

Having taken 93 shots for seventeen holes in the 1994 French Open at the National course in Paris, Sweden's Anders Forsbrand ran out of balls on the 18th. He had lost five balls in water and two more in deep rough in a round which included a nine at the 12th and a ten at the particularly unlucky 13th. His exit from the tournament came after he had already played five shots on the 18th and still faced a 115-yard pitch over water in order to reach the green. In many ways, it was a merciful release.

A Snake in the Grass

At the 1985 South African Masters, Vaughan Tucker reprimanded his caddie for moving his ball without permission. The caddie clearly did not take kindly to the ticking-off for after disappearing into the rough, he returned brandishing a snake which he angrily waved in Tucker's face.

Irwin's Aberration

Playing the par-3 14th in the third round of the 1983 Open at Royal Birkdale, Hale Irwin left his putt no more than an inch from the hole. But as he went to tap the ball in, he took his eye off it and missed the ball completely. The one-stroke penalty which he incurred was to prove more costly than even he could have imagined at the time. For at the end of four rounds, Irwin finished joint second – one stroke behind winner Tom Watson.

Equally careless was Max Faulkner at the 1962 Open at Troon. Playing the 11th, he succeeded in tapping the ball against his foot and ended up taking a miserable eleven for the hole.

A Dent in the Trophy

During the 1932 Walker Cup match at Brooklyn, Great Britain's Leonard Crawley managed to dent the cup when his wayward drive to the 18th hit the trophy which was on display outside the clubhouse.

Dangerous to Know

Those who think the most dangerous weapon available to US Presidents is the nuclear attack button have obviously never seen them with a golf club in their hands. Former Vice-President Spiro Agnew set the standard (one of his eccentric drives laid out Doug Sanders at the Bob Hope Classic) and it is good to know that more recent incumbents of high office are keeping up the good work. In February 1995, Bill Clinton played his immediate predecessor, George Bush, and Gerald Ford in the Bob Hope Invitation Tournament at Indian Wells, California. Amid rumours that all paramedics' leave in the area had been cancelled, Bush got off to a lively start when his drive on the 1st hole hit an elderly San Diego woman on the bridge of the nose and shattered her glasses. After being given first aid on the spot, the woman was taken to the Eisenhower Medical Center to receive ten stitches. Then on the 14th Bush struck a spectator on the buttock while Ford, anxious not be left out, drew blood from a woman's finger after his ball hit her on the 17th. Afterwards Bush, with commendable understatement, described his round of 92 as *'comme ci, comme ça'*.

In April 1996 President Clinton decided that he wanted to drop in at the Orinda Country Club near San Francisco for a friendly fourball. The exercise meant secret service agents checking the course, carrying out wholesale security checks on the clubhouse staff and demanding seventeen carts – two for the President and his playing partners and the rest for security staff. The men's locker room was cleared, a fourball playing behind the presidential group had their clubs and bags scanned by an X-ray device and two marksmen followed the Clinton match from trees either side of the fairway. After all that preparation, Clinton forgot his golf shoes and no replacements could be found. He ended up shooting 84.

Lost Open on a Technicality

The 1876 Open at St Andrews finished with David Strath tied for first place with Bob Martin but Strath was in trouble over an incident at the 17th, the famous Road Hole. The rules of golf state that no one shall play to a green with players on it but Strath was accused of having played his approach to the 17th before the green had cleared. Furthermore it was claimed that his ball had hit a player who was still putting. The player who had been hit demanded Strath's disqualification but officials ruled that Strath and Martin should play off for the title while Strath's alleged infringement of the rules was discussed. However, Strath flatly refused to take part in any play-off until a decision was reached over his possible disqualification. Not prepared to be dictated to, the officials forgot about the play-off and awarded the trophy to Martin.

Ball Eaten by Cow

Playing the 10th hole at Guernsey in 1963, S. C. King saw his ball land safely on the fairway while his partner, R. W. Clark, disappeared into deep rough. After helping Clark to locate his ball, King returned to his own . . . and found it being eaten by a cow. The following day, the pair played the course again and were on the lookout for hungry cows when they reached the 10th. This time it was King who drifted into the rough while Clark hit the fairway. Remembering the events of the previous day, Clark took the precaution of placing a protective woollen hat over his ball before setting off to find his partner's drive. On his return, Clark discovered that the cow had eaten his hat.

Watch the Birdie

In 1937 Densmore Shute of the United States retained his US PGA title, largely as a result of the misfortune which befell Harold McSpaden. The latter had a four-foot putt for victory at the final hole but was disturbed by photographers, missed the putt and lost the first extra hole.

The Long Wait

South Africa's Denis Watson missed out on the 1985 US Open title when he was penalised two strokes for waiting too long for a putt to drop into the hole. At the 8th hole on the first round at Oakland Hills, Watson's twelve-foot putt came to rest on the lip of the cup, but instead of tapping it in, he waited in the hope that it would fall in of its own accord. Sure enough, twenty-five seconds later the ball finally tired of defying gravity and dropped into the hole but by then Watson had exceeded the time allowed for such acts and incurred his two-shot penalty. He was left to curse his ill-fortune three days later when his 72-hole score placed him just one stroke behind winner Andy North.

Another hard-luck story at the same event belonged to T. C. Chen of Taiwan who, like Watson, finished one shot off the lead. Chen was actually four ahead of the field after four holes of the final round but at the 5th, while trying to play out of the rough, his club became entangled in thick grass on the follow-through and he was adjudged to have hit the ball twice, thereby suffering a one-stroke penalty. The incident clearly had an adverse effect on his game and he slipped to a 77.

The Curse of the Extra Letter

Previewing the 1945 Curtis Cup match, the women's golf magazine *Fairway & Hazard* concluded with a patriotic message for British team captain Baba Beck. It should have read: 'And so, Mrs Beck,

Good Luck and bring back to Britain that coveted Trophy.'
However, a misprint meant that the final sentence began: 'And sod
Mrs Beck . . .'

An Unfortunate Oversight

In spite of all his years of experience, Tony Jacklin was disqualified
from a British Seniors event in 1994 when, in trying to play out of a
bunker, the ball bounced back and hit him in the chest. Unaware that
there was a penalty for such an occurrence, fifty-year-old Jacklin
filled in the wrong score on his card and was duly thrown out of the
tournament. Appropriately the incident happened on the 13th hole.

A Soggy Signing

Coming off the 18th green at the Congressional Country Club
following a practice round in 1976, Gary Player suddenly found
himself surrounded by young autograph hunters. So eager were they
for the South African's signature that they accidentally pushed him
into a lake.

Another man to receive an unexpected drenching was Alan
Waters, professional at Worplesdon Golf Club in Surrey. Given a lift
in a golf cart by club captain Alec Justice during a mixed foursomes
competition, Waters was alarmed when the cart veered off line and
deposited him in the water at the Pond Hole. It was believed to be the
only time the professional had gone into the pond.

A Helping Hand

Before Britain joined forces with Europe, British victories in the
Ryder Cup were about as frequent as snowfalls in the Sahara. But
one memorable success occurred in 1933 when Britain defeated the
United States by a solitary point at Southport and Ainsdale. The star
of the singles matches from the British point of view was Abe

Mitchell who trounced Olin Dutra 9 and 8. At one point Mitchell won eight holes in a row including one where Olin, having been laid a stymie, tried to loft his ball but instead knocked Mitchell's into the hole.

In the Nick of Time

Celebrating his triumph in the 1981 Open, Bill Rogers could afford to look back with amusement on the fact that he very nearly wasn't allowed to take part. For he came within thirty seconds of being disqualified from the first round for being late on the tee after his car had been held up at a level crossing. Rogers thought he had allowed himself plenty of time to get to Royal St George's, Sandwich, but, just a mile from the course, he was delayed half an hour by the crossing gates. Sweeney Todd's customers never had a closer shave.

If the gods smiled on Bill Rogers, they frowned on Neil Coles, who was disqualified from the 1997 Seniors PGA Championship for missing his 11.50 a.m. tee time by five minutes. Coles maintained that he had been told he had a 12.50 start.

Former US Open champion J. J. McDermott didn't just get the wrong time for the qualifying rounds for the 1914 Open at Prestwick, he got the wrong week. Having journeyed all the way across the Atlantic, he arrived in Scotland just as qualifying was finishing.

Wallet Stolen

While playing the final hole of the 1936 US Open at Baltusrol, Leslie Madison discovered that his wallet had been stolen. Madison and a team of willing helpers searched for the thief for a quarter of an hour but neither the wallet nor its $55 contents were found. The delay did nothing for the nerves of Madison's playing partner, Harry Cooper, who proceeded to blunder away his chances to finish second, two strokes behind winner Tony Manero.

Struck by Lightning

Lee Trevino, Bobby Nichols and Jerry Heard were all struck by lightning during the 1975 Western Open at Butler National Golf Club, Oak Brook, Illinois. They recovered in hospital from their ordeal.

Faldo up a Palm Tree

Nick Faldo was disqualified during the final round of the 1999 Players Championship at Sawgrass, Florida, after being given incorrect advice by playing partner Corey Pavin. Faldo was already enduring a torrid time when he fired his approach to the 6th hole into a palm tree to the right of the green. A renowned expert on the rules of golf, Faldo said afterwards: 'I thought the ball was lost and I was going to play another from the same spot when Pavin persuaded me that I could drop a ball under the tree.' In fact, Faldo should have played his approach shot again. By dropping under the tree, finishing the hole and then teeing off at the 7th, he left tournament officials with no alternative but to disqualify him. Informed of the decision, he said to Pavin with a smile: 'You gave me a wrong ruling, partner.' Pavin admitted his error. 'I felt bad that I had made a mistake but it was an honest one. The same thing happened to me about eight or nine years ago at Palm Springs and I obviously got a wrong ruling then. I guess I learned the easy way. But the bottom line is that it is up to the player to call for a ruling.'

It was by no means Faldo's first disqualification. He dropped wrongly out of a ditch in a 1980s European Open at Sunningdale, and was thrown out of an event in Bali in 1993 when leading by six shots for removing a piece of coral from a bunker. He was also penalised at the 1994 Open at Turnberry for playing the wrong ball. After a first round in which he had been repeatedly outdriven by playing partner Jim McGovern, Faldo assumed that the same thing had happened again at the 17th and didn't bother to identify his ball before hitting it. It all added up to a miserable round of 75.

The Longest Drive

A member of the John O'Gaunt Club at Sutton, near Biggleswade in Bedfordshire, produced arguably the longest drive in British golf – one of forty-two miles. His tee shot sailed out of bounds and, instead of landing on the green, it landed on the greens – or to be precise a box of cabbages being transported on a passing vegetable lorry. The lorry was on its way to Covent Garden market in London and when the cabbages were unloaded there, the golf ball fell out. His recovery shot would have been worth watching . . .

A Lost Soul

Scotland's George Duncan won the 1920 Open at Deal despite taking a potentially disastrous six on the last hole of the first round. Just as Duncan was driving at the 18th, a lone spectator wandered aimlessly across the course out of view from the tee. Although Duncan couldn't see the trespasser, a steward could and immediately shouted, 'Fore!' The warning call came with Duncan in mid-swing and caused him to drag the ball into the rough. Wisely, the spectator vanished before Duncan could express his feelings with a three-iron.

Mixed Feelings

Dr A.W. Reid enjoyed an up-and-down sort of round when playing at Rotorua, New Zealand, in 1964. Ecstatic after getting a hole-in-one at the 110-yard 6th, he was playing his approach shot on the next hole when he was hit on the head by a ball driven from the 8th tee and knocked unconscious.

Unluckily Bunkered

Teeing off on the 10th hole at the Army Golf Course in Meerut, India, Faisal Qureshi saw his wayward drive bounce into the pocket of a fellow golfer, Maqbool Singh, who was playing the 4th hole. The rules stipulated that the second shot had to be played from where Maqbool was standing which, unfortunately for Qureshi, happened to be in a bunker.

With just five holes to play in the final of the 1912 Amateur Championship at Westward Ho!, Abe Mitchell was leading John Ball by two holes. Mitchell looked set to consolidate his position at the short 14th as his drive sailed towards the green, only for it to hit an open umbrella being held by a woman spectator. Mitchell could only watch helplessly as his ball, instead of landing on the green, was diverted into a bunker. The ricochet cost Mitchell the hole and he never recovered from this stroke of misfortune, eventually losing at the second extra hole.

Caddie's Question Cost the Hole

The fourball match at the 1971 Ryder Cup between Arnold Palmer and Gardner Dickinson for the United States and Bernard Gallacher and Peter Oosterhuis for Great Britain was marred by an unsavoury incident at the par-3 7th. Palmer had just played his tee shot when Gallacher's caddie, an American named Jack McLeod, called out: 'Great shot, what did you hit?' To which Palmer replied: 'A five-iron.' However, McLeod's innocent inquiry had broken the rules as technically he had asked his opponents for advice. As a result, the Americans were awarded the hole by the referee and went two up on their way to a 5 and 4 win.

An earlier caddie calamity took place in the third round of the 1946 US Open at Canterbury Golf Club, Ohio, when Byron Nelson's caddie, Eddie Martin, accidentally kicked his player's ball while climbing under a spectator rope on the edge of the 15th fairway. Martin's mistake cost Nelson a one-stroke penalty and ultimately the Championship, for after 72 holes, Nelson was tied for first place with Lloyd Mangrum but lost out in the play-off.

Rat Surprise

Playing in the second round of the 1968 Open at Carnoustie, Britain's John Morgan was bitten by a rat while addressing his ball on the 10th fairway.

Grapefruit Split

Attempting to play over a grapefruit tree at California's Eldorado Country Club in 1977, William Collings caught his shot a little thin and succeeded only in embedding his ball in a grapefruit.

Snapped His Putter

One of the most remarkable matches in the epic 1987 Ryder Cup contest at Muirfield Village, Columbus, Ohio, was the singles clash between Eamonn Darcy for Great Britain and Europe and the United States' Ben Crenshaw. Darcy was two up as they left the 6th green whereupon Crenshaw banged his putter into the ground in frustration and snapped the shaft. This left the American with something of a problem – namely twelve holes to play and no putter. For the rest of the round he putted with either his one-iron or the leading edge of his sand wedge and his improvisation was so successful that at one point he actually overhauled Darcy to take the lead. But he couldn't keep it up to the finish and Darcy battled back to win by one hole and help his team to a 15–13 victory.

Broke Down on Tee

England's Richard Boxall was forced to withdraw from the 1991 Open at Royal Birkdale after collapsing with a stress fracture of the leg on the 9th tee. Boxall was driving off during the third round when he suddenly heard a loud crack which ended his participation.

Mike Reasor decided to play on in the 1974 Tallahassee Open

despite being able to use only one arm. Having qualified for the final two rounds, Reasor injured his shoulder in a riding accident but because all those who completed the tournament were given automatic entry into the next PGA tour event, he elected to carry on using only his right arm. His handicap was reflected in his scores for the two closing rounds – 123 and 114.

Obstruction on Green

With most rounds of golf, an obstruction on the green amounts to little more than a leaf or a twig but when N. Bathie played the 11th hole at the Downfield course in Dundee in 1938, he was confronted by the remains of a wooden shelter. The shelter had been dumped on the green by a freak whirlwind which had also spun Bathie round just as he was about to play his approach shot. It is not known whether he was able to pick out a line to the cup through the debris.

A pro-am tournament which preceded the 1978 Hawaiian Open was livened up when a small plane crash-landed on the 18th fairway. The aircraft eventually came to rest some fifty yards short of the green where a group were putting.

One Club Too Many

Bob Dickson was denied victory in the 1965 US Amateur Championship after being penalised four strokes for having one club too many in his bag. This seemed a particularly harsh decision since the club wasn't even his, he had only carried it for a few holes and he hadn't actually used it. Dickson missed out on the title by one stroke.

Balls Collided in Mid-air

In the course of the 1980 Corfu International Championship, Sharon Peachey saw her drive collide in mid-air with a ball from a competitor playing a different hole. Not only did Ms Peachey lose vital yardage but her ball ended up in a pond.

Amateur Antics

The Hon. Michael Stott had an unenviable record in the Amateur Championship which included being disqualified on two separate occasions. His first transgression took place in 1910 when he was ruled out of the third round for failing to arrive on the 1st tee in time. Chastened by that experience, he resolved to be more punctual in future but incurred the wrath of officialdom again in 1924. This time he was a mite unlucky. Due to repeated slow play, the first starting times were running some forty minutes late so Stott calculated that he had a good half an hour to play with when it came to his tee-off time later in the day. However, he had neglected to take into consideration a forty-five-minute interval part-way through the programme which allowed the starting times to catch up. So when his name was announced, he was nowhere to be seen. Disqualification followed as sure as night follows day and a man with a bucket follows the Trooping of the Colour.

The 1922 Amateur Championship at Prestwick saw a competitor disqualified because he caught the wrong train. The hapless golfer boarded a train at Ayr, certain that it would be stopping at Prestwick, and was thus more than a little dismayed when it rattled through the station and headed off up the coast towards Troon. Observing that the track ran alongside the course, he even resorted to shouting from the carriage window that he would be back as soon as he could. He was as good as his word but that cut no ice with the committee. On reaching Troon, he sped back to Prestwick, only to find that he had been eliminated for having missed his starting time.

Chased by Bull

In the 1981 Coca-Cola Tournament at Ayr Belleisle, Scottish professionals George and Angus McKay were chased by a runaway bull. The pair had reached the 5th green when they became aware that the beast had escaped from a field adjoining the course. At first the bull seemed happy just to watch but as George stood nervously over a five-foot putt, the animal made its move. The men didn't stop to recite rules about course etiquette but beat a hasty retreat into a nearby toilet, leaving the bull to prowl around the edge of the green. Some time later, after the course superintendent had managed to coerce the bull back into its field, George returned to the green and holed his putt.

Costly Theft

At the 1972 Penfold Tournament at Queen's Park, Bournemouth, Christy O'Connor Jnr took a penalty for a lost ball, unaware that it had, in fact, been stolen by a young boy. The penalty meant that instead of winning the tournament outright, O'Connor finished up in a tie for first place and had to take part in a play-off which, continuing his misfortune, he naturally lost.

The Trials and Tribulations of Charles Whitcombe

In the 1924 Open at Hoylake, Charles Whitcombe, one of the leading home contenders, was disqualified for playing the wrong ball. Deep in the rough at the 14th on the third round, Whitcombe located what he thought was his ball, but on eventually holing out, he discovered that he was mistaken and had played someone else's ball instead. The following year Whitcombe retired in the final round of the Open at Prestwick after what the *Guardian* described as 'a disconcerting experience with two dogs on a tee'.

Doctor's Dismay

In 1936 a Dr Tucker of New Orleans put his name down for a hole-in-one tournament. He was so fired up with enthusiasm that as soon as he had put pen to paper, he marched straight out to the competition hole to stake his claim. And to his delight, he achieved a hole-in-one. Dashing back to the clubhouse to impart the joyous news, he was somewhat deflated to be informed that the competition didn't begin for another two weeks.

6 Athletics

What a Refreshing Change!

After a magnificent run in the 1938 Natal marathon, South Africa's Johannes Coleman stormed across the finishing line at Alexander Park, Pietermaritzburg, confident that he had shattered the world record. At the time it stood at 2hr 26min 42sec and, as he had entered the park, Coleman's own watch had shown 2hr 23min. So on bursting the tape for his fourth success in the race, he eagerly sought out chief timekeeper Harold Sulin for confirmation, only to find Sulin and his colleagues sipping tea in the park refreshment room. The red-faced officials humbly apologised for their absence, saying that nobody had expected any of the runners to arrive back so soon. Consequently, Coleman's record could not be ratified. The bewildered athlete said: 'I laughed but I felt like crying, because it must have been my fastest-ever marathon.'

Hounded out of Contention

Competing in the 1904 Olympic marathon at St Louis, the African runner Lentauw lost precious time when he was chased off the course and through a cornfield by two large dogs. As a result of the unscheduled detour, he could only finish ninth.

Yifter the Non-Shifter

The great Ethiopian distance runner Miruts Yifter (nicknamed 'Yifter the Shifter') missed the start of his 5,000 metres heat at the 1972 Munich Olympics because he was still in the toilet. His inability to tear himself away meant that he had to wait another eight years for the chance of 5,000 metres gold. Ethiopia boycotted the 1976 Olympics and so it was not until 1980 that Yifter was finally able to claim the crown.

That was by no means Yifter's first mishap in the 5,000 metres. Competing for Africa against the USA in 1971, he forged into the lead and, seemingly timing his run to perfection, sprinted for the line . . . where he discovered that there was still a lap to go. Utterly spent, he could do no more than jog around the last lap as Steve Prefontaine of the States surged past him to win.

Missed Opportunity

Miruts Yifter wasn't the only competitor to miss out at Munich. Americans Eddie Hart and Rey Robinson, who were among the favourites for the men's 100 metres, failed to appear for their second-round heats because their coach had misread the starting time. Waiting for the team bus at the Olympic village, Robinson was watching television when he suddenly realised that the athletes on screen were lining up for the race he should have been in.

A Hot Contest

Arguably the most gruelling race in Olympic history was the cross-country event at the 1924 Games. Run over a distance of around 10,000 metres on a swelteringly hot day in Paris, it claimed so many casualties that hours after the finish, the Red Cross were still scouring the route in search of lost runners. Competitors dropped like flies, overcome either by the heat or by poisonous fumes which billowed from an energy plant adjoining the course. And for good measure, sections of the circuit were knee-high in thistles. The majority of those who made it to the finish were in a sorry state. Aguilar of Spain collapsed on entering the stadium and hit his head on a marker, while Sewell of Great Britain headed off in the wrong direction. When he was shown the error of his ways, he promptly collided with another runner with the result that both men fell and failed to finish. Amid the mayhem, Finland's Paavo Nurmi took gold and helped his country to win the team event. But even the ice-cold Finns struggled. Henrik Liimatainen was just thirty metres from the finish when he suddenly ground to a halt. In a state of delirium, he turned round and started staggering back the way he had come, only to be stopped in his tracks by the screaming crowd. For what seemed like an eternity, he stood with his back to the finish before regaining his composure, turning round again and walking over the line.

The Wrong Man

After being presented with the bronze medal for the men's 100 yards at the 1962 Commonwealth Games in Perth, Australia's Gary Holdsworth was asked to hand it over to team-mate Mike Cleary instead. Although photographic evidence had not been called for on the day of the race, a few days later a jury of appeals studied a print of the finish and decided that the bronze medal had gone to the wrong man. 'You're joking, aren't you?' raged an indignant Holdsworth. 'My time was listed faster.' However, the photo showed Cleary a good two inches ahead of his compatriot. As a compromise, both men were awarded a bronze.

Went to Pot

The modern pentathlon at the 1984 Olympics in Los Angeles was a close-fought affair but when Sweden's Svante Rasmuson pulled clear in the final event, the 4,000 metres cross country, he seemed assured of victory. But just 20 yards from the finish, he had the misfortune to stumble over a potted plant, placed there by the Los

Angeles organisers to brighten up the course. Before he could get to his feet, he had been passed by Italy's Daniele Masala who went on to snatch the gold.

A Cunning Plan

While out on a training run over the course of the 1932 Olympic marathon in Los Angeles, Britain's Samuel Ferris hatched a cunning plan. He spotted a huge milk advertisement about a mile from the finish and decided to use it as a marker for his final push. Alas on the day of the race, the sign was masked by a grandstand and so Ferris didn't see it. Consequently he began his final effort too late and his charge through the field left him with silver instead of the anticipated gold. Entering the stadium, he was a full minute behind the eventual winner, Juan Carlos Zabala of Argentina, and although he closed with every stride, he was still nineteen seconds adrift at the finish.

Making a Stand

When Wendel Motley won the men's 440 yards at the 1966 Commonwealth Games in Kingston, Jamaica, he refused to stand on the winner's podium after being told that the Trinidad and Tobago flag could not be raised because the rope had broken. The medal ceremony was postponed until the next day.

Which Way?

Coming to the end of the marathon in the 1954 European Championships in Berne, Russian athlete Ivan Filin powered into the stadium clear of Finland's Veikko Karvonen. But once inside the stadium, the Soviet runner turned the wrong way and lost over 100 metres before realising his error. By the time he had got back on course, the best he could manage was third place.

The Fates Conspired

Javelin thrower Bruce Kennedy was doomed never to take part in Olympic competition. In 1972 he was selected for the Rhodesian team for the Munich Olympics but pressure from the black African nations brought a ban on Rhodesia's participation. He was chosen again in 1976 but his native country was still not allowed to compete. The following year he acquired US citizenship and duly qualified for the American team for the 1980 Moscow Olympics, only for the States to boycott the Games in protest at the Soviet invasion of Afghanistan. The luckless Kennedy finally made it to the 1984 Olympics in Los Angeles . . . as a stadium usher.

One Lap Too Soon

There were few more deserving winners at the 1930 Empire Games, staged at Hamilton in Canada, than New Zealand's Billy Savidan. For his victory in the 10,000 metres was achieved in spite of a blunder by a track official who accidentally turned over one flip card too many on the laps-remaining counter. As a result, Savidan, thinking he was on his last lap, sprinted down the home straight whereupon he was informed that there was still a lap to go. By then he had stopped and didn't know whether or not to believe the news he was receiving. But when watching team-mate Ossie Johnson confirmed the awful truth, Savidan had little option but to set off again, hotly pursued by England's Ernest Harper who had closed the gap significantly amid the confusion. In a heroic effort, Savidan managed to summon the energy for another lap and held on for the gold before collapsing in the dressing room. To add insult to injury, when he stood on the victory podium, the band mistakenly played 'Land of Hope and Glory', the English anthem.

Dropped a Clanger

At the start of the final lap of a 5,000 metres heat in the 1978

Commonwealth Games, the official rang the bell and it promptly fell off its stand.

Calendar Chaos

Preparing for the 1896 Olympics in Athens, the United States team reckoned they had left nothing to chance. After spending sixteen and a half days at sea, they arrived in the Greek capital at 9 p.m. on 5 April, allowing, so they thought, another twelve days before the competition commenced. But to their horror they were awoken at four o'clock the next morning by the sound of a brass band announcing the start of the Games. In their calculations, the Americans had forgotten that Greece still used the Julian calendar and was thus eleven days in advance.

Short Course Championships

At the 1912 Polytechnic Harriers marathon in London, the runners were directed the wrong way on entering the stadium and therefore completed only 480 yards on the track instead of 840. So the winning time of Canada's James Corkery couldn't be recognised as a world record because it was short of the full marathon distance.

There was a similar mishap in the women's marathon at the 1995 World Championships in Gothenburg. The runners were supposed to complete four laps of the Ullevi Stadium before heading off on to the road but for some reason they did only three. Furthermore, nobody spotted the mistake until long after the finish. So the winning time of Portugal's Manuela Machado was utterly meaningless.

Blank Looks

The Jamaican national track championships of 1966 had to be delayed because nobody remembered to bring the starting pistol.

The Legend of Dorando Pietri

When the organisers of the 1908 Olympics in London decided to add an extra 385 yards to the marathon distance so that it could finish directly in front of the royal box at the White City, they could scarcely have imagined the furore it would create. After all, what's an extra few yards when you've already run twenty-six miles? For Dorando Pietri, the answer was an awful lot. The race was run in intense heat but all looked well when Pietri, the small, moustachioed Italian, was first to enter the stadium. However, he started to falter when he lost momentum on the downward ramp leading on to the cinder track and was then directed left instead of right as he had been expecting. The confusion caused him to stumble . . . 385 yards from the finish. He scrambled to his feet but by now his legs had completely gone and, to screams from the 100,000 crowd, he fell four more times as he bravely endeavoured to negotiate the final part-lap. His last fall was just short of the line. Perhaps deciding that such a harrowing spectacle was not fit for the king, or maybe out of a genuine desire to help the stricken Italian, chief race organiser Jack Andrew jumped to Pietri's aid and helped him across the line. As Pietri was taken away on a stretcher, John Hayes of the United States became the second man home, half a minute after Pietri's assisted finish. While the Italian team celebrated what they saw as a noble victory, the Americans lodged a protest, as a result of which Pietri was disqualified. The following day, a fully recovered Pietri insisted that the officials should have left him alone because he was certain that he could have finished without their help, and a contrite Andrew maintained that he hadn't actually helped Pietri but had merely caught him as he fell at the tape. As it turned out, the luckless Italian became infinitely more famous than the race winner. Pietri was presented with a special inscribed gold cup as compensation for missing out on the medal and was fêted in his homeland with poems and festivals. There were even songs written about him, including one by Irving Berlin. The world loves a gallant loser.

They Felt Run Down

Enthusiastically doing some last-minute training on the day before the 1930 Commonwealth Games marathon in Hamilton, English record holder Harry Payne was hit by a car and had to miss the race. There was a similar tale of woe in the following year's Port Chester marathon where the favourite, James Henigan of the United States, could only finish second after being involved in a collision with a car while in the lead.

Champagne Charlie

Leading with just two miles to go in Dorando Pietri's 1908 Olympic marathon, South African Charles Hefferon made the fatal mistake of accepting a drink of champagne. Far from reviving him, the alcohol merely served to disorientate him and cause discomfort. A dizzy mile later, he was struck down by stomach cramps and could only take the silver medal.

Strike Off the Band

At the medal ceremony for the 1964 Tokyo Olympics marathon, won by Abebe Bikila of Ethiopia, the stadium band didn't know the Ethiopian anthem so they played the Japanese one instead. Twelve years earlier, officials at Helsinki had been equally embarrassed when Luxembourg's Josef Barthel emerged as the surprise winner of the Olympic 1,500 metres. Not expecting Luxembourg to win a medal at anything, the organisers had failed to take the precaution of providing the band with the score for the country's national anthem. So at the medal ceremony, the musicians hurriedly improvised a tune which sounded nothing like the Luxembourg anthem. But nobody was any the wiser.

Digging for Defeat

In the days before starting blocks, competitors had to dig their own starting holes for sprint races, which was all very well provided they knew where to excavate. Preparing for the men's 200 metres final at the 1932 Olympics, America's Ralph Metcalfe was told by Los Angeles track officials to dig his holes some four feet further back than they should have been. He eventually finished third behind fellow countrymen Eddie Tolan and George Simpson but, without having had to cover the extra distance, he would have taken silver. He was offered the chance of a rerun but patriotically declined because he didn't want to jeopardise the host country's 1–2–3.

Down to Earth with a Bump

As Britain's first astronaut, Helen Sharman became something of a celebrity in her home city of Sheffield. So when the organisers of the 16th World Student Games, which were being staged in Sheffield's Don Valley Stadium in the summer of 1991, were looking for someone famous to feature in the opening ceremony, who better than the local girl made good? Sharman's task was to light the symbolic Games flame to declare proceedings officially open but those same feet which had coped so ably with the vagaries of outer space let her down badly on terra firma. While performing her duties, she tripped over a red carpet at the stadium and managed to extinguish the flame.

Helen Sharman's embarrassment in Sheffield was matched only by that of three Mozambican athletes who were competing in the Games. Looking for somewhere nearby to go on a training run, they found a nice stretch of smooth tarmac, seemingly unaware that it was in fact the hard shoulder of the M1. When the police spotted them, they escorted the mystified runners to the safer confines of a local sports ground.

Bad Timing

Storming into the White City stadium at the end of the 1946 AAA marathon, Donald McNab Robertson and Squire Yarrow were alarmed to find that the steeplechase was still in progress on the track. Trying to pick their way through hurdles, confused officials and the steeplechase runners, the pair still managed to fight out a close finish with Yarrow just snatching the verdict. But there is little doubt that McNab Robertson's celebrated sprint finish was somewhat blunted by having to cope with the athletic equivalent of a contraflow system.

Snap!

Making his way to the 1906 Olympics in Athens, Canadian pole vaulter Ed Archibald contrived to lose his pole on the train journey through Italy. Sympathetic Olympic officials provided him with a few replacement models but when one broke and nearly impaled him, he went off the idea and returned home before he ended up as a Greek kebab.

A Hurdle Too Far

Celebrating his victory in the 400 metres hurdles final at the 1974 Commonwealth Games, England's Alan Pascoe decided to jump an extra hurdle by way of an encore. With one eye on the crowd as he tried to wave to the Christchurch family with whom he had been staying while in New Zealand, he proceeded to make a complete hash of jumping the hurdle from a standing start and ended up in an undignified heap on the track. To compound his embarrassment, he then tried again with the same result. As the crowd held its breath, he approached a third hurdle but this time instead of trying to jump it, he casually flicked it away with his hand. The crowd roared its approval. A red-faced Pascoe, who had clearly underestimated his tiredness, said afterwards: 'The adrenalin was rushing to my head but my legs wouldn't go with me. I missed the first hurdle and I couldn't believe it. I was embarrassed, and the motto of the hurdles is that if you miss a hurdle, you go right back afterwards and make it. That was my second mistake.'

One in the Eye

Athletes manage to come up with all manner of excuses to explain away a poor performance. For example, Ahmed Salah of Djibouti, who finished third in the 1988 Olympic marathon in Seoul, said he would definitely have won but for the fact that his shoelaces were too tight.

But the gold medal for originality must surely go to American 400 metre hurdler Boyd Gittins who was eliminated from the 1968 US Olympic trials when a pigeon dropping hit him in the eye and dislodged his contact lens just before he was about to jump the first hurdle. He did manage to win a run-off in order to qualify for the team but even in Mexico his troubles weren't over and he had to withdraw from his first-round heat because of a leg injury.

Waiting for a Train

A marathon runner's worst nightmare is to get stuck behind something over which he or she has no control, such as a broken-down lorry or, in the case of the 1907 Boston marathon, a train. The course crossed a railroad track at South Framingham and, as luck would have it, a long train appeared on the scene just as the field approached the crossing. The first nine runners, including the eventual winner, Canada's Thomas Longboat, managed to scramble across in front of the train but the rest were left kicking their heels. Among this latter group were Robert Fowler and John Hayes who, once the train had finally passed, chased hard after Longboat. They made up a lot of the lost ground but the gap was too great and they had to settle for second and third place respectively . . . all because they caught the train.

Hammer Blow

At the 1978 Commonwealth Games in Edmonton, a wayward hammer throw caused consternation by landing perilously close to the Queen who was on a trackside visit. The missile sailed over the heads of photographers covering her tour of inspection and almost hit a CBC cameraman. As a result the hammer competition was postponed until the royal party had left the stadium, forcing the competitors to hang around aimlessly. When the organisers of the next Games in Canada – Victoria in 1994 – were asked what day the hammer event would be, they replied: 'Any day the Queen isn't there.'

The Tender Trapp

Standing contentedly on the podium after coming third in a 200 metres college event in the United States, James Trapp of Clemson University was suddenly left reeling after being hit on the head with the trophy. The unintentional culprit was race winner Dave Braunskill who, in the euphoria of victory, stood on the number one position, held the cup aloft and completely forgot to avoid the man next to him. As a result of the blow, Trapp required stitches and treatment for concussion.

The Long High Jump

It was a tense moment for Germany's Hans Liesche in the 1912 Olympic high jump competition. Needing to clear 6ft 4in to equal the best jump of Alma Richards of the United States, Liesche had already failed twice and was left with just one more attempt. Slowly and surely he composed himself for the third effort but just as he was about to begin his run-up, the gun went off to signal the start of a track race. After waiting patiently for the race to end, Liesche once again set about getting himself in the right frame of mind but no sooner was he ready than the Stockholm stadium band began to play.

By now, his nerves were in shreds. But he couldn't delay much longer and, sure enough, after nine minutes a Swedish official told him to hurry up. The dispirited German made a token run at the bar but, not surprisingly, failed miserably.

A Dogged Performance

Forty-three-year-old Englishman Jack Holden triumphed in the marathon at the 1950 Empire Games in Auckland despite running in bare feet for the last eight miles after his running shoes had been soaked by a sudden downpour. He also had to contend with a dog which began snapping at his heels three miles from the finish. Despite Holden's best attempts to shoo the animal away, it persisted in following him and at one point nearly tripped him up. Race officials eventually succeeded in guiding the dog out of the way, enabling Holden to progress unhindered.

Less fortunate was John J. Kelley of the United States, competing in the 1961 Boston marathon. The race became very much a head-to-head between Kelley and Finland's Eino Oksanen, although for part of the race they were also kept company by a stray dog. The hound repeatedly got in their way, causing them to break stride, until at seventeen miles, Kelley fell over the dog and had to be helped up by another runner. The lost time cost Kelley the race as he eventually finished second, just twenty-five seconds behind Oksanen. Afterwards the Massachusetts Society for the Prevention of Cruelty to Animals announced that for future events it would station a fleet of vehicles around the course to round up any stray dogs. For John J. Kelley, it was not a moment too soon.

Lost in the Translation

American Loren Murchison was left at the start of the 1920 Olympic men's 100 metres final in Antwerp because he didn't understand French. When the starter said '*prêt*' (French for 'get set'), Murchison thought the runners had been told to stand up and was just in the act of relaxing his body and rising to his feet when the gun went off. Left trailing by ten yards, he finished plumb last.

The Unkindest Cut

The 1954 Commonwealth Games mile in Vancouver was billed as a showdown between England's Roger Bannister, the first man to break four minutes, and Australian John Landy, the new world-record holder. But on the eve of the final Landy trod on a photographer's light bulb and needed four stitches in a gashed foot. Landy was still determined to run but the handicap allowed Bannister to win comfortably.

Olympic Chaos

The 1948 Olympic 10,000 metres ended in chaos, mainly due to the brilliance of Emil Zátopek. The Czech runner had lapped all but two of his rivals, thereby causing confusion among the London officials who were unsure as to how many laps were left. In a state of panic, they announced the start of the final lap one circuit too soon. Fortunately Zátopek was alive to the situation and carried on running but the others didn't and finished a lap early. In the ensuing mayhem Severt Dennolf of Sweden found himself relegated from fourth to fifth while sixth place was originally awarded to Belgium's Robert Everaert until the runner himself pointed out that he had actually dropped out of the race five laps from the finish.

But of course any blunder the British can make, the Americans can do bigger and better, as had been proved by the Los Angeles Olympics of 1932 where the 3,000 metre steeplechase descended into farce. The problem arose when the regular lap-checker was taken ill at the last minute and his inexperienced replacement forgot to change the lap count at the end of the first circuit. First to cross what should have been the finish line at the end of the race was Volmari Iso-Hollo of Finland, but instead he found no tape and a lap counter reading one to go. Thinking he must have miscalculated, he kept on running and won comfortably, but behind him, Britain's Thomas Evenson overtook Joseph McCluskey of the United States on the extra lap to take the silver. When it emerged that officialdom was at fault, McCluskey was offered a re-run the next day but he declined the offer because he was too exhausted.

The Forgotten Athlete

Trailing home almost thirty-nine minutes behind the previous finisher in the marathon at the 1979 Pan American Games at San Juan, Puerto Rico, plucky Wallace Williams of the Virgin Islands was horrified to find the stadium locked. Everybody had forgotten about him and gone home.

The Decking of Decker

It has to be said that the only time South African import Zola Budd truly endeared herself to the British public was when she inadvertently tripped America's Mary Decker in the final of the women's 3,000 metres at the 1984 Olympics. The incident, one of the most controversial in Olympic history, occurred around the 1,700-metres mark. Budd, running in bare feet as was her wont, was in the lead with Decker right behind and trying to squeeze through on the inside. As the two came close, the American hit one of Budd's legs, knocking Budd slightly off balance. Five strides later, they bumped again and, as Budd landed awkwardly, Decker tripped on Budd's right heel and fell to the ground. As Decker, hot favourite for the gold, sat sobbing at the side of the track, Budd continued in the face of hostile booing from the partisan Los Angeles crowd and despite the fact that her heel had been badly gashed by Decker's spiked shoe. Budd finished unplaced but her attempts to apologise to Decker afterwards met with a frosty reception. 'Looking back, I should have pushed her,' said the distraught American.

False Start in a Marathon!

If there is one athletics event which should never see a false start it is the marathon, yet that is precisely what happened back in 1900. The scene was the Boston marathon, the field for which was graced by a strong Canadian presence. Unfortunately the visiting Canadians were so wound-up that they began sprinting the moment starter John Graham had finished his official speech and before he could actually start the race.

Blume's Bloomer

At the 1960 West German Athletics Championships, German long jumper Manfred Steinbach had his fourth leap measured at 8.14 metres, just a centimetre short of Jesse Owens' world record which had stood since 1935. Sadly for Steinbach, the strength of the following wind was then announced as 3.2 metres per second – considerably in excess of the permissible level of 2.0 metres – and so the distance could not be entered in the record books. However, Walter Blume, the official in charge of the long jump, was later said to have admitted in private that, owing to an oversight, there had been no wind gauge reading for that particular jump. Apparently afraid of confessing in public to the mistake, Blume had allegedly invented a high reading which would render any record invalid. To add weight to the theory, it emerged that the wind measured on all of Steinbach's other jumps that day never exceeded 1.1 metres.

Expensive Acclimatisation

To prepare himself for the heat of Rome where he won the 50km walk at the 1960 Olympics, Britain's Don Thompson converted his bathroom into a veritable sauna. Over a period of eighteen months leading up to the Games, Thompson ensured that the smallest room was also the hottest room, so much so that he generated a gas bill for

£9,763. He returned home from his Olympic triumph to find that the gas had been cut off.

Baton Blunder

A golden opportunity for Nazi propaganda at the Berlin Olympics of 1936 presented itself in the final of the women's sprint relay. The German quartet were strongly fancied and were nine yards clear at the final changeover when Marie Dollinger handed the baton to Ilse Dörffeldt . . . who promptly dropped it. The Germans' disqualification allowed the United States team to take the gold. Hitler was not amused.

A Real Sickener

Paavo Nurmi of Finland certainly received a warm welcome at the end of his Olympic 10,000 metres triumph in Antwerp in 1920. For the runner-up, France's Joseph Guillemot, promptly vomited all over him. Guillemot's discomfort had been caused by the fact that he had just eaten a substantial lunch when he heard that the start time of the race had been brought forward from 5.30 p.m. to 2.15 p.m. at the request of the King of Belgium.

These Shoes Weren't Made for Running

Among the favourites for the 5,000 metres at the 1978 Commonwealth Games was Rod Dixon of New Zealand but his chances were spiked when his running shoes were stolen shortly before the start of the race. The start was delayed for fifteen minutes while Dixon hunted around for a replacement pair. In the end, he accepted an offer from English 800 metres runner David Cook but it was quickly apparent that the new shoes weren't to Dixon's liking. He limped home a distant seventh and, in dismay, hobbled straight on to the dressing room without breaking stride.

Another runner who mourned the loss of a shoe was Sergei Skrypka of the Soviet Union, competing in a heat of the 3,000 metres steeplechase at the 1972 Olympics in Munich. Despite losing a shoe with six laps remaining, he kept in touch with the leaders until coming to the final water jump where his bare foot slipped on the wet barrier causing him to fall headlong into the water. He may have been eliminated but at least he didn't need a post-race shower.

Greeks Bearing Gifts

Three miles from the finish of the 1896 Olympic marathon in Athens, Australia's Edwin Flack was so exhausted that he was in danger of collapse. A Greek spectator was asked to support him but the delirious Flack, thinking he was being attacked, repaid the generosity by punching the poor man to the ground. Wisely, Flack retired soon afterwards.

Watch the Birdie

Leading the 1994 New York marathon in the closing stages through Central Park South, Mexico's German Silva accidentally strayed from the course by following a camera motorcycle. By the time he had returned to the route, he was fifty yards adrift with less than a mile to run. However, by a superhuman effort he overhauled fellow countryman Benjamin Paredes to win by two seconds.

There was not such a happy ending for nineteen-year-old Swede Ernst Fast at the 1900 Olympic marathon in Paris. With under four miles to go, he was comfortably ahead until he and his accompanying cyclist took a wrong turning. By the time he had recovered, his hopes of victory had vanished and he had to settle for third place.

Otherwise Engaged

The incompetence of the officials at the 1932 Los Angeles Olympics has already been touched upon but they surpassed themselves during the men's discus. The lead was being held by John Anderson of the United States when France's Jules Noël unleashed a mighty effort with his fourth throw which appeared to land beyond the flag marking Anderson's best. However, all the discus officials were so engrossed in the pole vault competition which was taking place nearby that none of them saw precisely where Noël's throw had landed. They did offer the Frenchman an extra throw by way of apology but he was unable to produce another long one and finished out of the medals in fourth position.

Relay Choker

Athletes should always stick to what they're best at and in the case of former British discus champion Gerry Carr that meant field rather than track events. But in 1962 Carr was persuaded to run in a special 'heavyweights' relay for University College, Los Angeles, against Stanford University. Sadly old habits die hard and, running the first leg, he squeezed the baton so tightly that it broke.

Premature Celebration

Certain that victory was his, Canada's Alex Wilson threw up his arms in triumph a yard from the finish of the men's 800 metres final at the 1932 Olympics. But as he eased down, he had reckoned without a blistering spurt from Britain's Tommy Hampson who powered through to snatch the decision on the line. Wilson never did win Olympic gold.

Petered Out

Nearly half a century after Dorando Pietri's gallant effort in London, another marathon, this time on the other side of the world, ended with the leader staggering all over the track in a desperate, but ultimately fruitless, attempt to reach the finish unaided. The race was the 1954 Commonwealth Games in Vancouver and the athlete in question was England's Jim Peters. Once again the race was run in searing heat, resulting in a number of athletes suffering from sunstroke. Indeed another English runner, Stan Cox, had been eliminated after running straight into a telegraph pole. But no. 349, Peters, pressed on and entered the stadium twenty minutes ahead of the field. Dehydrated and suffering from severe heat exhaustion, he now began to pay for his suicidal pace. Reeling all over the track, his legs unable to support him, he fell on no fewer than ten occasions, each time just about managing to pick himself up. The crowd couldn't bear to look. 'Stop it. For God's sake someone help him,' shouted English high jumper Dorothy Tyler. Finally Peters saw what he thought was the finish line and tried to jog towards it but it was the finish line for the mile on the other side of the track. He still had 200 yards to go. At this point, he collapsed into the arms of team trainer, Mick Mayes, and was disqualified. Roger Bannister later wrote: 'No one who saw the tragic gallantry of his futile attempts to reach the finish wanted the painful exhibition to continue, yet no one seemed to have the authority to remove him from the race.' As Peters was ferried to hospital, the marathon was won by Scotland's Joe McGhee, himself so drained by the heat late in the race that he twice rebounded from trees after running into them.

A Wasted Journey

Wym Essajas was justifiably proud of being the first person chosen to represent Surinam in Olympic competition when he was sent to take part in the 800 metres at Rome in 1960. Alas, a breakdown in communications meant that he was told that the heats were in the afternoon instead of the morning. After spending the morning resting and building himself up for the challenge which lay ahead, he arrived at the stadium only to be told that the 800 metres heats were over. Thus the despondent Essajas returned to Surinam without having competed.

Traffic Jam

Leda Diaz de Cano of Honduras was so far behind the rest of the field in the 1984 Olympic women's marathon – twenty-seven and a half minutes at twenty kilometres – that officials persuaded her to retire so that they could reopen the streets of Los Angeles to traffic.

So Near But Yet So Far

With a gold medal for the women's 1500 metres at the 1970 Commonwealth Games in Edinburgh almost within touching distance, Sylvia Potts of New Zealand dramatically fell just two yards from the tape. By the time she had picked herself up and walked over the line, she was ninth, the gold having gone to England's Rita Ridley instead. 'I didn't trip,' said the hapless Potts afterwards. 'My legs just couldn't carry me any further. I was just run out.' By way of compensation, she was given the honour of carrying the Queen's Baton into the stadium for the opening ceremony of the 1974 Games in Christchurch. This time she managed to stay on her feet.

Wottle Woe

After storming to victory in the 800 metres at the 1972 Olympics in Munich wearing his familiar golf cap, Dave Wottle of the United States committed the grievous sin of forgetting to take it off during the playing of 'The Star-Spangled Banner' at the medal ceremony. Wottle was so mortified by his oversight that he was reduced to tears and made a formal apology to the American people.

Smoky Bacon Gets in Your Eyes

In 1991 it was reported that Scottish sprinter Euan Clarke was having to miss a number of engagements after cutting his eyeball while attempting to wipe the sweat from his forehead with a crisp packet.

Medal Muddle

In the days before photo finishes, no race was ever closer than the men's 440 yards final at the 1938 Empire Games in Sydney. The athletes concerned were England's Bill Roberts and Bill Fritz of Canada and it was a full fifteen minutes before officials declared Roberts to be the winner. Then, after further deliberation, they suddenly announced that they had changed their minds and were giving the gold to Fritz instead. However, the Canadian's joy was short-lived as, believe it or not, the officials reversed the decision yet again and returned the gold to Roberts. If he had any sense, he got out of Australia as fast as he could before the race officials had another change of heart.

Dead Slow

At the inaugural Boston marathon in 1897, the eventual winner, John McDermott, was nearly run over by cars in a funeral procession. An exasperated McDermott was forced to slow down suddenly to avoid a collision. He carried on but it was reported that several of the horseless carriages stalled.

7 Rugby

Selectors Chose Wrong Player

Arnold Alcock of Guy's Hospital was selected to play for England against South Africa in 1906 . . . but purely because of a clerical error. The selectors had originally pencilled in the name of Lancelot Slocock, who played for Liverpool, but the notice of selection was mistakenly sent to Alcock instead. In view of the fact that he was way out of his depth, it is scarcely surprising to learn that it turned out to be Alcock's only cap while the superior Slocock went on to play for his country eight times.

Injured Leaving Dressing Room

All set to take the field for the 1969 international with Scotland in Paris, France's Jean-Pierre Salut tripped as he was running up the stairs from the dressing room to the pitch and broke his ankle. He thus enjoyed the dubious distinction of being carried off before he had even made it on to the pitch.

Rain Stopped Play

A torrential downpour at St Helen's, Swansea, prior to the start of the

Wales–England international on 18 January 1903 filled the brass band's instruments with water and forced them to stop playing.

Referee Refused Entry to Ground

There was tremendous anticipation in Wales for the 1936 international with visitors Ireland. Wales were in line for the championship while Ireland had their hopes on the Triple Crown and the showdown attracted a huge crowd to the principality. One man who had considerable difficulty gaining admission was the match's English referee, Cyril Gadney. When Mr Gadney arrived at the entrance to the ground and announced that he was the referee for the big game, the gateman flatly refused to believe him and dismissed him as an impostor, saying that the same trick had been tried by countless others that day. As kick-off time neared, Welsh Rugby Union officials became increasingly worried about the non-appearance of the referee. Just as they were thinking about making contingency plans, they spotted him in the queue outside the ground paying to get in. With faces as red as their team's shirts, the officials ushered Mr Gadney inside so that the match could begin on schedule.

Ambulance Stuck on Pitch

Rugby players in New Zealand are used to pitches which are more like paddy fields but the surface for Taranaki's game against the British Lions in 1977 was exceptionally damp. Never was this better illustrated than when Taranaki scrum-half Dave Loveridge sustained a nasty knee injury. Given the squelching mud, the obvious procedure would have been to have removed Loveridge by stretcher but someone decreed the injury to be so serious that an ambulance needed to be brought on to the pitch. The inevitable happened – the ambulance got stuck in the mud and play was held up for eighteen minutes while players and spectators struggled to extricate the stricken vehicle.

Ball Stolen

The West Wales Challenge Cup final of 1877 between Cardiff and Llanelli was abandoned after the crowd stole the ball.

Coach Driver Got Lost

The coach drive to Wembley for the Rugby League Challenge Cup final affords players time to relax and soak up the atmosphere of the big occasion. But there was precious little opportunity for relaxation as the Bradford Northern team bus set off for the Twin Towers in 1947, mainly because the driver seemed to have no idea where he was going. At first nobody was any the wiser but as three o'clock drew nearer and they still seemed to be getting no closer to Wembley, questions began to be asked – especially as some players were convinced that they had passed the same junction three times. In the end the driver had to admit that he was hopelessly lost and that there was as much chance of them ending up in Worthing as Wembley. Fortunately help was at hand in the rotund shape of prop forward Frank Whitcombe, holder of an HGV licence. Relegating the driver to the back of the bus, Whitcombe took the wheel and steered his team-mates safely to the stadium in time for kick-off.

The King is Dethroned

On the British Lions' 1989 tour to Australia, the final Test in Sydney was won thanks to a monumental clanger dropped by, of all people, the great David Campese. Eschewing safety tactics, the Australian winger elected to try to run the ball out from behind his own line, but the pass he threw to Greg Martin was positively suicidal and allowed the Lions' Ieuan Evans to pounce for the try which won the match 19–18 and the series. Campese was roundly pilloried in the Australian press and plummeted overnight from 'Wonderman' to 'Blunderman'.

Bitten During Game

Nowadays stories about players being bitten by opponents during games of rugby are all too commonplace but the fate of George Podmore was altogether different. He was bitten by a dog during a game. The occasion was the 1873 Varsity match and Podmore, an Oxford forward, had to leave the field for treatment to his wound. Cambridge profited from his absence by storming to victory, giving rise to the theory that the dog's owner had light-blue blood.

Spot the Blunder

In 1901 Lord Ranfurly, the Governor of New Zealand, generously offered a trophy to the New Zealand Rugby Union. The offer was accepted and a trophy was commissioned from England. When it arrived, everyone commented on what a handsome shield it was . . . apart from one small thing. The centrepiece depicted soccer goal-posts and a round ball! The engravers were told to try again.

Confusion Over the Score

After Wales had gone over for a try at Twickenham in 1933, Vivian Jenkins' kick at goal went, according to the Daily Telegraph, 'at least a yard outside the right-hand post'. The English touch-judge signalled that the kick had failed but his Welsh counterpart, filled with patriotic pride, put his flag up to indicate that the kick was successful. The referee didn't blow his whistle, suggesting that he took the word of the Englishman, but the scoreboard registered a goal to Wales. And the scoreboard continued to carry the wrong score for the rest of the match so that the spectators left thinking Wales had won by six points whereas in fact they had won only 7–3.

A Fit of the Giggles

The second Test between the All Blacks and the visiting Springboks in 1937 was chiefly memorable for an unconventional display by the South Africans' giant prop forward Boy Louw. Following a blow to the head, he was left badly concussed and lost all sense of normality. Apart from no longer having much idea as to what he was doing, the concussion also gave him a continuous fit of the giggles which proved unnerving for team-mates and opposition alike. In the middle of these bouts of laughing, Louw would frequently break off and ask his captain, Danie Craven, what was happening and what he should do. Trying to give him a sense of purpose, an exasperated Craven suggested that Louw should try to stop the All Black prop, Dalton, from coming through the lineout. Obeying his leader's every word, Louw gleefully charged into Dalton at the next lineout while the referee's back was turned. 'Was that what you wanted?' giggled a delighted Louw, childlike, to his captain. 'No, Boy,' replied Craven, 'but it will have to do.' In spite of the handicap they were carrying, the Springboks managed to win 13–6 but it is doubtful whether Boy Louw remembered much about it.

Embarrassing Misprint

In the matchday programme for the 1980 international between France and Ireland, the surname of Irish back row Colm Tucker was spelt with an F instead of a T.

Ref Walked Off

When the Bristol–Newport game on 14 September 1985 erupted into a mass brawl in the first half, referee George Crawford decided he'd had enough and walked off. A local official took his place for the remainder of the match.

Something Missing

Having travelled fifty miles to play North Wales rivals Porthmadog in 1966, Colwyn Bay eagerly took to the field alongside their hosts, the referee and his touch-judges. It was only as the teams lined up for the kick-off and the referee prepared to put his whistle to his mouth that anyone realised that a vital ingredient of the game was missing. There was no ball. Unable to locate a spare, the referee had no choice but to abandon the match.

And even when a ball is provided, there is no guarantee that it will prove satisfactory. When Wales entertained New Zealand at Swansea in 1924, the referee, Colonel John Brunton, insisted on delaying the kick-off because he was unhappy with the match ball. The hard-to-please colonel then rejected two more balls before finally deigning to accept the fourth that was offered to him.

But the preparations for that match were exemplary compared to those made by the United States in 1976. Playing their first rugby union international since defeating France in the final of the 1924 Olympics, the US took on Australia in Los Angeles. However, the Americans hadn't done their homework. The pitch was neither long enough nor wide enough and was wrongly marked. And the game couldn't be started because the ball hadn't been inflated properly. Following an appeal over the public address system, a pump was found and the match finally got under way, Australia running out the 24–12 winners.

Too Much Bubbly

There are about as many teetotal rugby players as there are Dutch mountaineers, and in the early days of touring, generous hospitality ensured that the champagne flowed freely – sometimes with adverse effects. The first major rugby tour to visit these shores from the southern hemisphere was undertaken by New Zealand who set sail for Australia and Britain over the winter of 1888–89. The tour was the brainchild of English businessman Tom Eyton who lived in New Zealand. The idea was for an all-Maori squad of twenty-six but the organisers could only find twenty-two Maoris of a suitable standard and made up the numbers by inviting four others who looked a bit like Maoris. The British weather was something of a shock to their system, and in the game against Carlisle the rain and sleet were so unrelenting that the tourists' backs wore raincoats in the second half. However, the fixture with Middlesex, played on the estate of Lord Sheffield, was altogether more agreeable even though several of the New Zealanders probably had little recollection of it afterwards. For the pre-match lunch was so sumptuous and the drinks so liberal that many of the visitors were incapable of playing. To ensure that there was no risk of them sobering up, Lord Sheffield sent out his servants at half-time with more champagne.

It was a similar story when the British Lions toured South Africa in 1896. Of twenty-one games played, the Lions won nineteen, lost one and drew one. The draw came against Western Province in the third match of the tour and the tourists' poor performance was undoubtedly alcohol-related. Before the game the Lions had lunch with the South African Prime Minister, Sir Gordon Sprigg, and although the players were told to restrict themselves to four tumblers of champagne each (a remarkably generous restriction!), the bubbly flowed so freely that most of the team were totally incapable by the time they took the field. In the end, they were lucky to escape with a 0–0 draw. Later in the tour a sober Lions beat Western Province 32–0.

Corby must have taken a leaf out of the Lions' book on their 1989 tour of the north of England although it is doubtful whether club finances quite stretched to champagne which, in view of the amount of alcohol consumed, was probably just as well. After a particularly heavy night, Corby staggered on to the field the following day to play Whitby – but found themselves 80–0 down with just seven minutes of the second half gone. At that point the referee abandoned the game, ruling that most of the Corby players were too drunk to continue. They were thus left with little option but to drown their sorrows in the bar.

Collided with Goalpost

With minutes to go in the 1938 championship decider at Twickenham and with England trailing Scotland by 18 points to 16, England winger Hal Sever was put through for what seemed certain to be the winning try. With plenty of space outside, he instead elected to cut inside and ran smack into one of the goalposts. The impact caused him to drop the ball which Scotland eagerly picked up breaking away for the championship-clinching try.

Injured in Bed

John O'Meara missed out on playing for Ireland against Wales at Lansdowne Road in 1954 after ricking his back while sleeping in the team hotel on the night before the game.

Luck of the Draw

In the days before shiny balls were used for cup draws, the Rugby League used cardboard discs to determine the pairings for the Challenge Cup. For the draw for the first round of the 1923–24 competition, thirty-two discs were placed in the bag. All went smoothly until the last tie was announced – Salford at home to . . . nobody. There were no discs left in the bag. As worried officials checked through to find out which team was missing, it became apparent that, while in the bag, Hunslet's disc had somehow stuck to the base of Swinton's. The League immediately gave Hunslet the only available space – the away tie with Salford. Hunslet protested and demanded a re-draw but the League insisted that the draw, for all its flaws, had to stand.

Rugby union fared little better with the draw for the 1995 World Cup which had to be made three times before meeting requirements. The original draw was made in January 1993 but provoked complaints from Australia and New Zealand who felt that teams from the same pool should not meet again until the final. Taking this on board, the organisers made a second draw in April but here a printing error crept in which meant that teams from the same pool would meet before the final after all. They finally got it right with a third draw the following month.

Wounded Refs

It's not only players who get injured in rugby union matches – referees are equally at risk, particularly if they happen to be in the wrong place at the wrong time. Frenchman Robert Calmet became entangled in a ruck just before half-time in the 1970 England–Wales international and broke a leg. A replacement took over for the second period.

Three years later, Ken Pattinson, only just appointed to England's panel of referees, took charge of the France–Scotland game at Parc des Princes in Paris. Sadly he tore a calf muscle after only fifteen minutes of his first international and had to be replaced by a French referee, François Palmade.

One referee who might have been better advised to have left the field was Frenchman Dr Alain Cuny, who officiated at the Wales–Scotland match in 1975. Half an hour from the end he injured a leg muscle and was reduced to hobbling around a long way behind the play. As his grip on the game diminished, it was suggested that he come off but, presumably in the belief that doctor knows best, he insisted on seeing it right through to the finish. It was his last international.

Equine Opponent

The East Coast Rugby Football Union on North Island is one of the smallest rugby unions in New Zealand. Founded in 1921, in their early years they had difficulty fielding a representative team and would often recruit players from the local pub minutes before a game. Once on tour in the North Island, East Coast suffered so many injuries that the team's overweight, middle-aged bus driver was invited to play. But he was positively slim compared to one who turned out for East Coast's game against the Junior All Blacks. With the action at the other end of the field, the players turned round to see that a horse had wandered on to the pitch and was grazing quietly near the 22-metre line. They played round it . . .

Game Interrupted by Air Raid

The Rugby League international between England and Wales at Oldham on 9 November 1940 was brought to a temporary halt by the sound of air-raid sirens. The match resumed after a short break and England went on to win 8–5.

Couldn't Get Time Off Work

When Frank Clayton was selected for the first New Zealand tour to Australia in 1884, the bosses at the bank where he worked didn't believe him and refused to give him time off. He was never chosen again. Meanwhile, Canterbury scrum-half Peter Harvey was considered too important to the nation to join the All Blacks' tour of Britain in 1905. The New Zealand Prime Minister refused to allow Harvey to travel because he was the only qualified lip reader in New Zealand.

Lost All Sense of Direction

Brunei rugby player Dick Dover had never doubted his own pace. He was sure that with the right kind of pass and a clear run, he had the legs of most opponents – it was just that such opportunities were few and far between. But then, playing for Kukris against Panaga, he seized his moment when the ball broke loose from a scrum. Sprinting away, he showed blistering speed and ran fully seventy-five yards to touch down unchallenged. Nobody could get near him . . . or rather, nobody wanted to get near him. For disorientated by the wheeling of the scrum, Dover had run the wrong way and had touched down under his own posts instead of those of the opposition. No wonder his team-mates shook their heads in dismay.

A Lightning Strike

The second rugby union Test between the United States and France at Colorado Springs on 20 July 1991 was abandoned just after half-time when the scoreboard was struck by lightning. France were leading 10–3 at the time.

Killed by Rhino

Newton Abbot and England forward Denys Dobson had an unfortunate habit of making headlines for the wrong reasons. Capped six times by his country, he began by earning notoriety for being the first player to be sent off in a major match for using 'obscene language' directed at the referee. This transgression, which took place during the British Lions' tour of Australia and New Zealand in 1904, landed Dobson with an eight-month suspension. He later worked in the Colonial Civil Service and decided to start a new life in Nyasaland as a farmer. It was there in 1916 that he made his second headline when he was trampled underfoot by a rhinoceros – the only England rugby international known to have met his death by such means. On hearing the news, his former headmaster apparently remarked that Dobson's fend always was a bit weak . . .

Lost on Way to Match

Blackheath forward Philip Newton got lost on his way to Swansea and missed England's international against Wales in 1882. To rub salt into the wound, his replacement, Gregory Wade, scored three tries.

Out of Thin Air

The third-round Rugby League Challenge Cup tie between Swinton and Castleford in the 1927–28 season was a closely fought affair, but with one of the Swinton players receiving treatment off the pitch, Castleford looked to press home their numerical superiority. Swinton held firm and even committed men forward themselves but this looked to be their undoing when a breakaway opportunity presented itself and Castleford descended en masse towards the Swinton line. It seemed a certain score but suddenly a Swinton man appeared from nowhere to make a try-saving tackle. As the downcast Castleford players scratched their heads wondering where on earth the tackler had come from, they received an unlikely answer – it was the man who had been off the field injured. Seeing Castleford break away, he had defied the pain to run back on to the field unannounced and launch himself at the man with the ball. Castleford's protests fell on deaf ears and their sense of injustice was heightened when they lost the game. However, the incident did lead to a change in the rules so that in future injured players had to get permission from the match officials before returning to the field.

Clutching at Straws

Playing for Ireland against England in 1958, fly-half Mick English allowed his opposite number Phil Horrocks-Taylor to run past him for the match-winning try. Asked by his team-mates what had gone wrong, English replied: 'Well, the Horrocks went one way, and the Taylor went the other, and I was left holding the hyphen.'

Ref in a Hurry

Referees have been known to make the odd error regarding time-keeping but invariably it's only a matter of a minute or two. But former England international Adrian Stoop, who was officiating at the East Midlands–Barbarians fixture at Northampton in 1921, came up with what must surely be a world record when he blew for full-time fourteen minutes early. Either his watch had a mind of its own or he had a train to catch! In fact, he didn't get away early at all because when the mistake was discovered, he and the players were dragged out of the bath to complete the match.

In May 1985 Scotland rounded off their tour of Canada with a 79–0 drubbing of the Alberta President's XV at Calgary, equalling their record victory. And the Scots would surely have set a new national record had the referee, obviously sympathetic to the Canadians' plight, not blown for time a full five minutes early.

Another referee with time-keeping problems was John Cail who took charge of New Zealand's game against Yorkshire on the Maoris' 1888–89 tour of Britain. When his watch failed, he went into the crowd and borrowed one from a spectator.

Stole Goalposts

Bridgend RFC were none too happy about having to leave their Brewery Field home in 1948 to make way for a rugby league club. But the union boys got their revenge by creeping back in the dead of night to steal the goalposts.

Two Men Short

The first rugby union international between England and Wales took place at Blackheath in 1881. Wales were somewhat ill-prepared for this momentous occasion and arrived in London to find that they were two men short on account of their invitations having gone astray. They managed to make up the numbers by recruiting two Varsity players with Welsh qualifications but could never bridge the gulf in class and were crushed by eight goals and six tries to nil. The result proved such a humiliating experience for the Welsh that the fixture was not repeated the following year.

On the Blind Side

In the heat of combat, rugby union players occasionally lose clumps of hair, teeth, even bits of ear. But they're not often parted from a glass eye. Yet when Silverhill Colliery from Nottinghamshire met Daw Mill of Warwickshire in a 1993 Coal Board Cup tie, the game was held up for several minutes while a search was conducted for a Silverhill player's artificial eye. It was the property of 14-stone forward Steve Bush who had lost the sight of his left eye following a pit accident three years earlier. Now as he put all of his considerable weight behind a scrum, the false eye fell out and sank into the turf. Referee Peter Llewellyn said: 'I saw this player walking round staring at the ground. I asked, "What have you lost?" When he said, "My eye", I thought we had a major injury on our hands.' Despite scouring every blade of grass in the immediate vicinity, the wandering eye could not be found, leaving Bush to play the rest of the match with an empty socket. Although this must have been a somewhat disconcerting sight for the opposition, Daw Mill managed to turn a blind eye to it and ran out 17–8 winners.

Fans Left in the Dark

One of the first rugby union matches to be played under lights was a fixture between Hawick and Melrose in 1879. A crowd of 5,000 gathered for the occasion at Buccleuch Park despite a night of driving snow. But the clubs' hopes of making a financial killing out of the match were wrecked by inadequate security which allowed a good proportion of the spectators to creep in without paying. So as soon as the game ended, partly to save money on electricity but also perhaps partly out of spite, officials switched off the lights, leaving the homegoing fans to slither, slide and fall over each other in the darkness and slush.

A Question of Priorities

England players were puzzled when referee John Reardon stopped their game with Mid-West at Cleveland, Ohio, on 13 June 1982 early in the second half with England close to the try line. The referee explained that he had been instructed to stop play because the local television station that was covering the game was screening adverts at that point and didn't want its viewers to miss any of the action. Although operating in the constant fear that their best moves could be halted by a TV ad for peanut butter, England still managed to win 53–7.

Opponents Were Out

For part of their centenary tour to New Zealand in 1975, Ireland had arranged to drop in and play a game against Fiji. However, the planned engagement had to be scrapped because, when the Irish team arrived on the island, they were told that the Fijians were on tour in Australia . . .

Royal Flush

When his shorts tore during the international against England at Twickenham on the 1947–48 tour, Australian captain Trevor Allen scorned the time-honoured convention of waiting for a ring of players to surround him so that he could change with a modicum of privacy. Instead he simply cast the old shorts aside in open play and, with buttocks gleaming and his jockstrap clearly visible, trotted twenty yards to receive a new pair from an attendant. The incident, performed in full view of royalty, caused mutterings of disapproval within the rugby union world for weeks afterwards.

Forgot to Touch Down

The turning point of the 1896 England–Ireland international at Leeds was when England's Ernest Fookes was put in for a try under the posts but failed to touch down before running out of play beyond the dead-ball line. The lapse allowed Ireland to win 10–4.

French winger Patrick Estève was guilty of a similar aberration in the match with England at Twickenham in 1985. After crossing the try line in the corner, Estève tried to simplify the conversion attempt by running round and touching down near the posts. But before he could do so, he was tackled by an England player and dropped the ball. The lost try proved crucial since the game ended in a 9–9 draw.

More deserving of sympathy was Irish centre Jack Arigho whose crossing of the line for a try against Scotland in 1929 prompted scenes of wild celebration from the Lansdowne Road crowd. The trouble was that in their excitement the spectators swarmed on to the pitch, thus preventing Arigho from running round under the posts. While he managed to touch down for the try, the unnecessarily difficult conversion was missed and Scotland proceeded to win 16–7.

The Lord Moves in Mysterious Ways

Due to meet mighty Wigan in the 1989 JPS Trophy, struggling Runcorn Highfield Rugby League Club were further crippled by a players' strike which forced them to field nine amateurs. So stretched were their resources that they also had to name their coach Bill Ashurst, a forty-one-year-old born-again Christian, as one of the substitutes. He came on in the second half but was sent off eleven minutes later for head-butting. Runcorn lost 92–2.

Tour Tragedy

The British Lions' 1888 tour to Australia and New Zealand was tinged by tragedy and misunderstanding. Not only did they lose their captain, R. L. Seddon, who was drowned in a boating accident on Australia's Hunter River, but they also discovered on arrival that of the thirty-five matches they were due to play Down Under, nineteen were Australian Rules games. The Australians clearly thought their game was much the same as rugby union but it was like putting Tim Henman on a squash court and expecting him to get on with it.

And things didn't improve when the Lions reached New Zealand, where they encountered the sort of hazards you just don't expect to find at Twickenham. A report of Wellington's match with the Lions stated that 'Budge played well, and only missed securing a force down for Wellington when the ball caught in the telephone wires which ran across the field.' Another feature to be found at a New Zealand rugby ground in the nineteenth century, this time at Nelson, was a thick may hedge which ran parallel to the touchline. During one game a Nelson player was thrown head first into the hedge but, according to contemporary reports, 'seemed not at all disconcerted and picked the thorns out of his head as the opportunity offered'.

Last-Minute Disappointment

It was a dream come true for Birkenhead Park winger Wilfrid Lowry when he was selected to play for England against Wales in 1920. As the big day finally arrived, there was no more excited England player in the dressing room. And he was positively glowing with pride when he donned the national shirt and ran out on to the pitch for the official pre-match team photograph. Then as he made his way back to the dressing room with his colleagues for the final team-talk, he was suddenly informed that he wouldn't be playing after all. Was it something to do with the photo? Had his profile left something to be desired? Was he pulling a funny face? No, his position was going to Harold Day because the latter was deemed better suited to the heavy conditions. Lowry's disappointment was alleviated somewhat when he was selected – and played – against France two weeks later. But it was to prove his only international cap.

A Muted Celebration

The first Rugby League World Cup was staged in France in 1954 and was won by Great Britain. The trophy was presented by the French Rugby League but the victorious British team found difficulty in having the traditional celebratory drink out of it because the trophy leaked where the handles joined the body.

Referee All at Sea

Appointed to referee the Ireland–New Zealand international in Dublin in 1935, Scotland's W. A. Allan thought he had set off from his homeland in plenty of time. But he had reckoned without the tempestuous weather, and when the game kicked off, he was still stranded at sea, sheltering from a storm. His place was taken by R. W. Jeffares, son of the secretary of the Irish Rugby Football Union.

Disappearing Act

When the Ivory Coast under-19 squad flew home from Gatwick after competing in the 1999 Junior World Cup, they did so without twelve of their players who had done a vanishing act in Britain. One made a break for it after the final in Llanelli, five more disappeared at the end of a banquet in Cardiff and within a few days another six had gone AWOL in a move which brought a whole new meaning to elusive running. As police and immigration officials sought twelve large, French-speaking youths last seen wearing distinctive blue tracksuits, a Home Office spokesman admitted: 'We have no firm information at all on their whereabouts. They are now liable for arrest.'

Going . . . Gone

The undisputed star of North Auckland's 35-point victory over Buller for New Zealand's Ranfurly Shield in 1972 was All Blacks half-back Sid Going. And while Buller couldn't keep tabs on Going, they did at least have the consolation prize of his boot. For when Going lost one of his boots in a tackle, Buller lock Orlando Nahr, following through, scooped it up and tucked it into his shorts out of sight. With none of the North Auckland team seeing where it went, Going was forced to play on with one boot.

John Roberts played with no boots at all for Cardiff Athletic against Chepstow in 1937. When he turned up at the ground, he realised he had forgotten his boots but so keen was he to regain his place in the Cardiff first team that rather than pull out, he chose to play in stockinged feet.

Missed the Train

Over *la lune* at being selected to play for France against Scotland in 1911, Gaston Vareilles eagerly accepted the chance to travel to the game by train with his new team-mates. But the excitement of the occasion had left him feeling a little empty in the stomach so when the train pulled into Lyon, Vareilles decided to jump off and buy a sandwich. Exactly how long the train was supposed to stop at Lyon remains something of a mystery but suffice to say that by the time Vareilles had queued patiently for his French bread, paid for it and returned to the platform, he was just in time to see the train and his team-mates disappearing into the distance. With no alternative means of transport, the luckless Vareilles missed the match. It comes as no surprise to learn that he was never again picked to play for France.

New Rule Floors Ref

Referee Gareth Simmonds apologised to Neath after allowing the dropped goal by Emyr Lewis which enabled Llanelli to win the first SWALEC Cup at Cardiff in May 1993. The goal – twenty-four minutes into the second half – put Llanelli 21–18 ahead, a position they held right to the final whistle. But it should never have been allowed since it was contrary to new laws introduced that season. The dropped goal came immediately following a free-kick but the new regulations stipulated that the ball must first be touched by an opposition player. Being unlucky losers was not quite the prize Neath had been hoping for.

Knocked Out by Flour Bomb

The Auckland Test which closed the Springboks' 1981 tour to New Zealand was marked by repeated anti-apartheid demonstrations. Even before the match got under way, a bogus referee sneaked on to the pitch, stole the ball and booted it into the crowd, causing a delay while a replacement was found. And during the game a light aircraft flew overhead, dropping leaflets and flour bombs in almost equal numbers. One of these bombs scored a direct hit on the head of burly New Zealand prop Gary Knight and knocked him out cold.

Amended Result

The British Lions' shock Test win in South Africa in 1938 nearly didn't make it into the record books because nobody believed the score. The Lions' triumph at Cape Town was their first in that country since 1910 and came in a game that nobody back home expected them to win. Among the doubters was a London news agency reporter who, knowing a fair bit about the game and aware that the Lions were trailing 13–3 at half-time, refused to believe the final score which was wired to him and which read: South Africa 16, the British Lions 21. Thinking that the scores must have been transposed, he changed it to South Africa 21, the British Lions 16.

An even more dramatic misinterpretation was by a fledgling radio broadcaster from Warrington who convinced the entire town that one of their number had been killed during the 1928 Rugby League Challenge Cup final with Swinton. When two first aid men rushed on to the pitch to attend to Warrington scrum-half Billy Kirk, the reporter jumped to the conclusion that they were clergymen and that

Kirk was dead. Seeing the men cover Kirk's face and carry him off on a stretcher merely served to confirm the intrepid reporter's worst fears. While the man at the mike relayed the sombre news to his listeners, Kirk was well on the road to recovery.

Tackled by Boxer Dog

During the third Test between New Zealand and the British Lions in 1971, the All Blacks' Howard Joseph was heading for the try line when he tripped over a boxer dog which had strayed on to the pitch. The ball ran loose, the chance was lost and the Lions went on to win 13–3.

Tricked Out of a Cap

Full-back George Nepua was all set to represent New Zealand on the All Blacks' tour to Britain in 1927 until someone sent the selectors a bogus telegram saying that Nepua was unavailable. The hoax wasn't uncovered until the team had sailed.

Plan Backfired

Salford were hot favourites to win the 1939 Rugby League Challenge Cup final at the expense of Halifax but were undone by the pre-match plans of their own manager, Lance Todd. Coming to the conclusion that what his players needed in the week before the big game was fresh air and countryside, Todd took them training into the back of beyond. The barn which he had hired as accommodation didn't have any baths, and over half of the team caught colds. Many of the Salford players were still feeling under the weather by the time they walked out at Wembley. Tired and weak, their noses did more running than their legs and they crashed to a shock 20–3 defeat.

Injured While Celebrating . . .

South Africa reserve forward Howard Watt suffered a hairline fracture of the right ankle after jumping up and down in the grandstand to celebrate his team's victory over New Zealand in the second Test of 1937.

. . . and Injured on Deck

To keep in shape and pass the hours on their voyage aboard the *Windsor Castle* on its journey to Britain, the 1931 Springbok tourists practised their handling movements on the ship's deck. But this soon proved a costly exercise. Three practice balls disappeared overboard and, in trying to prevent another one from going over the side, Jock van Niekerk hurt his knee so badly that his tour was ruined and his career was brought to a premature end.

8 Horse Racing

A Case of Mistaken Identity

Veteran trainer Reg Hollinshead was left with egg on his face when the wrong horse was saddled up for a race at Southwell in 1996. Hollinshead had two runners at the meeting on 8 January – Taniyar and Loch Style, both bay geldings. Taniyar was entered in the 12-furlong Waterford Median Auction Stakes with Loch Style due to run in a seven-furlong seller later in the afternoon, but a mix-up resulted in Loch Style running in place of the superior Taniyar . . . and over a much longer distance. The error only came to light after Loch Style, made 5–2 second favourite on the strength of Taniyar's form, had returned to the unsaddling enclosure, having been beaten over forty lengths in seventh. 'They are of a similar size and shape,' explained an embarrassed Hollinshead. 'I'm afraid we did not realise we had saddled the wrong horse. The penny didn't drop even when he ran badly although the jockey, Ray Cochrane, told me the horse wouldn't have stayed one mile in a horsebox!'

Sick in the Saddle

Among the rank outsiders for the 1919 Grand National was the locally trained All White. The horse's usual jockey, Robert Chadwick, was injured about a week before the race and so All

White's connections hastily sought a jockey who could ride at 9st 10lb. The only one available was a T. Williams who is believed to have been French although it has to be said that Williams is not exactly a common surname in Provence. Anxious to make the weight, Williams fasted religiously for days on end and on the day of the big race thought it was safe to sample some seafood from a stall at Aintree. The intake of mussels and cockles may not have upset the scales but they certainly upset his stomach. With All White in a challenging position after jumping Becher's on the second circuit, Williams suddenly pulled the horse to a halt at the side of the course. There, spectators were amazed to see the jockey leaning from his mount to be violently sick. As soon as he had cleared out his system, Williams set All White off in pursuit of the leaders once more but could never hope to make up the lost ground. The partnership eventually finished fifth, victims of a deadly seafood cocktail.

Early Post

In October 1989 jockey Ray Goldstein travelled all the way from Lewes in Sussex to partner his only ride of the day, Indian, in the Grunhalle Handicap Chase at Carlisle. The effort looked like proving worthwhile as the 11-10 favourite accelerated into the lead close to home. But then Goldstein, mistaking the winning post, dropped his hands too soon and was caught on the line by Trafalgar Blue. It must have been a long journey home.

The Luckless McDonough

During the inaugural years of the Grand National, few jockeys suffered as much misfortune as William McDonough. In the first year of the race, 1839, when it was still known as the Grand Liverpool Steeplechase, McDonough partnered an Irish horse called Rust. They were going along quite nicely until McDonough opted to run wide in search of better ground. Suddenly horse and jockey found themselves deliberately hemmed in by a crowd of spectators who clearly had their money on another entrant. McDonough and Rust were only allowed to continue when the rest of the runners were virtually out of sight. By then, pursuit would have been futile and the hapless Rust was pulled up. Seven years later, McDonough took the ride on Lancet. This horse was also handily placed in the race until a mounted spectator galloped into him knocking McDonough from the saddle. Given his luck, it will come as no surprise to learn that William McDonough never did ride the winner of the Grand National.

Dozed Off

On 18 May 1994 jockey Graham Bradley took a nap in his car and missed the start of a race at Worcester. To make matters worse for Bradley, who was fined £100 by the stewards, the horse he should have ridden, Macedonas, went on to win the Handley Castle Novices' Chase partnered by Bradley's replacement, Simon McNeill. Bradley lamented afterwards: 'I was here an hour and a half before racing and I had a doze in the car. When I woke up, I was a minute too late to weigh out.'

An Error of Judgement

The 1927 Cambridgeshire was a curious event all round. The hot favourite was 4–1 chance Weissdorn but his interest in racing disappeared the moment he found himself drawn next to the filly Kitty II who happened to be 'in season'. Throughout the race Weissdorn refused to leave her side which might not have been too damaging had she been anything other than a 100–1 outsider. Instead the lovers trailed in together at the rear of the field. But the real drama lay up ahead amid claims that the real winner of the race had only been placed third by the judge. The problem for the judge was that the runners had split into two groups with Medal and Niantic heading the field on the stand side and Insight II crossing the line first on the far side. Most observers thought that Insight II had won – his jockey reckoned he had got home by a good half a length – but the judge announced a dead heat for first place between Medal and Niantic with Insight II a full length away in third. To compound the confusion, he later amended the distance between the joint winners and the third horse to a neck. Photo-finish cameras couldn't come soon enough.

But even modern technology does not automatically rule out the human error factor. In June 1980, having announced Summary as the winner of the Walmer Handicap at Folkestone, judge Graham Wemyss admitted that he'd misinterpreted the photograph of the finish. So he reversed the decision, making King Hustler the new winner with Summary relegated to second. Bets were paid out only on the original result however.

Then on Easter Monday 1986 a horse called Play The Knave was declared the winner of a race at Hereford, but after studying the photo-finish print, the judge, Peter Roffe-Silvester, realised that favourite Castle Warden was clearly in front at the line. So half an hour after awarding the race to Play The Knave, Mr Roffe-Silvester announced that he was amending the result. Bookmakers who had to pay out twice on the race were predictably unhappy at the shambolic outcome. Mr Roffe-Silvester tendered his resignation a few days later.

The Devon Loch Affair

Almost every year the Grand National throws up a hard luck story but nothing captured the public's imagination quite like the Devon Loch mystery of 1956. Having jumped impeccably throughout, Devon Loch, owned by the Queen Mother, trained by Peter Cazalet and ridden by Dick Francis, was clear on the run-in until, with just fifty yards to go, he inexplicably spreadeagled on the flat. The crowd's cheers, so vociferous in anticipation of a royal winner, turned to stunned silence as ESB passed the stricken Devon Loch to claim the National. As the Queen Mother tried to console Francis, theories circulated as to what had caused Devon Loch to slip up in such dramatic circumstances. Some suggested that the horse had been confused by the water jump on the other side of the rail and had tried to take a leap over a non-existent fence; others thought he may have been unnerved by the deafening roar of the spectators. Whatever the reason, there was at least a silver lining to this particular cloud since the intrigue surrounding the finish fired Dick Francis's imagination and helped him on his way to a highly successful career as a thriller writer.

Devon Loch wasn't the first horse to come to grief on the Aintree run-in. There was a similar incident back in 1917 during the War National Steeplechase, the wartime version of the Grand National. Limerock, ridden by Bill Smith, had galloped into a commanding lead from the last fence but, with the race apparently won, he collapsed and fell a matter of yards from the winning post.

Carberry's Clanger

On board Sallie's Girl in the New Stand Design Team Slaney Novice Hurdle at Naas in Ireland at the start of January 1999, Paul Carberry made the fatal mistake of not riding out a finish because he thought there was still a circuit to go. All up the home straight, Carberry kept Sallie's Girl tucked in behind Glazeaway, hard ridden by Conor O'Dwyer. Seeing O'Dwyer rousting his mount along, Carberry even shouted to him that there was another circuit left, but it was Carberry who had miscalculated. As the hard-held Sallie's Girl passed the post three-quarters of a length in arrears and still full of running, Carberry realised to his horror what he had done. The lapse cost him a suspension of ten racing days.

Foiled by a Dog

Three days after winning the 1835 St Leger, Queen of Trumps was turned out again at Doncaster, this time in the three-runner Scarborough Stakes. Pitted against two opponents better suited to giving rides on Scarborough beach, Queen of Trumps was backed down to 1–10 favourite. Victory seemed a formality. And as the race unfolded, favourite backers appeared to have little cause for concern. But just as Queen of Trumps was moving out to deliver her challenge with 100 yards to go, she was suddenly brought to her knees by a bulldog which had run on to the course. While stunned racegoers struggled to come to terms with what had happened, Ainderby ran on to claim a hollow victory.

There was another canine intruder during the 1926 Derby. Swift and Sure was closing in on the leaders when a dog ran into his path and nearly brought him down. The horse finished fourth but would undoubtedly have been placed but for the intervention of man's best friend.

One dog which got on to a course without affecting the result was a greyhound that took part in the closing stages of the Tote Each Way Handicap Hurdle at Lingfield on 21 December 1985. The dog – an ex-racer owned by Mrs Vi Cowan – slipped its leash and chased the horses home, eventually passing the post in a highly creditable fourth place. The excitement proved too much for the dog's owner who, after trying to retrieve the errant hound, collapsed and was given first aid.

Shutting the Stable Door . . .

One of the great Grand National horses around the turn of the century was Manifesto, a winner in 1897 and 1899. And he was only deprived of a hat-trick by the carelessness of a stable boy. Prior to the 1898 race, Manifesto had been sold for the princely sum of £4,000 to Mr J. G. Bulteel who had put the horse in the care of a new trainer, Willie Moore. But with just a week to go to the National, Manifesto got loose when the door of his box was left open by a stable boy. After exploring his new surroundings and strolling around the yard, Manifesto tried to jump a gate but ended up badly bruising his fetlock. As a result he had to miss the race. When he realised his mistake, the stable boy is said to have fled the scene in terror.

Feeling Sheepish

Riding in a National Hunt race at Wye, jockey Aly Branford was deposited over the running rail on being parted from his mount. Medical staff rushed to the scene but when the ambulance arrived, Branford was seen to be twitching ominously. It transpired that, in addition to breaking his collarbone, he had landed on a live electric sheep wire.

The Mildmay Jinx

The Hon. Anthony (later Lord) Mildmay looked set to spring a major surprise in the 1936 Grand National on board the 100–1 outsider Davy Jones. The front-running Davy Jones had the rest of the field struggling and rounded the home turn well clear of his rivals. But disaster lay ahead because Mildmay had failed to take the precaution of knotting the end of his reins. At the second last Davy Jones made his only mistake and pecked slightly on landing. It was nothing serious but it was enough to cause the buckle of the reins to come undone and, with no back-up, Mildmay suddenly found himself powerless to steer the horse. Consequently Davy Jones veered left at the final fence and ran out, scattering spectators before him and leaving Reynoldstown to win for the second successive year. It was scant consolation to Mildmay that the Aintree authorities decided to name the ordinary chase course after him.

Mildmay's Aintree jinx struck again in 1948. Some months before that year's National, the intrepid jockey had broken his neck in a fall at Folkestone and since then had been prone to attacks of cramp in the neck. Of all the moments for the condition to return, it chose precisely when Mildmay was up with the leaders in the National on Cromwell. After clearing Becher's second time around, Mildmay's head suddenly slumped forward so that his chin rested on his chest. His neck gripped by cramp, he became little more than a passenger as Cromwell ploughed on over the formidable fences. It was to the credit of both horse and rider that, despite such a handicap, Cromwell still managed to finish third.

Ironically, with echoes of Mildmay himself twelve years earlier, there was another crazy drama between the last two fences of the 1948 National. Although Cromwell was plugging on bravely, he was no match for First of the Dandies, Sheila's Cottage and the 100–1 shot Zahia. And at the second last as Zahia, partnered by Eddie Reavey, ranged up alongside First of the Dandies, there seemed likely to be a shock result. Perhaps Reavey simply wasn't expecting to find himself in front without anybody to point the way home but approaching the last he took the wrong course and steered Zahia wide of the fence. In the end, it was Sheila's Cottage who profited from Reavey's howler although there was one last sting in the tail for winning jockey Arthur Thompson. When he went to visit Sheila's Cottage after the race to thank her for her efforts, she expressed her gratitude for the ride he had given her by biting off the top of his finger.

Flight of Fancy

The Orchard Portman Selling Handicap Hurdle at Taunton on 9 November 1995 ended in chaos as six horses were disqualified for taking the wrong course at the final flight. With jockey Michael Clarke lying injured from a fall on the first circuit, the final hurdle was dolled off. The jockeys should have gone round the outside of the hurdle but the culprits, led by Tony McCoy on first-past-the-post Little Hooligan, got it into their heads that they should bypass the hurdle on the inside and in the process nearly mowed down a group of ambulance personnel. The first to go the right way was Jamie Osborne on fifth-placed Safe Secret who, despite finishing over eighteen lengths behind Little Hooligan, was promoted to first place. Faez, the original eighth, was moved up to second. Safe Secret's trainer, Roy Brotherton, said: 'I saw her disappear off the TV screen and wondered where Jamie Osborne had gone, but fair play to him – he got it right.'

Gone Grazing

There are some days when even horses decide it is simply too nice to race and that a lush green field looks altogether more enticing than carrying someone you hardly know round tight bends at breakneck speed. Such an occasion occurred at the 1952 Goodwood Cup for which Aquino II had been backed down to 2–1. Aquino II was something of a character anyway and had been fitted with blinkers in an effort to instil some degree of concentration, but on this brilliantly hot day, nothing would persuade the horse to race. No sooner were they off in the long-distance event than Aquino II tried to turn round and head back to the paddock. Frustrated in that manoeuvre, the horse ran on for a furlong before swerving violently out into the centre of the course and attempting to pull up. The poor jockey managed to galvanise the horse into some form of forward movement until, reaching the bend leading out of the straight, Aquino II spotted from behind its blinkers an adjacent field of long grass, dappled with pretty wild flowers. This was the place to be and so when a gap in the railings appeared, the hotly fancied runner calmly ambled off the course and into the meadow where it grazed contentedly, watching the other runners sweat out the remaining two miles.

Another reluctant participant was Inkerman, a runner – if that's not too strong a word for it – in the 1863 Grand National. Having already got rid of jockey Smith, Inkerman wandered off at the Canal Turn and promptly disappeared. After connections had spent hours searching in vain for the missing horse, Inkerman was eventually located late that night grazing in a field several miles from Aintree ... and no doubt wondering what all the fuss was about.

Finished Too Soon

Unlike Paul Carberry who didn't ride a finish in the mistaken belief that there was still a circuit remaining, jockey Richard Hughes landed in hot water in August 1996 for riding a finish a circuit too soon. Partnering Mapengo in the 1¾ mile Shelton Trenching

Systems Handicap at Wolverhampton, Hughes had his mount in front from the off and was well clear when he eased the five-year-old down passing the post. At that point, he was overtaken by the rest of the field starting the second circuit! The horse's trainer, John Cullinan, said of Hughes: 'He did not acquaint himself with the distance of the race.'

Strangely enough, there was a repeat performance at the same track fifteen months later when Carl Lowther was banned for five days after riding a finish a circuit too soon on Naval Games in the 1m 7f Frost Claiming Stakes. Inevitably the horse finished unplaced.

Picnic Panic

Whereas recent Grand Nationals have occasionally seen protesters gather at the first fence, the 1871 event witnessed a more tranquil sight. For sitting beneath the rail of the first fence were a party of picnickers. Indeed they were feasting so merrily that they were totally oblivious to the fact that the race had started and that twenty-five horses were thundering towards them. It was only when they could almost see the whites of the horses' eyes that they realised they had better get out of the way and scrambled to safety. It is not recorded whether they left behind any cucumber sandwiches. The Aintree public behaved equally badly at the end of the race. The winning horse, The Lamb, lost most of his white tail to souvenir hunters, and the winning owner, Lord Poulett, was relieved of his pocket watch.

Dragged Across the Finish Line

National Hunt jockeys are renowned for their courage and their ability to stick like glue in the saddle but rarely have those qualities been put to a sterner test than at Newton Abbot on 28 August 1984. The jockey in question was Mr Stuart Kittow who was partnering a horse called Tango Shandy in a novices' chase. As is common in such races, there was widespread carnage, with the result that before long there were only two horses left standing – Tango Shandy and Legal Session. And when Legal Session too fell some way from home, the result appeared a foregone conclusion. Alas, as Mr Kittow and Tango Shandy approached the final obstacle in splendid isolation, the saddle slipped. This caused the horse to make a catastrophic blunder at the fence but somehow the partnership remained intact. However, the impact on landing saw Mr Kittow lose his irons and he was reduced to hanging on grimly around the horse's neck along what must have seemed an interminable run-in. With no saddle at all now, Mr Kittow clung on for dear life until, just a few yards from the winning post, he was unshipped and slipped to the ground. Still determined to claim the prize, the plucky jockey desperately held on to the reins as he was dragged across the finish line. Since he had retained some form of contact with the horse as it passed the post, Mr Kittow reasoned that he was a worthy winner, a fact with which the judge concurred. However, the stewards took a less sympathetic view and disqualified Tango Shandy. Instead the spoils went to Legal Session who had been remounted to finish a distant second. Deprived of victory, Mr Kittow at least had the satisfaction of being heartily cheered to the unsaddling enclosure although that particular facility was somewhat superfluous in this case.

Two years later, similar misfortune befell jockey Roger Charlton down the road at Devon and Exeter. He was cruising to the winning post on Amantiss when, just yards from the line, the horse suddenly decided to deposit Charlton on the turf. Although Amantiss passed the post first it was *sans* jockey and so the race went to the second horse home – Slip Up!

Sheep on Course

The start of the Ulster Derby at Down Royal in July 1988 was delayed after a flock of sheep wandered on to the course. And the following May runners at Beverley had to wait in the paddock until a bullock could be removed from the course.

Pile-Ups

Although riderless horses are very much the norm in the chasing game, pile-ups in flat racing are mercifully rare. Even suffragette Emily Davison's dramatic dash across the course to pull the king's horse Anmer to the ground during the 1913 Derby failed to affect the other runners. But in the 1962 race, seven horses, including the favourite Hethersett, hit the ground as the field came down Tattenham Hill. The Epsom stewards later blamed the accident on too many horses of a poor standard being allowed to enter the big race. They reported: 'The general opinion of the jockeys was that too many horses were falling back after six furlongs and the remainder closing up, and in the general scrimmage some horse was brought down, the rest falling over that horse. The stewards accepted that view and regret that such a large number of horses not up to classic standard were allowed by their owners and trainers to start.'

In 1989 the St Leger was transferred from Doncaster to Ayr when the Yorkshire course was declared unsafe following two incidents earlier in the meeting. On the first day, jockeys Paul Cook, Ian Johnson and Ray Cochrane were injured in a pile-up two furlongs from home. The course was declared safe for racing, but two days later Billy Newnes was leading the way on Able Player in the Laurent Perrier Rose Champagne Stakes when his horse too crashed to the ground near the two-furlong marker. Subsequent inspection uncovered a sizeable hole in the course and the remainder of the meeting was abandoned. The appearance of the hole was blamed on subsidence in the drainage system.

At Goodwood on 27 July 1994, three jockeys were sent hurtling to the ground in two separate falls around the three-furlong mark. Jimmy Quinn was floored after his mount Haitham was brought down after clipping the heels of another horse and then later in the afternoon bunching in the seventeen-runner Tote Gold Trophy led to Michael Kinane and Wendyll Woods being unseated from Eurolink Chieftain and Virtual Reality respectively. Glorious Goodwood had never seen anything like it.

Day Trip to Bangor

For Midlands trainer Sally Oliver, a trip to Bangor marked a first. She had never been there before and had to look it up on an atlas to find out precisely where it was. In one respect, it was to prove a profitable day since one of Mrs Oliver's horses came home first at the tiny Shropshire course of Bangor-on-Dee. But when the stewards held an inquiry into the race and appealed for the trainer to come forward, she was nowhere to be found. The reason was simple: Sally Oliver had gone to the wrong Bangor, some 100 miles away on the North Wales coast.

A Day to Remember

Saturday 26 November 1988 was certainly a day to remember for jump jockey Chris Warren – but for all the wrong reasons. Having been sidelined for five weeks with a broken collar bone, Warren was excited about returning to action that day on Allied Force in a novices' hurdle at Newbury. But the day started badly when he woke to find that his car had been stolen during the night. Although the vehicle had been smashed up and left abandoned several miles away, he at least had the consolation of discovering that his riding gear had not been touched and so, after retrieving his equipment from the car, he hurriedly organised a lift to Newbury. He cut it so fine that another jockey had already changed into his colours in readiness for the ride but Warren managed to get the leg up on Allied Force in the nick of time. He shouldn't have bothered. Allied Force fell at the first and as Warren crashed to the ground he smashed the same collar bone again.

Wipe Out

After a hard race such as the Grand National, horses are generally pampered when they return to their stables. But nobody could have blamed trainer Frank Bibby if he harboured less than charitable thoughts towards his horse Wickham who took part in the 1910 National. For Wickham's erratic on-course behaviour succeeded in putting out of the race not only himself but also his two stable-mates. Yet things had started so promisingly for the Bibby yard. Nearly half the twenty-five runners were eliminated over the first three fences but the Bibby trio – 66–1 shot Wickham and the more fancied Caubeen and Glenside – were still bowling along nicely. But then Wickham set to work. First he collided with Caubeen, knocking both horse and jockey 'Tich' Mason to the ground, then at the fence before Becher's, he ran across Glenside, bringing Glenside down and falling himself. All three runners wiped out at a stroke. Consolation for Bibby came in the following year's National when Glenside, who was blind in one eye, triumphed at 20–1.

Travelling Light

Hogmanay was disqualified from first place in the Netherkelly Novices' Chase at Huntingdon on 29 November 1988 after jockey Richard Rowe had returned 14lb light. He had weighed out at 11st 11lb but weighed in with only 10st 11lb. Despite carefully studying the film of the race, the stewards were unable to see any point where the lead weights had fallen from the saddle. The stewards' adviser confessed: 'It's a complete mystery where the missing stone has gone.'

Dead Heat

In July 1923 jockey Frank Hayes rode 20–1 shot Sweet Kiss to victory in a steeplechase at Belmont Park in the United States. But when friends and connections rushed to congratulate him, they found Hayes slumped forward, dead in the saddle. He is believed to be the only deceased jockey to win a race.

Handicapper's Howler

In 1931 Windsor stewards fined the handicapper, Mr Kenneth Gibson, the sum of £10 after he admitted a mistake when calculating the weights for the Ivor Nursery, run at the Berkshire track on 19 September. When the weights for the race were first published, Lord Ellesmere complained that his horse, Attractive, had been set to give 29lb to Wantalot despite the fact that Wantalot had beaten Attractive earlier in the month by half a length when receiving only 13lb. Mr Gibson confessed that he had overlooked that result.

An Unexpected Detour

Ridden by a Mr Crickmere, Dragsman looked all over the winner of the 1843 Grand National until he swerved sharply at the last fence before the home straight, jumped a gate at the side of the course and bolted down a lane. Clinging frantically to the horse's neck, Mr Crickmere eventually managed to regain some semblance of control and brought the wayward beast to a halt. He took Dragsman back to the fence and the partnership rallied to finish third.

The Starter with a Stutter

The 1830 running of the Duke of Richmond's Plate at Goodwood was blighted by a succession of false starts, largely attributable to the fact that the man chosen to set the runners and riders underway was afflicted with a fearful stutter. Apparently whenever he became excited – which he was apt to do on big occasions – the stutter became so bad that he was scarcely able to speak at all. After the race was finally run, William Arnull, the senior jockey present, was asked by the stewards to explain the reason for the tardy start. 'The fault lay chiefly with the starter,' he replied. 'He is just like an old firelock which fizzles ever so long in the pan before it goes off, and when he did get the word out, there was no knowing whether he said "Go!" or "No!"'

Over-Confident

It seemed certain to be a lucky first ride at Sedgefield for amateur jockey Paul McMahon when he cruised to the front on Masnoon in the Hope Inn Handicap Chase in December 1989. Having brought his horse alongside long-time leader Lacidar at the last, McMahon was able to glance back confidently as Masnoon strode clear on the run-in. But instead of passing the winning post, McMahon suddenly took the wrong course and steered his mount towards the water jump, leaving the prize at Lacidar's mercy. Not surprisingly, McMahon's welcome as he dismounted was not so much warm as heated.

Life in Mars

After romping home by eight lengths in a race at Ascot in August 1979, No Bombs was disqualified for having eaten a Mars Bar! A routine dope test revealed traces of two mild stimulants, caffeine and theobromine, acquired from a Mars Bar which the horse had snatched from his stable boy on the way to the races. Trainer Peter Easterby lamented: 'That's the most expensive Mars Bar ever – it cost £4,064 in prize money.'

The curse of the Mars Bar reared its head again in September 1986 when four-year-old gelding De Rigueur, 20–1 winner of another race at Ascot, was disqualified after being given a Mars Bar by a stable girl on the day before the race.

Swapped Mounts Mid-Way Through the Race

Riding at Southwell in 1953, Irish jockey Mick Morrissey enjoyed the distinction of changing mounts half-way through a two-mile chase. Morrissey had set off on board 20–1 shot Knother, but five fences from home his horse ploughed into the back of the fallen favourite, Royal Student. The impact catapulted Morrissey into the air and he landed on the back of the riderless Royal Student as that horse was in the process of getting to its feet after its fall. And so Morrissey struck up a new partnership and safely steered Royal Student over the remaining four fences, although the pair came in last.

Jockey Bill O'Neill attempted a similar feat in the 1924 Grand National. Having already parted company with his own mount, Libretto, O'Neill saw the favourite, Conjuror II, come to grief when sent sprawling by a loose horse at Becher's second time round. Climbing into the saddle on Conjuror II, O'Neill set off in pursuit of Libretto. On reaching that horse, O'Neill swapped mounts for a second time and resumed his original partnership. Alas there was no happy ending. No sooner were Libretto and O'Neill reunited than the horse fell again.

Epsom Sorts

Anyone thinking that today's Derby crowds are boisterous should bear in mind what used to happen on the course back in the eighteenth century. An illustration of just how undisciplined the crowds could be then comes from a report on the first day of the October meeting in 1776. It describes how a horse was winning comfortably until the spectators took a hand. 'Just before he came in at the winning post, being crossed by a gentleman on horseback, the rider was thrown; but his leg hanging in the stirrup, the horse carried his weight in, and won miraculously without hurting his jockey.'

At the end of the 1815 Derby, the Epsom crowd were so angry with jockey J. Jackson who had been beaten into second place on the 7–2 favourite Raphael that they dragged him from the saddle and attacked him.

Blinded by the Sun

After making all the running to beat Local Councillor by a length and a half in a selling hurdle at Market Rasen in January 1983, Headway was disqualified because jockey Gordon Holmes had accidentally strayed from the course. As Headway turned into the home straight, Holmes was momentarily blinded by the sun with the result that the horse crashed through a plastic doll marker. The incident was seen by Chris Pimlott, riding the runner-up, and he objected. Holmes admitted: 'Because of the sun, I didn't see the doll and hit it slap bang in the middle.'

The Wrong Choice

Legendary jockey Steve Donoghue was desperate to end his career with a winner. And so when it came to his last-ever ride – in the Final Plate at Manchester on 27 November 1937 – there was no shortage of offers from trainers. He was torn between two horses – Pegomas, who had won the corresponding race the previous year, and Lord Derby's Highlander who had finished third that day. On that occasion they were racing at level weights but in 1937 Highlander was set to receive 10lb. Taking the form book into consideration, Donoghue rejected the offer to ride Pegomas and instead opted for Highlander, a decision which caused the latter to be backed down to 4–5 favourite. Unfortunately for Donoghue, history repeated itself and Highlander was once again beaten into third place by Pegomas.

The National That Never Was

The 1993 Grand National should have been a proud day for sixty-four-year-old Captain Keith Brown who was starting the race for the fifth and final time, but it was to turn into a nightmare played out in front of millions on the worldwide TV stage. Captain Brown's troubles began when Animal Rights protesters assembled at the first fence, causing the start to be delayed by more than ten minutes. When the thirty-nine runners did eventually come into line, the starting tape went up too slowly and caught under the horses' hooves. Captain Brown immediately flourished his red flag to indicate a false start and recall man Ken Evans, positioned 100 yards further up the track, raced out into the middle of the course to wave his red flag and send the runners back.

With steady rain falling, horses and jockeys were growing increasingly restless at the start. Captain Brown tried again but once more the tape failed to rise properly, half-strangling Richard Dunwoody on board Won't Be Gone Long, who was unable to go anywhere. Realising that the start was improper, eight more jockeys quickly pulled up their mounts but the rest of the runners raced away in earnest. This time there was no sign of the recall man – it was later said that he hadn't seen the Captain's flag on the second occasion. As the field pressed on, an attempt was made to call a halt to proceedings at The Chair but the jockeys merely thought that the officials running on the course with traffic cones were more protesters. Some riders pulled up at half-way but others went the distance.

At the end of the two circuits, Jenny Pitman's 50–1 outsider Esha Ness was first past the post, but this was the Grand National that never was and the race was soon declared void. Esha Ness's jockey John White was understandably distraught. 'It wasn't until I saw fellow jockey Dean Gallagher standing on the ground past the finish and he shouted that there had been a false start, that I realised anything was wrong. Afterwards I was numb with shock. Valet John Buckingham tried to get me to weigh in, which gave me another flash of hope, but the Aintree officials wouldn't let me sit on the scales. Later I had a quick drink with owner Patrick Bancroft, who was in a terrible state, then jumped in the car and drove straight home to Lambourn. It was all over the news but I couldn't watch. The house was besieged by journalists and even David Frost wanted me to appear on his show the next day. But I just wanted to forget about the whole nightmare experience.' As recriminations continued for weeks to come, the principal culprit in the fiasco that was the 1993 Grand National was found to be the slack elastic on the starting tape.

The 1993 event was not the first National to be beset by starting difficulties. In 1951 starter Leslie Firth released the tape while over half the runners were facing the wrong way. In the mad scramble to catch up, horses fell like ninepins and only two were left standing after Valentine's on the second circuit – the eventual winner, Nickel Coin, and Royal Tan.

The Least Successful Race Meeting

A four-day meeting at Kelso in 1803 attracted just three runners with the result that every race was a walk-over.

Only marginally more successful was the final day's racing at Derby on 9 August 1939. Although there were nineteen nominated entries for the Hartington High-weight Handicap, all withdrew, leaving the 'race' to be declared void and the £300 prize money to go begging.

Forgot to Weigh In

Jockey Gerry McEnhill lost a race on Adirondack at Down Royal, Ireland, in July 1981 because he failed to weigh in after winning. The course bookmakers were so angry that they went on strike for the rest of the meeting.

Mercer Misery

Even the most experienced jockeys can get caught out in a finish . . . as Joe Mercer will testify. Cruising in front on 1–3 favourite Mujbil in the Heathorn Two-Year-Old Stakes at Bath in June 1984, Mercer looked round twice, saw no danger and dropped his hands close to the winning post. However, he had reckoned without Ninattash, given a determined ride by Trevor Rogers to snatch victory on the line. Reeling from a £500 fine, Mercer explained: 'I was trying to win easily and just got caught.' Ironically he had just come back from an eight-day suspension imposed by the Longchamps stewards for mistaking the winning post when second on Mourjane in the Prix Dollar.

Teething Troubles

At the turn of the century, Diamond Jubilee was a talented but temperamental customer. Whereas other horses tucked into oats and hay, Diamond Jubilee favoured a diet of human flesh. Naturally enough, this didn't exactly endear him to jockeys or stable lads. In 1899 the experienced Jack Watts, stable jockey to trainer Richard Marsh, decided he'd had enough of Diamond Jubilee's aggression and vowed never to ride him again. The following year, a few days before the Two Thousand Guineas, Watts's replacement, 'Morny' Cannon, dissolved the partnership after an incident at exercise when the horse grabbed hold of him with his teeth and pushed him to the ground. Fast running out of jockeys, trainer Marsh gave the ride to the horse's stable lad, Herbert Jones, who amazingly struck up such a rapport with the animal that together they won three classics, including the 1900 Derby. Another stable lad was less fortunate – Diamond Jubilee bit his finger clean off.

Travel Sick

Trainer David Elsworth was fined £55 in 1989 for sending his horse Kpjes late into the paddock for a race at Wincanton. He'd had to stop his car on the way to the races so that his four-year-old daughter Jessica could be sick.

Carried Out

Backed down to 11–2 second favourite for the 1998 Cheltenham Gold Cup, See More Business lost out in the most unfortunate circumstances. When Cyborgo went lame just before the seventh fence, jockey Tony McCoy pulled the horse wide of the obstacle and in the process inadvertently forced See More Business and Indian Tracker to run out. The disappointment manifested itself in a heated after-race exchange between Paul Nicholls, trainer of See More Business, and Cyborgo's trainer Martin Pipe. An indication of just how unlucky See More Business had been came when he won the Gold Cup the following year.

Wyndburgh Woe

One of the most remarkable riding performances in the history of the Grand National was that of Tim Brookshaw on Wyndburgh in the 1959 race. Despite having to ride the last mile and a half without irons, Brookshaw still managed to finish a gallant second to Michael Scudamore and Oxo. Brookshaw had enjoyed a great ride until tackling Becher's for the second time when, on the steep landing side, his off-side stirrup broke. To even things up Brookshaw slipped his other foot from the remaining iron and pressed on. Although unable to give Wyndburgh as much assistance as he would have liked, Brookshaw kept the horse in contention and at the finish was beaten by just one and a half lengths.

The same fence had caused similar heartbreak in the 1882 National. Approaching Becher's for the second time, Eau De Vie, ridden by Dan Thirlwell, was clear of her rivals and seemingly full of running. But on landing, a stirrup leather broke loose and the horse veered off into the crowds, putting her out of contention. Proof of how unlucky the horse had been came when Thirlwell steered her to a fifteen-length win the very next day in the Sefton Steeplechase.

But these riding misfortunes paled into insignificance compared to that of Harry Brown who rode the 9–1 favourite The Bore in the 1921 Grand National. Rounding the home turn, The Bore appeared likely to justify his favouritism but the horse fell at the second last and Brown suffered a broken collar bone. While Shaun Spadah came home alone, Brown bravely remounted The Bore and, despite the fact that his right arm was hanging limply at his side, somehow guided the horse over the final fence to finish a remote second.

There were only four finishers that year and the fourth-placed Turkey Buzzard had been remounted by Captain 'Tuppy' Bennet no fewer than three times. Turkey Buzzard's owner, Mrs Hollins, was so angered by the Captain's treatment of the exhausted horse that after the race she chased him round the paddock with her umbrella.

Course Confusion

The Prince of Wales Novices' Chase at Chepstow on 5 December 1987 was declared void after the field took the wrong course and crashed through a running rail. Marker dolls had been wrongly positioned on the chase course, causing the runners to be diverted on to the hurdles course. The Chepstow racecourse executive decided to pay out a share of the prize money to the owners of the twelve horses in the non-race.

Five years later the Waterloo Hurdle at Haydock Park had to be re-started after the second hurdle had been erroneously blocked off and all the runners had bypassed it. The fault was found to lie with a groundsman who had accidentally turned over two pages in his racecard. Thinking the race was a chase, he had put the marker dolls at the wrong obstacle.

Spooked!

At Royal Ascot in 1988, Ile de Chypre was well clear in the King George V Handicap but then the horse suddenly swerved sideways 100 yards from the finish and dumped jockey Greville Starkey to the turf. The cause of the incident was subsequently found to be a 'sonic gun', designed to look like an ordinary pair of binoculars. Its inventor was duly prosecuted.

An Unhappy Career

Few horses endured such a miserable career as L'Africain, owned by a Frenchman named M. Vailland. The horse was cast in his box on the way to Aintree for the 1865 Grand National and had to miss the race. Although he ran the following year, he never fulfilled his potential, principally because he was trained incompetently. One contemporary wrote: 'They watered him when he was not thirsty, tempted him with beans when he was not hungry, pulled at him and raced him in the wrong places.' The horse's last owner was a sausage-maker and it is assumed that L'Africain was eventually eaten . . .

Tangled in the Tape

Owned by Sir John Rutherford, Solario was strongly fancied for the 1925 Derby but his chances evaporated when he got tangled up in the starting gate and lost valuable ground. As proof of the horse's ability, he went on to win the St Leger later that year and as a four-year-old lifted both the Coronation Cup and the Ascot Gold Cup.

Wrong Number

The French horses Nupsala and stable companion Nord A. C., were forced to miss the 1988 King George VI Chase at Kempton Park on Boxing Day because confirmation of their entry details was faxed to the wrong number by trainer François Doumen's office. This was particularly hard on Nupsala who had won the race the previous year.

Ambulanceman Injured

Riding at Fakenham once, Jeremy Hindley suffered a crashing fall and cannoned into one of the course ambulancemen who sustained a broken leg. The unfortunate medic was conveyed to hospital in his own ambulance.

Comedy of Errors

Back in the days when he was riding as Mr John Lawrence, Channel 4 racing stalwart Lord Oaksey suffered an experience which probably haunts him to this day. It was in December 1964 that Lawrence partnered Pioneer Spirit in an amateur riders' chase at

Cheltenham. As the pair jumped the second last, seven of their eight opponents had departed and they were a furlong clear of the only other horse standing. However, it was the first day's racing at Cheltenham's new course and, looking ahead of him on the turn, Lawrence saw a flight of hurdles. Not realising that the rails would guide him round to the steeplechase fence, the noble Lord wrongly jumped to the conclusion that he was on the wrong course, pulled Pioneer Spirit to a halt and began retracing his steps. By the time he realised his mistake, the other horse had swept past him and gone on to win. On eventually reaching the finish, Lawrence was roundly booed by the crowd and fined £25 by the stewards.

But his problems didn't end there. In yanking Pioneer Spirit to a standstill, Lawrence had put his back out so when he arrived home he ran himself a soothing hot bath. He recalled: 'Just as I was turning on the tap, my sister telephoned to commiserate. We talked for much too long, the bath overflowed and the ceiling fell into the dining-room!'

Spectator Interference

Second favourite Peter Simple finished third in the 1842 Grand National but would have been much closer had the crowd not got in the horse's way after the Canal Turn, resulting in his rider Mr Hunter being unseated. The jockey remounted but Peter Simple was unable to catch Gay Lad and Seventy Four.

In the 1856 National The Forest Queen had made every yard of the running until fate intervened at Becher's on the second circuit. As the mare was about to take off at the mighty fence, a spectator suddenly ran across her path. The ensuing collision put The Forest Queen out of the race.

During the Compton Welter Handicap at Northampton on 14 November 1901, a man suddenly ran across the track, causing three of the runners to unseat their jockeys. The man – a carpenter by trade – sustained fatal injuries and one of the jockeys, Sam Loates, broke a thigh and a collar bone.

And during the Ribblesdale Stakes at Royal Ascot in 1994, James

Florey, a twenty-one-year-old student from Bracknell, ran on to the course and straight into the path of the filly Papago. Luckily neither were hurt in the collision. Florey said afterwards: 'I couldn't even remember seeing a horse, let alone hitting one.'

Burke's Law

Hob Green, a first winner in Britain for Irish apprentice Robbie Burke, was disqualified after passing the post first at Newmarket in October 1992 because Burke had claimed the wrong allowance – 5lb instead of 3lb.

Ran on Strongly at the Finish

The Duke of Portland's horse Roche Abbey clearly had plenty in hand when winning the 1909 Singleton Plate at Goodwood. Indeed the horse was still so full of running at the end of the race that it galloped on way past the post, deposited its jockey and disappeared over the brow of The Trundle. The disconsolate rider dusted himself down and returned to civilisation but was unable to weigh in since the saddle which he was supposed to be carrying had last been seen heading for the Hampshire border.

Leger Wait

The start of the 1819 St Leger was such a farce that five runners missed it altogether and the stewards ordered a rerun. The connections of Antonio, who had won the original race, declined to take part in the rerun, insisting that their horse had won fair and square. So for the next fortnight there were two winners of the St Leger, both pressing their claims to the prize. Eventually the Jockey Club declared the rerun invalid and announced that Antonio was the winner after all.

Black Country Shambles

The Castlecroft Selling Handicap Hurdle, run at Wolverhampton on 7 November 1988, degenerated into a veritable shambles when nine of the eleven runners took the wrong course. Irate punters besieged the weighing-room, demanding that the race should be declared void after jockeys Jonathan Lower, on Brigadier Blake, and Trevor Wall, on Trematon, had led the other runners on to the chase course. Lower and Wall were each fined £100 for failing to acquaint themselves with the layout of the course. The trouble occurred on the bend in front of the stands where a strip of rail separated the hurdles and chase courses. Willie the Moon, a 66–1 outsider, was leading the field at the time with Brigadier Blake almost upsides him. Keith Sims, on Willie the Moon, correctly kept to the right of the rail but the rest of the runners, with the exception of Hallowed at the rear of the field, veered left on to the chase course. As jockeys realised their mistake, they turned and went back to take the correct route although five soon gave up the ghost and pulled their mounts up. In the confusion, Willie the Moon and Hallowed got clean away and the latter went on to win by twenty-five lengths at the handy price of 14–1.

Mad at the Hatter

Lester Piggott was none too pleased at being delayed for over half an hour at the London heliport prior to his 1983 Derby ride on Teenoso after a racegoer's top hat had blown into the helicopter's rotor blades. Fortunately for all concerned, Piggott made it to Epsom on time and partnered Teenoso to victory.

Punters' Pal Pilloried

For the most part, Willie Carson was popular with punters because he was a whole-hearted trier who would give his horse every assistance from the saddle. But there was an occasion at York in

1984 when racegoers were after his blood. Carson was on board the even-money favourite, the Queen's Rough Stones, in the four-runner BBC Radio Humberside Stakes on 10 October. When the stall gates opened, the colt reared up, swung round and momentarily trapped his head over the barrier of the adjoining stall. By the time Carson had extricated him, Rough Stones was a furlong behind the other runners. As Carson trailed in last, a few punters expressed their anger and one attempted to throw a pint of beer over the jockey. 'It was just one of those things that happen in racing,' explained Carson afterwards.

Unwanted Attention

In the 1937 Grand National, Jack Fawcus had a traumatic ride on Cooleen, the horse being repeatedly attacked by the riderless Drim who had fallen at the first fence. Time and again, Fawcus got Cooleen into a challenging position, only for the intimidating teeth of Drim to loom large alongside. Poor Cooleen lost vital ground fending off the aggressor and was eventually beaten three lengths into second place by Royal Mail.

The Racehorse on Platform 2

Due to run in the 4.15 at Plumpton on 26 October 1988, Our Sedalia decided to take jockey Dale McKeown for an unscheduled journey. The horse bolted on the way to the start, crashed through two sets of rails and ended up on the platform of the adjacent railway station. As alarmed passengers looked on, McKeown managed to pull her up before too much damage was done and before she could be prosecuted for attempting to travel without a valid ticket. She even made it back to the course in time for the race but the exertion had clearly taken a lot out of her and she was pulled up.

The Luckless Filly

Throughout 1943 the diminutive filly Ribbon found herself cast as the eternal bridesmaid in that year's big races as Lady Luck defiantly turned her back on her. First up was the One Thousand Guineas where Ribbon's lack of stature proved decisive in her neck defeat to the bigger Herringbone. In the Oaks her chances seemed to have been scuppered at the start when Noontide veered across in front of her, leaving her facing the wrong way as the rest of the runners set off. Although many lengths in arrears, Ribbon bravely went in pursuit and began to work her way through the field until just Why Hurry stood between her and the most improbable of victories. Alas, the winning post came a couple of strides too soon and Ribbon was again beaten by a neck. Next came the St Leger where most observers – including her trainer, Jack Jarvis – thought Ribbon was robbed of the victory she so richly deserved. After getting anything but a clear run, little Ribbon appeared to get up by a neck from her old rival Herringbone. Only one person on the course seemed to disagree with that verdict but unfortunately the person in question was the judge, Major Petch, who awarded the race to Herringbone by a short head.

Determined to end her career with a win, Ribbon's owner Lord Rosebery had her entered for the Jockey Club Cup at Newmarket in October but on her way out to the course she was frightened by a passing jeep. She reared up and fell before getting to her feet and galloping off into the centre of Newmarket town. She was eventually recaptured and although she bore scratches and a small cut, she did not appear to be lame and was therefore allowed to take her chance in the race. However, the ordeal had clearly taken a lot out of her and she ran well below par, finishing down the field. And so she retired with her reputation as a tragic heroine still intact.

Mystery Tour

Due to run one day at Folkestone, Tony Hide's filly Magnetic Point was mistakenly loaded into a horsebox bound for Southwell instead.

The blunder was not discovered until the horse was within half a mile of the Nottinghamshire course, by when it was too late to get her down to Kent in time for the first race.

Chance Ride Ended in Disaster

When champion steeplechase jockey Gerald Wilson picked up a last-minute ride on Prince Memnon in the final race of the day, the Cowley Hurdle at Cheltenham on 2 November 1938, he could not have foreseen the repercussions. For the horse fell and Wilson broke two ribs, causing him to miss a special dinner being held in his honour that night by the directors of the Cheltenham course.

Took a Short Cut in the Fog

One of the most unusual disqualifications in recent times was that of American jockey Sylvester Carmouche who was banned from riding in Louisiana for ten years after being found guilty of taking a short cut in dense fog to win a race at the Delta Downs track in January 1990. Riding the 23–1 outsider Landing Officer, Carmouche was claimed to have dropped his horse out of the race near the start, hidden in thick fog and then rejoined the pack towards the completion of a circuit in the one-mile race. Two jockeys in the race reported that no horse passed them at any time but Carmouche retorted: 'They never noticed me.'

The Whole Field Fell at the Last

All four runners in the Chilton and Windlestone Working Men's Club Handicap Chase at Sedgefield in September 1989 came to grief at the final fence. Grange of Glory landed on top of the fence; Invisible Thief fell just before the fence; Clonroche Stream ran into Invisible Thief and unseated its rider; and Hatsu-Girie, seeing the commotion ahead, wisely refused. Just when racecourse officials were beginning to despair of finding a winner, jockey Andy Orkney dragged Grange of Glory from its precarious perch, remounted and rode to the finish.

The three-mile Ovingdean Steeplechase at Plumpton on 17 December 1892 had witnessed a similar reluctance to finish. None of the three runners were exactly bursting with enthusiasm but the 20–1 outsider Covert Side seemed particularly uncooperative and when he refused to go beyond half-way, his jockey rode him sedately back to the paddock ready for unsaddling. However, on arriving in the paddock, the jockey learned that the other two runners were also persistently refusing to jump the obstacles and so he decided to give Covert Side one last chance. They returned to the course and somehow negotiated the fences to record an unlikely win although at a pace more akin to a funeral procession than a horse race.

Off Early

A race at Beverley in July 1991 was declared void after starter Major John Mangles set the runners off over a minute early.

The Race with Three Different Winners

In ordinary circumstances, the only time there can be three winners to a race is in the event of a triple dead-heat, but the Rathnure Handicap Chase, run over three miles at Wexford on 3 March 1988, was a law unto itself. The confusion was caused by pacemaker Lady Daffydown who went the wrong side of a marker on the first circuit and the rest of the field followed. However, jockey Pat O'Donnell on Derrygowan realised his mistake, pulled the horse up, returned to the marker and took the correct course. Obviously the manoeuvre cost him any chance of victory in the actual race but he was confident of success in the stewards' room. And sure enough the first nine horses to finish were disqualified so that Derrygowan, who had trailed in tenth and last, was awarded the race and first, second and third prize money.

But that wasn't quite the end of it. The connections of Mullaghea, who had originally finished sixth, were adamant that their horse had also taken the right course and, after studying a film of the race, the stewards concurred and Mullaghea was reinstated. So Mullaghea became the new winner with poor Derrygowan relegated to second. Some might say it could only happen in Ireland . . .

Carnage at the Canal Turn

A record field of forty-two set out for the 1928 Grand National. Yet there were only two finishers and one of those had to be remounted after the final fence. The reason for the incredibly high casualty rate was an incident involving Easter Hero, ironically the classiest horse in the race, at the Canal Turn which was then a stiff open ditch, one of the most feared fences on the Aintree course. Approaching it, Easter Hero was momentarily distracted and swerved, baulking the horses around him, before landing on top of the fence and falling back into the ditch. Horse after horse ploughed into the mêlée, hopelessly unable to jump the fence. The only ones who got a clear passage were those on the extreme outside, among them 100–1 shot Tipperary Tim. With over thirty of the field coming to grief at that one fence, there were only two left standing running to the last – Tipperary Tim and the American horse Billy Barton. Tipperary Tim held a slight advantage but his sole opponent gave him the race anyway by slipping up on landing. Billy Barton was remounted to finish a forlorn second. The fiasco prompted a huge outcry for improvements to be made to the course, the most notable of which was the filling in of the open ditch at the Canal Turn.

After 1928, everyone concerned hoped that history would never repeat itself but in 1967 there was another mass pile-up, this time at the twenty-third, the fence after Becher's and just about the smallest obstacle in the National. The mayhem was caused by two horses refusing and swerving across the course. As jockeys found themselves on one side of the fence with their horses on the other, only rank outsider Foinavon, ridden by John Buckingham, managed to clamber over, and that was simply because the horse had been so far back in the field that Buckingham was able to pick a path through the fallen animals. The others, led by favourite Honey End, eventually set off in hot pursuit but by then Foinavon was long gone. The 100–1 no-hoper went on to win by fifteen lengths, to the astonishment of his owner Cyril Watkins and trainer John Kempton who weren't even there to greet him. They had gone to Worcester instead to watch a more fancied runner.

Easter Hero, villain of the 1928 National, featured in another bizarre incident later that year. At the Grand Steeplechase in Paris, he was ridden by Dick Rees, a jockey renowned for enjoying the finer things in life. But on this occasion it appeared that Rees had wined and dined a little too well before racing and was therefore not exactly at his best. Without his usual alertness and strength, he allowed Easter Hero to refuse at the water jump in front of the stand and was promptly thrown off. Dragging himself to his feet, Rees made a derogatory gesture in the direction of the crowd and, facing the stand, proceeded to urinate in full view of the spectators. Remarkably, the French crowd warmed to this show of defiance and began chanting, *'Vive l'Anglais!'*

Beyond Recall

The Yorkshire Handicap at Ripon on 4 August 1980 was thrown into chaos and confusion by an over-zealous recall man who insisted on waving his red flag even though the stalls had opened perfectly satisfactorily. Eight of the fourteen jockeys simply ignored the red flag and raced on, but the other six pulled their horses up. The stewards promptly declared the race void and reopened it an hour later. Five turned out for the rerun – four who had been pulled up plus the original winner, Wynburry. Not surprisingly the second race went to one of the fresh horses, Swaying Tree, leaving Wynburry as a winner with no prize.

The Man with no Horse

There are numerous occasions in the annals of racing when victory has turned to defeat as the result of interference from a riderless horse. But Newton Abbot on 14 December 1992 witnessed what may well have been a first when a mount was brought down by a horseless rider. The race looked to be at the mercy of Wheal Prosper, ridden by Mick Fitzgerald, until they fell at the last when well clear. This left Hywel Davies on board the nearest challenger Troubador Boy with only the final fence to jump to claim the prize. Troubador Boy cleared the fence well enough but touched down just as a dazed Mick Fitzgerald staggered to his feet from the earlier fall. The ensuing collision sent Troubador Boy crashing to the ground and out of the race. The horse's trainer, Tim Thomson Jones, said: 'Mick hobbled into the weighing room looking for a bit of sympathy but all he got was an earful from Hywel.'

Race Card Muddle

At a meeting at Killarney in 1989, punters were puzzled when the 8.00 race was run at 7.30 and vice versa. They found themselves backing horses which weren't due to run for another half-hour or, worse still, horses that had run half an hour earlier. It emerged that the race order had been printed wrongly on the official race card.

The Masterplan

The finish of the Sidney Phillips Novices' Chase at Ludlow on 23 November 1989 was a titanic battle between the odds-on favourite Gay Edition, ridden by David Hood, and I Like It A Lot, partnered by Bruce Dowling. They were neck and neck on the run-in but the jockeys must have become so engrossed in the struggle that they forgot which way they were going and instead of coming over to the stand side, they went on to jump the first fence of the next circuit. This left the way clear for Career Bay, a distant third, to snatch a surprise victory. Winning trainer Derek Haydn Jones, tongue firmly in cheek, insisted that the success was by no means unexpected. 'It was all a planned strategy,' he said. 'We thought we'd let the first two get lost and then come to win the race.'

9 Overthrows

Missed the Sled

The Canadian number two team competing in the four-man bobsled at the 1992 Winter Olympics at Albertville would have been well advised to have devoted a little more time to practising their start. As the quartet set off on one run, Chris Farstad slipped while trying to jump into the sled and ended up in the wrong seat – that which was supposed to be occupied by Jack Pyc. Seeing this, Pyc hesitated fatally with the result that he never quite managed to get into the moving sled. As his bewildered team-mates headed off down the course, Pyc slid along helplessly behind it until he was rescued by an obliging spectator. With Pyc having missed the boat – or in this case the sled – the Canadians were disqualified for arriving at the finish a man short.

The Canadians were not alone in their misfortune that year. In the same event Soviet team member Aleksandr Bortyuk also slipped at the start and, when he made a desperate dive into his seat, he finished up facing the wrong way. With the sled in full flow, there was nothing he could do about it and so the Russians completed the course with Bortyuk facing one of his team-mates.

Lineswoman Fell Asleep

South African tennis player Abe Segal had reached match point in his 1964 Wimbledon men's singles first-round match with Clark Graebner of the United States when Graebner hit a ball which landed well beyond the baseline. Segal waited for the inevitable call of 'Out!' which would signal his passage to the next round, but none was forthcoming. All eyes on court number three turned to the lineswoman, Dorothy Cavis Brown . . . who was sitting in her chair fast asleep. As newspaper cameramen clicked into action, a kindly ball boy woke her up. But it was too late to spare her blushes. She was suspended from duty and shortly afterwards gave up umpiring.

Misread Finish

In the sprint finish at the climax to the 1961 Tour of Flanders cycling race, Italy's Nino Defillipis forged ahead and raised his arm in victory. But in his jubilation, he had misread the finish line which was actually further along the road than he had thought. Britain's Tommy Simpson took advantage of the Italian's error to snatch the prize.

Indecent Exposure

Germany's Hildegard Schrader won the women's 200 metres breast-stroke final at the 1928 Amsterdam Olympics despite a potentially embarrassing moment when the straps of her bathing suit broke. While her fellow competitors clambered out of the pool after the race, the discreet Ms Schrader remained in the water until the straps were fixed.

At the 1991 World Student Games in Sheffield, gymnast Raewyn Jack of New Zealand had points deducted after her leotard rode up too high during her exercise.

In the ladies' singles at Wimbledon in 1936, Britain's Dorothy Round encountered bra strap problems during her quarter-final match with Hilde Sperling of Denmark. Miss Round was the number one seed and firm favourite to recapture the title which she had won two years previously but in the course of the first set her bra strap snapped and she was refused permission to leave the court to carry out repairs. She fiddled with it endlessly but, never quite sure whether a call of 'Out!' referred to a shot or her cleavage, she became so distracted that she lost in straight sets.

Swine Fervour

Mike Tereui, a weightlifter from the Cook Islands, had prepared himself rigorously for the 1990 Commonwealth Games and was determined that his body would be in peak condition for the event. Unfortunately he forgot himself one day when he saw a pig raiding his vegetable patch. In his eagerness to teach the porky trespasser a lesson, he threw a punch at the animal and ended up badly damaging his hand – an injury which severely hampered his chances at the Games.

Sad Farewell

Six-times Wimbledon ladies' singles champion Suzanne Lenglen bade an acrimonious farewell to the tournament in 1926 following a breakdown in communications. The French star had specifically requested that she should not be scheduled to play her singles match with Evelyn Dewhurst on the same day as an important doubles match in which she and fellow French girl Diddie Vlasto were up against Elizabeth Ryan and Mary K. Browne. Lenglen never read the newspapers during Wimbledon and so it came as something of a shock when Vlasto told her late on the morning of the match that the referee, Frank Burrow, had arranged for her to play her singles shortly before the doubles. Apparently Lenglen tried to contact the referee but when her attempts failed, she refused to play. After arriving at Wimbledon late, she left again with her unopened tennis bag on the roof of her car. The committee rescheduled her doubles match for the following day (Thursday) but she and Vlasto lost. And when she was booed on court for a mixed doubles match on the Saturday, Lenglen promptly withdrew from that competition and the singles and returned to Paris. She never hit another ball at Wimbledon.

An Alarming Interruption

In the course of the 1981 World Snooker Team Cup, referee John Smyth nipped out one morning to buy a new battery for his travel alarm clock. He put the clock in his jacket pocket and forgot all about it. However, it returned to haunt him with a vengeance that afternoon when the alarm went off while he was officiating at a match between John Spencer and Paddy Morgan. Play was halted while an embarrassed Smyth rummaged around to locate the off button.

Lost in the Post

The four Turkish freestyle wrestlers who had won gold at the 1948 London Olympics – Celá Atik, Yasar Dogu, Nasuh Akar and Gazanfer Bilge – were unable to defend their titles in 1952 because their federation forgot to post their entry forms.

Too Cold for Huskies

Britain's first husky sled championships, scheduled to take place in Kielder Forest, Northumberland, in February 1993, had to be called off because it was too cold for the dogs. Two years previously the National Outdoor Skating Championships at Bury Fen, Cambridgeshire, were cancelled because of too much snow. Conversely the 1995 World Skiing Championships, due to begin in Sierra Nevada at the end of January, were cancelled due to lack of snow. Despite bringing in over 100 snow machines, the organisers still couldn't rescue the event.

Spectator Distractions

At the end of a tense rally during the 1912 Davis Cup rubber in Melbourne between Britain's James Parke and Rodney Heath of Australia, Parke hit the ball deep to Heath's backhand and, hearing a cry of 'Out!', stopped playing. However, the call had not been made by a linesman but by a spectator. Heath sportingly offered to replay the point but Parke declined. The unsavoury incident cost Parke the game but he fought back to take the match.

In the 1949 Davis Cup European zone final in Paris, Italy's Marcello del Bello was distracted at match point by a shout from a spectator. He never recovered and lost 10–8 in the fifth set to France's Marcel Bernard. But the Italians had the last laugh, winning the tie 3–2.

That Sinking Feeling

When the yacht *One Australia* sank in March 1995 during the Americas Cup race off San Diego, it was the first sinking in competition in the event's 144-year history. It wasn't something to shrug off either – the yacht cost a cool £1.2 million. No doubt the owners were insured.

Sinkings occur slightly more frequently in the University Boat Race – when Cambridge went under in heavy waters at Barnes Bridge in 1978, it was the sixth sinking in the race's history. Before that Oxford had sunk in 1951 in the most dramatic fashion. Winning the toss, Oxford chose the choppy waters of the Surrey station, convinced that these tactics would pay off in the latter stages of the race. But it never got that far. Within the first minute, half the Oxford boat was waterlogged and while Cambridge steered for the calmer water of the Middlesex shore, Oxford sank lower and lower in the water. By the time Cambridge reached Fulham Football Ground – two and a half minutes into the race – Oxford had officially sunk. The race was rerun two days later and fittingly Cambridge won.

In the 1912 Boat Race, both crews sank! Cambridge went down off Harrod's, and after pressing on for a while in the choppy river,

Oxford too took on so much water that they decided to head for the sanctuary of the shore. There the crew disembarked and the boat was emptied of water and refloated with the intention of continuing to the finish. But, when the time came to take to the water once more, there was no sign of the number two, C. E. Tinné. It later transpired that he had spotted a friend on the shore and had gone off for a chat. When the elusive Tinné did eventually return to the fold and Oxford got going again, it was a waste of effort since the umpire immediately announced that he had called a 'no race'. There was a re-row which Oxford won. The newspapers made great play of the double sinking. Two weeks later, they were carrying news of another, even more dramatic sinking . . . that of the *Titanic*.

Picture of Misery

Britain's cyclists were unluckily beaten into second place in the team time trial at the 1956 Melbourne Olympics when Billy Holmes crashed into a photographer who had strayed on to the course. The collision forced Holmes to change a wheel – a delay which cost him two and a half minutes and meant the British team missed out on the gold medal by just one second.

A photographer also wrecked the chances of Swedish speed skater Ake Seyffarth at the 1948 Winter Olympics at St Moritz. Seyffarth lost valuable time on the final lap of the 5,000 metres event when he brushed against the prying lensman who had jumped on to the ice to get a better picture. The contact destroyed Seyffarth's rhythm and he could only finish a disappointing seventh.

Fellow countryman Gillis Grafstrom would have sympathised. Three times a winner of the Olympic men's figure skating gold, Grafstrom was strongly fancied to complete a four-timer at the 1932 Winter Olympics at Lake Placid. The Swede's exploits had made him something of a hero, not only in his homeland but all over the world, and it was decided to record his latest efforts for posterity by means of a movie camera. Alas the camera literally proved Grafstrom's downfall during the compulsory figures. For it was allowed too close to the action and part-way through his routine,

Grafstrom collided with it and fell so heavily that he suffered mild concussion. The fall ultimately knocked the champion back into second place behind Austria's Karl Schafer.

Team Orders

France's René Vietto was denied victory in the 1934 Tour de France because he twice had to defer to his team captain Antonin Magne. First, when Magne broke a wheel, Vietto gave him one of his but had to wait five minutes at the roadside for a replacement. On the very next day Magne again broke a wheel and called out to Vietto who was ahead. Vietto dutifully rode back, gave the captain his wheel and once more endured a lengthy wait by the roadside. These setbacks cost Vietto dear and he could finish only fifth in the overall reckoning. It will come as no surprise to learn that the winner was Antonin Magne.

Dive to Disaster

Competing in the 1983 World University Games at Edmonton, Alberta, young Georgian diver Sergei Chalibashvili attempted a difficult three-and-a-half reverse somersault in tuck position. On the way down he smashed his head against the board and was rendered unconscious. He died from his injuries a week later.

Pulled Muscle

The 1936 Wimbledon men's singles final between Britain's Fred Perry and Baron Gottfried von Cramm of Germany was a match that never got into its stride. Von Cramm had already experienced an attack of leg cramp before the start and then on his first serve of the match he felt a muscle go in his right thigh. For the rest of the afternoon the German was a mere passenger as Perry romped to the easiest of straight-sets wins, 6–1, 6–1, 6–0. As the vanquished von

Cramm was finally put out of his misery, he relayed a message of explanation – and apology – to the crowd who had been deprived of a great tennis spectacle by his unfortunate injury. At the end of the match the umpire told the spectators: 'I have been asked to announce that Baron von Cramm pulled a muscle in his thigh in his first service game, and he much regrets that he was not able to play better.'

A more dramatic exit from court was made by Earl Buchholz of the United States in his men's singles quarter-final at Wimbledon in 1960. Playing on an unusually hot afternoon, Buchholz was leading Australia's Neale Fraser 6–4, 3–6, 6–4, 15–14 when he was struck down by cramp. The agony caused him to miss six match points and when Fraser levelled at 15-all, Buchholz collapsed for a second time. Unable to continue, the American was carried off and retired. Fraser went on to win the title.

Hare Too Slow

At the inaugural greyhound meeting at Wembley Stadium on 10 December 1927, a dog called Palatinus managed to catch the hare before the race had even finished. The race was re-run.

Drunk in Charge

The Swedish modern pentathlon team at the 1968 Olympics in Mexico were stripped of a bronze medal when one of their members, Gunnar Liljenvall, failed an alcohol test. The Swedes had finished third but were disqualified when the test results came through. Liljenvall protested that all he'd had to drink were two beers to steady his nerves before the shooting section . . .

Blacked Out

Competing in the super-heavyweight category of weightlifting at the 1974 Commonwealth Games, twenty-one-year-old New Zealand bank clerk Graham May took time to prepare himself for a colossal lift of 187.5kg. All looked to be going well but as he jerked the bar over his head, he blacked out and crashed off the stage on to the floor. Meanwhile, the weight ran loose, forcing officials and fans to dive for cover. Happily May recovered to take gold.

The Slippery Slope to Failure

The Tour of Flanders cycle race was famous for its long climbs on cobbled hills, among which was the 600-metre Koppenberg. But in 1987, after twelve years as part of the race route, the Koppenberg was dropped when Denmark's Jesper Skibby fell on the slippery slope and was run over by the race director's car.

Red-Faced Redskin

The National League championship play-off was one of the highlights of the 1945 American Football season with the east division winners, Washington Redskins, coming up against the west division winners, Cleveland Rams. A key player for the Redskins was Slingin' Sammy Baugh, a man with a reputation as a great thrower. But on this occasion Sammy's expertise was to desert him in spectacular fashion. During the first quarter, finding himself under pressure near his own line, he stepped back into the end zone and prepared to deliver one of his arrow-like passes. It was the kind of thing he'd done a thousand times before and all eyes turned to the far end of the field in search of a likely recipient. However, his throw travelled only a few yards since it hit the back of his own goalpost and dropped in the end zone, giving the Rams two points. At the final reckoning, Washington had lost by one point, 15–14.

A Puzzling New Game

Tennis was first introduced to the United States in 1874 when it was played on a court at the home of William Appleton at Nahant, a suburb of Boston. The locals, hearing that it was a new game from Britain, gathered round and watched it under the impression that it was cricket.

Thirty Yards from Glory

The defending champion in the Alpine Combined (one downhill and two slalom runs), Austrian skier Hubert Strolz looked certain to retain his crown at the 1992 Winter Olympics in Albertville, France. He was in the lead when less than thirty yards from the finish of his second slalom run he lost his balance, missed a gate and was disqualified. Afterwards he said ruefully: 'I was already at the finish in my thoughts.'

Putting a Dampener on Things

In 1989 the Toronto Blue Jays proudly unveiled their new stadium, the Skydome, the first in Canada to have a retractable roof. Unfortunately the opening ceremony was interrupted by a sudden downpour which caught everyone unawares. Naturally enough, none of the spectators had thought to bring umbrellas and in the thirty-four minutes it took to put the hi-tech roof in position, all present were soaked to the skin.

The Mystery of the Empty Chair

The 1903 Davis Cup witnessed a tense encounter between Laurie Doherty of Britain and Bill Larned of the United States. In the fifth and deciding set, the score was 4–4 but Doherty was 15–40 down on his own service when Larned hit what appeared to be a clear winner. The umpire awarded the point and the game to Larned who started to change ends but Doherty queried whether his serve had been in. At this, the umpire turned to the linesman for confirmation, only to find an empty chair. It transpired that the linesman had been obliged to leave early in order to catch a boat and that nobody had even noticed that he'd gone. In the confusion, the match referee ordered the point to be replayed. Poor Larned could only look on in disbelief as Doherty fought back, not only to hold his serve but also to win two of the next three games to clinch the rubber and the Davis Cup for Britain.

Stroke Struck Down

With just fifty metres to go in the semi-final of the four-oared shell coxless rowing event at the 1928 Olympics in Amsterdam, the German men held a narrow but seemingly decisive lead. Then suddenly their stroke, Werner Zschieke, collapsed and slumped forward on to his oars. His stunned colleagues instinctively stopped rowing, allowing the British boat to overtake them and cross the line in first place. Furthermore, Britain went on to take the gold.

Off Key

Fifteen-year-old Cecilia Colledge's hopes of winning a gold in the women's figure skating at the 1936 Winter Olympics at Garmisch were shattered when the officials put on the wrong music. When the mistake was realised, the British girl had an anxious wait until they found the right music. She was so unnerved that she nearly fell in the first minute of her programme and finished up with the silver medal behind Norway's Sonja Henie.

Borrowed Bike

Nearing the finish of the 1934 Paris–Roubaix cycle race, Frenchman Roger Lapébie had the bad luck to suffer a puncture while in the lead. With no time for repairs, the resourceful Lapébie commandeered a replacement bike from a spectator and rode it across the finish line in first place. However, the race organisers took a dim view of his actions and disqualified him for an illegal change of bicycle.

Dropped Medal in Lake

Having won a gold medal in the single sculls rowing at the 1956 Melbourne Olympics, eighteen-year-old Russian Vyacheslav Ivanov then managed to drop it into the depths of Lake Wendouree. He was so mortified by his clumsiness that he dived to the bottom of the lake in a bid to retrieve the coveted medal, but it was nowhere to be found.

The same thing happened to another rower, Italy's Davide Tizzano, at the 1988 Olympics in Seoul. The Italians had just won the quadruple sculls event and celebrated by throwing one of the team, Tizzano, into the Han River, but when he emerged from the murky waters, it was minus his gold medal. Fortunately there was a happy ending on this occasion for after a fifty-minute search, a diver succeeded in locating the medal.

Irving Jaffee was parted from his medals for a different reason – poverty. The American won gold in both the 5,000 and the 10,000 metres speed skating at the 1932 Winter Olympics at Lake Placid but became so poor during the Depression that he felt it necessary to pawn the medals. Sadly even the pawnshop went out of business so that Jaffee and his proud possessions were never reunited.

Tractor Trouble

Preparing for their Challenge Cup final against Sheffield Steelers in March 1999, Nottingham Panthers' ice hockey team were forced to abandon a crucial training session two days before the game because the club's ancient ice-cleaning tractor broke down. With the ice in an unfit state, coach Mike Blaisdell had no option but to send the players home. Panthers lost the final 4–0.

A Hint of Foul Play

There was more than a suggestion of underhand tactics during the 1904 Tour de France. It was only the second Tour and, because of the widespread corruption and sabotage, many thought it would be the last. Routes were changed in secrecy by the organisers and some riders were given illegal lifts by car or motorcycle. Nails were thrown on to the road to wreck competitors' chances, especially if they didn't happen to be French, and pressure was exerted by spectators to ensure the result they wanted. On the second stage an open car drew up alongside the leaders, hustling them to the side of the road and the passengers, masked by goggles, warned the riders of the dire consequences should their favourite, Faure of St Etienne, fail to win. Then on a night stage in the mountains 100 men armed with sticks and stones attacked all but Faure. Italy's Giovanni Gerbi was knocked to the ground and even a rival Frenchman, Maurice Garin, was hit on the head with a bottle. In addition, some riders were deliberately given bottles of dirty drinking water to make them ill. One was fed a soporific which made him crash; another had his cycle frame cut with a file so that it collapsed as soon as he tried to ride it; and a third had his shirt filled with itching powder! It goes without saying that the winner was a Frenchman . . . but Henri Cornet rather than Faure.

The Italians gained their revenge the following year on the inaugural Giro di Lombardia race. Home rider Gerbi won by over forty minutes, his cause aided by Italian fans who threw tacks and even a bicycle into the path of two Frenchmen who were chasing him.

Italian Hopes Go Up in Smoke

The 1980 Davis Cup final between Czechoslovakia and Italy in Prague was a predictably volatile affair, no match more so than that between Tomas Smid and Adriano Panatta. The latter won the first two sets but Smid fought back as Panatta became embroiled in a succession of queries about line calls. With the score at 3–3 in the fifth set, play was held up for forty-five minutes while an Italian spectator was arrested and thrown out of the hall. The Czech police said the man (a lawyer) had broken the hall's no-smoking rule, but his friends maintained that he had been ejected merely for supporting his team. The incident reached such proportions that the Italian players refused to resume the match until the man was allowed to return to his seat. When play did eventually restart, ironically it was Panatta whose concentration had been destroyed. He quickly lost the set 6–4 and the match. And when Ivan Lendl defeated Corrado Barazzutti, the Cup belonged to the Czechs.

The Horse Whisperer

After finishing second in the individual dressage at the 1932 Los Angeles Olympics, Sweden's Bertil Sandström was disqualified and relegated to last for encouraging his horse, Kreta, by making clicking noises. Sandström insisted that the noise was his creaking saddle.

Fencing Tragedy

At the 1982 World Fencing Championships in Rome, the foil of Matthias Behr of West Germany snapped and pierced the mask of his Russian opponent, Vladimir Smirnov. The weapon penetrated the Russian's eyeball and went into his brain. Smirnov, the reigning Olympic champion, died from the injury nine days later.

Cold Comfort

In 1966 Frenchman Jacques Anquetil was on course for his sixth win in the Tour de France when a spectator stepped out and hurled a bucket of cold water over him. While this practice is welcomed by riders in the heat, Anquetil received his drenching high up in the Alps and it quickly started to take effect. Within minutes he was shivering and, gasping for breath, was ultimately forced to withdraw from the race the next day.

Bowls Brawl

Until recently the game of bowls was seen as a last bastion of gentlemanly behaviour in the sporting world. The only time there was any unrest was if the kettle was broken. There weren't any reports of flare-ups on the green, of bowlers seeking counselling or of rival supporters from Worthing and Bognor meeting on the seafront for a pitched battle with walking sticks and zimmer frames, taunting each other with their bus passes. But sadly there are signs that even bowls has fallen victim to yob culture. In March 1999 young England international and world number eight Les Gillett was attacked after a tournament at Bournemouth and left with a twisted tendon in his knee, a displaced rib and two jarred vertebrae, as a result of which he missed two weeks' practice. It can only be a matter of time before we have green invasions.

Crashed into Umpire's Chair

Australia's Roy Emerson looked in command of his Wimbledon men's singles quarter-final against fellow countryman Owen Davidson in 1966 when he coasted to the first set 6–1. But then in chasing a drop shot which most other players would have conceded, he slipped and crashed into the umpire's chair. Emerson never recovered from the tumble and Davidson won the next three sets for the match.

The Man in Black

The slalom event at the 1968 Winter Olympics at Grenoble took place in dense fog and threw up a mystery which would not have been out of place in a Victorian melodrama set in foggy London town. According to his own version of events, which was backed up by three witnesses, Karl Schranz of Austria was approaching the twenty-second gate when a strange figure in black suddenly emerged from the mists and walked across the course. Totally nonplussed,

Schranz immediately skidded to a halt. He then asked the referee for a re-run which, in view of the fact that there were people able to support the story, was granted. On the re-run Schranz did the fastest time of all and was declared the unofficial winner at the expense of France's Jean-Claude Killy. But the drama took another twist two hours later when Schranz was disqualified for having missed two gates just before his encounter with the mystery interloper. Schranz protested that if he had missed a gate, it was because he was distracted by the man in black. As arguments raged, Schranz's fans claimed the trespasser was a French policeman or a soldier who had deliberately tried to sabotage the Austrian's win in order to guarantee victory for Killy. For their part, the French reckoned Schranz had made the whole thing up after missing a gate.

Late Flight

A racing pigeon owned by the Duke of Wellington was released from a sailing ship off the Ichabo Islands, West Africa, on 8 April 1845. It flew across deserts, mountains and seas, defying storms, intense heat and Spanish air traffic controllers, until on 1 June, fifty-five days and at least 5,400 miles later and just a mile from its loft at Nine Elms, Wandsworth, it dropped dead.

Victory by Default

Belgian cyclist Karel Kaers had decided to use the 1939 Tour of Flanders as a training run for the Paris–Roubaix race which he considered to be more important. Accordingly he left instructions for his car to be left at the top of the Kwaremont climb, 140 kilometres after the start, so that he could pull out of the race at the half-way stage. Since he had no intention of finishing and was only going to ride half as far as the rest of the field, Kaers was able to set a blistering pace and by the time he reached the top of the Kwaremont, he was more than a minute ahead. His job done, he looked for his car but it was nowhere to be found. His manager had removed it. With no other means of transport, Kaers climbed back into the saddle and finished the race, maintaining his lead right to the end.

Played to the Wrong Whistle

With the score goalless, France were attacking the Belgium goal in a hockey match at the 1960 Rome Olympics when an Italian traffic policeman, on duty outside the ground, blew his whistle. Thinking it was the umpire's whistle, the Belgians immediately stopped playing, allowing France to score the only goal of the game.

Slippery Surface

The combination of drizzle and still-wet lines, which had been marked too close to the start of play on such a sultry day, meant that the Centre Court surface at Wimbledon for the 1986 ladies' singles final between Martina Navratilova and Czechoslovakia's Hana Mandlikova was far from ideal. Despite repeatedly finding difficulty in keeping her feet, Mandlikova built up a 5–2 lead in the first set, at which point she decided to change her shoes in the hope of obtaining better grip. But it was an ill-timed move. The interruption to her concentration proved fatal as Navratilova stormed back to 5-all before taking the set 7–6. She then won the second set 6–3, and with it the championship.

A Star Is Born

Roy Riegels earned his place in American Football folklore as a result of a highly individual move in the 1929 Rose Bowl. Playing as centre for California, Riegels collected a fumble from opponents Georgia Tech on their twenty-yard line and sprinted off on an electrifying run. The 53,000 crowd rose in unison. They had never seen anything like it before – Riegels was running the wrong way, towards his own goal! Finally, just a yard short of his own line,

Riegels was brought to earth by a tackle from team-mate Benny Lom. But the seeds of defeat had already been sown. As a result of Riegels' brainstorm, Georgia picked up two points which were to prove vital as they edged home 8–7. Riegels, who said afterwards that he thought the shouts from the crowd were yells of encouragement, became an unlikely all-American hero. He received a mountain of fan mail including a proposal of marriage in which he and his bride would walk up the aisle instead of down . . .

Equipment Binned

Having arrived in Canada in preparation for the 1976 Montreal Olympics, the Czech cycling team's medal hopes suffered something of a setback when all their wheels and spare tyres were inadvertently picked up by garbage collectors and crushed.

Poor Turn-Out

The Commonwealth Basketball Championships held in Malaysia in 1994 were a somewhat depleted affair. Australia and New Zealand wanted nothing to do with the event, Scotland and Northern Ireland withdrew at the last minute and Swaziland, Tanzania and Western Samoa simply didn't show up. This left just six countries, including such powerhouses as Singapore and Hong Kong. For those who care, Canada won from England and Nigeria.

Much Ado About Nothing

The final of the men's 1,000-metre sprint at the 1908 London Olympics was declared void after two cyclists suffered punctures and the other two exceeded the time limit. Following the departure of the British pair Victor Johnson and Charles Kingsbury to flats, France's Maurice Schilles beat another Briton, Ben Jones, in a sprint finish. But because their finish times were over the permitted 1min 45sec, they were disallowed and no medals were awarded.

Boat Race Won on Foul

The only time in which the Boat Race has ever been won on a foul was back in 1849. Starting on the Surrey station, Cambridge went into an early lead and took advantage of a strong tail wind to cross to Middlesex. However, as Oxford fought back, Cambridge tried to veer back over to Surrey and in doing so, were bumped. Oxford stopped rowing for a few seconds and although they were closing again at the finish, it was Cambridge who crossed the line first. But that was not the end of the matter. The rules at the time stated that if the leading boat – in this case Cambridge – departed from the water where it started and the two crews then came into contact, then the leading boat was guilty of a foul. So the umpire awarded the race to Oxford.

There have been a few cases of individual crew members being overcome with exhaustion during the Boat Race. In 1926 Oxford's Hugh Edwards, known as 'Jumbo', blacked out for several strokes at Chiswick Eyot and in 1957 P. F. Barnard, the Oxford number five, collapsed off Duke's Meadows. Legendary commentator John Snagge said of the 6ft 6in Barnard: 'He just broke down, couldn't take it. It was a very strange thing, he just sat there doing nothing.' Without Barnard's assistance, Oxford were beaten. In 1980 a third Oxford man, bow Steve Francis, stopped rowing after collapsing near Barnes Bridge. Consequently Oxford saw their comfortable lead dramatically reduced over the closing stages and their final winning margin was barely a canvas. While his team-mates celebrated, Francis was given oxygen.

Kept Eye on the Ball

In the final of the 1912 French covered-court tennis championship between André Gobert and William Laurentz, a Gobert service ricocheted off the frame of Laurentz's racket and hit him in the eye. Laurentz gallantly played on even though he had suffered a detached retina and eventually lost the sight in that eye.

During the Wimbledon mixed doubles competition the following year, defending champions Ethel Larcombe and Cecil Parke were a set up against Agnes Tuckey and Hope Crisp when a smash from Parke accidentally hit his partner in the eye. Miss Larcombe was forced to retire.

Brought Down by Motorcycle Cameraman

A motorcycle carrying a TV cameraman filming the leaders of the 1985 Liège–Bastogne–Liège cycle race caused chaos when it toppled over, brought down Australia's Phil Anderson and blocked the road. In the general mêlée, a small group of riders managed to squeeze through including the eventual winner, Moreno Argentin of Italy.

A Weighting Game

Competing in the 1952 Olympics in Helsinki, weightlifter Arkady Vorobyev of the Soviet Union was dismayed when his final lift in the light-heavyweight section was ruled invalid, condemning him to only the bronze medal. While the dejected Vorobyev got changed in his dressing room, his camp protested long and hard about the decision, maintaining that he had been made to hold the lift in question for longer than the statutory two seconds. After forty minutes of argument, Olympic officials agreed to let him have one more go. By the time his coach had informed him, the clock had already started and Vorobyev had to hurry back to the platform, ill-prepared for the most important lift of his life. Not surprisingly, he failed with the bonus attempt.

English weightlifter Louis Martin had a nasty scare during the 1966 Commonwealth and Empire Games. Going well in the middleweight class, Martin asked for a weight increase in pounds.

But Games officials thought he meant kilograms and he nearly did himself a permanent injury attempting the lift.

Unable to Perform

Supporters of France's Fabrice Guy, who won gold in the Nordic skiing at the 1992 Winter Olympics in Albertville, France, were so excited that they sang 'La Marseillaise' outside the doping control room. Because of the noisy distraction, it took poor Guy an hour to produce the required urine sample.

Snooker Rained Off

If ever a sport should be safe from adverse weather conditions, it's snooker but at the 1973 World Championships water came in through the roof of the City Hall, Manchester, and dripped on to the baize during the quarter-final between Fred Davis and Alex Higgins. Play was stopped while workmen carried out emergency repairs.

Mountain Fall

Leading the 1951 Tour de France, Dutch rider Wim van Est went off the road in the Pyrenees and fell more than 150 feet down the mountainside. Battered and bruised, he was hauled back to the road with the aid of a 'rope' made from tubular tyres. Despite this valiant effort, there was no way he could continue the race and he was forced to retire.

At least van Est lived to tell the tale but some riders have not been as lucky. In 1950 Camille Danguillaume of France was fatally injured when knocked down by a motorcycle during the French road championships at Monthléry; in 1969 another Frenchman, José Samyn, was killed after colliding with a programme seller during a race in Belgium; and in 1984 Portugal's Joaquim Agostinho died from a fractured skull following a collision with a dog on the Tour of Portugal.

Entire Team Overslept

Following a mix-up over start times, the entire German fencing team were asleep in their hotel when they should have been in action in the épée competition at the 1906 Athens Olympics. Roused from their slumbers, the Germans hurried to the fencing grounds but lost 9–2 to Britain. They should have stayed in bed.

Another late starter was snooker player Nick Pearce. The former Gloucester male model misread the start time for a qualifying match against Gary Ponting in the 1999 Embassy World Championships at Telford and arrived half an hour late for the opening session. Pearce was docked three frames as punishment but still won through 10–7.

To Start or Not to Start?

The starter for the 1903 Boat Race, a worthy by the name of Fred Pitman, elected to use an antique gun for the purpose. After he had shouted to the crews 'Are you ready?', he pulled the trigger, only for the weapon to stick at half-cock. Not sure whether or not the race was underway, Oxford hesitated and were nearly a length down by the time they started rowing. They never made up the lost ground, eventually going down by a margin of six lengths.

Bottled Out of Davis Cup

Due to travel to England for the 1906 Davis Cup, Beals Wright, the American number one, celebrated freely on the eve of departure, knowing that he had the transatlantic voyage on which to clear his head. Waking up in the team hotel the next morning, he felt that familiar dry sensation in the mouth which goes with excessive alcohol intake. He rang down for a bottle of soda water which duly arrived unopened. Since he didn't have a bottle opener, Wright, rather than ring down for one, decided in his haze to have a go at levering the top off with a toothbrush. The attempt was not an unqualified success since the neck of the bottle broke in his right hand, cutting him badly. Wright wasn't normally squeamish at the sight of blood – unless it happened to be *his* blood. So when he saw the red stuff spurting out from his gashed hand, he promptly fainted. And things got worse. On the voyage, the wound became infected. He developed blood poisoning and one finger eventually had to be amputated. Inevitably he missed the Davis Cup tie. It was an expensive drink.

Horse Attacked by Rider

In the modern pentathlon competition at the 1968 Olympics in Mexico City, West Germany's Hans-Jürgen Todt drew a particularly reluctant horse called Ranchero. The partnership didn't exactly hit it off and Ranchero took great delight in refusing three times. Todt was so furious at this display of wilful disobedience that at the end of the round he started attacking the horse and had to be dragged away by his team-mates.

Bike Got Lift from Man

Just over half a mile from the finish of the 1909 Tour de France, race leader François Faber of Luxembourg watched in horror as the chain on his bicycle broke. So he completed the stage by running with the bike on his shoulder and was fast enough on foot to retain his overall advantage.

Say It with Flowers

The first time Tim Henman really made a name for himself with the British tennis public was for the wrong reason – he was disqualified from Wimbledon 1995 for accidentally hitting a ball girl in a fit of temper. Playing in the first round of the men's doubles, Henman and Jeremy Bates were leading Henrik Holm and Jeff Tarango 7–6, 2–6, 6–3, 6–6 when Henman lost a point and angrily belted the ball towards the net. It so happened that ball girl Caroline Hall had chosen that precise moment to dart across the court and the ball struck her hard on the temple. Referee Alan Mills reacted by disqualifying Henman from all events at Wimbledon that year – the first time such a punishment had been meted out at the All England Championships. A repentant Henman repaired the damage by presenting the unfortunate ball girl with a bunch of flowers.

Coincidentally one of his opponents in that ill-fated doubles encounter, Jeff Tarango, was also in hot water at Wimbledon that year. Trailing 6–7, 1–3 to Germany's Alexander Mronz in the third round of the men's singles, Tarango conceded the match by walking off Court No. 13 following a stormy exchange with French umpire Bruno Rebeuh. As Rebeuh left the court, he found out what it was like to be Tarango'd when he was slapped by the American's irate wife Benedicte. Tarango was fined £10,000 for the impromptu walk-out. A month earlier he had been fined £3,400 at the French Open.

The Ultimate Jump

At the 1991 World Women's Figure Skating Championships in Munich, Midori Ito of Japan, a competitor renowned for her spectacular jumps, mistimed the take-off of her double toe loop, flew off the ice, sailed over the barrier and finished up in the crowd.

Beaten by Sunstroke

Britain's Roper Barrett should never really have started his Wimbledon men's singles final against New Zealander Tony Wilding in 1911. He began the match with a temperature of 102, looking drawn and grey, and was scarcely his usual athletic self on court. The *Daily Express* wrote: 'People who did not know looked upon his languid movements and long pauses between services as part of a cunning scheme of bluff to lure his opponent into the belief that he was already a beaten man.' But as he continued to lurch across the court, it became clear that it was no act. Remarkably Barrett won two of the first three sets but after losing the fourth 6–2, he finally admitted defeat in the battle against sunstroke and 'tottered blindly off court' to retire.

Pet Sounds

A family who went to cheer on their pet greyhound running in a race in Ireland in the early 1980s may have been better advised to stay away. For as the dog rounded the final bend, very much in touch with the leaders, it recognised the voices of encouragement coming from the side of the track, pulled itself up and, tail wagging, trotted over to the fence to greet its owners.

One Swallow Doesn't Make a Swimmer

Competing in the final of the ladies' 100 metres butterfly at the 1960 Rome Olympics, fourteen-year-old Carolyn Wood of the United States was lying a close second at the two-thirds mark. But her medal hopes evaporated when she accidentally swallowed a lot of water and became so disorientated that she had to stop swimming.

Hard Held

French cyclist Guy Lapébie could rightly claim to have been robbed of a gold medal in the 100-kilometre individual road race at the 1936 Olympics in Berlin. The records show that first place went to fellow Frenchman Robert Charpentier who dramatically overhauled Lapébie to win by 0.2sec after the latter inexplicably slowed down just before the line. But when a photograph of the finish was studied some years later, it revealed that Charpentier had pulled the unfortunate Lapébie back by his shirt.

Shorts Shortage

Troubled Budweiser League basketball club Worthing Bears plumbed new depths in April 1999 when star player Larry Coates refused to wear a pair of borrowed shorts and quit the team. Returning to the side after a thumb injury, Coates arrived for the game against Newcastle to find that there weren't any Bears trunks in his locker. Newcastle offered to lend him a pair but he refused and sat out the game. 'I'm supposed to be the best ball player,' he raged. 'I should be able to take a pair of shorts off someone who doesn't play.' Without Coates, Worthing lost 100–88.

Faulty Service

In her first-round ladies' singles match against Mrs L. Thung of Holland at Wimbledon in 1957, Miss M. de Amorim of Brazil got off to a somewhat shaky start on her own serve. Indeed she began by serving seventeen consecutive double faults. Mrs Thung went on to win 6–3, 4–6, 6–1.

Stripped of Gold

That winning feeling didn't last long for South African cyclist Henry Kaltenbrun at the 1920 Antwerp Olympics. After being hailed as the winner of the road race, he was just about to start celebrating in earnest when it emerged that the runner-up, Sweden's Harry Stenqvist, had been delayed for four minutes at a level crossing. Taking this lost time into consideration, the organisers reversed their original decision and declared Stenqvist the winner instead.

Pain in the Neck

Britain's Stephen Lee, ranked number nine in the world, was forced to withdraw from the 1999 British Open snooker tournament after damaging his back in a freak accident at his Trowbridge home. His manager Ian Doyle explained: 'Stephen got up suddenly to answer the phone and twisted the muscle leading from his shoulder to his neck.'

Ice Melted

The 10,000 metre speed skating event at the 1948 Winter Olympics at St Moritz became a lottery when the sun came out and turned the course to slush. The last skaters were the ones to suffer and no fewer than eight withdrew in the face of impossible odds. However, the last skater of all – Richard Solem of the United States – was determined to give it a go. Doing more paddling than skating, he completed the course in 26min 22.4sec – almost nine minutes behind the winning time.

The Bull's Revenge

Spanish bullfighter José Culberto was so busy playing to the crowd after apparently killing a bull in 1985 that he didn't notice the dying animal stagger to its feet. The bull proceeded to exact a full and bloody revenge by sinking its horn into Culberto's heart and killing him.

Hair Loss

United States tennis prodigy Venus Williams was docked a point at the 1999 Australian Open Championships at Melbourne when a string of beads dislodged from her dreadlocked hair and scattered around the court. Playing fellow American Lindsay Davenport, Williams was trying to fight her way back into the match after losing the first set 6–4. Early in the second set, a few beads fell out and umpire Denis Overberg warned Williams that he considered their detachment from her hair to be a distraction and called a 'let'. Then at break point on her own service, the same thing happened again. Although the service was good, umpire Overberg immediately awarded the point and therefore the game to Davenport, giving her a 3–0 lead. Backed by the crowd, Williams protested but the umpire would not be swayed. 'It was the first time I've been docked a point in eight years of playing in beaded dreadlocks,' moaned Williams afterwards. 'I don't think it was a very fair call.' But Davenport responded: 'The noise of the beads falling on the court did distract me.' However, the incident seemed to distract Williams more and she failed to win another game, going down 6–4, 6–0. 'I lost my focus after that,' she admitted.

Wrong Directions

The 1949 Paris–Roubaix cycle race ended in farce when the leading group of three – including France's André Mahe – were given wrong directions by race officials when looking for the entrance to the Roubaix Vélodrome. The trio were eventually forced to carry their bikes into the stadium through a turnstile – it is not recorded whether they actually had to pay – and lost so much time that they were overtaken by the main pack, led by Italy's Serge Coppi. After much discussion and not a little acrimony, the organisers opted for compromise and awarded the race jointly to Coppi and Mahe.

Something Fishy

The National Ambulance Servicemen's Angling Championships, staged at Kidderminster in 1972, proved something of a disappointment. After spending five hours on a canal side, pitting their wits man against fish, the 200 ambulancemen had managed to catch precisely nothing. It was only then that a passer-by informed them that all the fish had been moved to other waters three weeks previously.

Rowing Row

It is uncanny how so many claims of sabotage in sport seem to revolve around the French. Whereas in the Tour de France and other cycling events they have sometimes been the perpetrators, they appeared to have been the victims in the men's rowing competition at the 1984 Olympics in Los Angeles. For part-way through their eights race, one of the French crew lost an oar when his oar-lock gate broke. Considerably handicapped, the French missed qualification, but as accusations of dark deeds began to emerge, they were reprieved and allowed to move through to the final. Even with a full complement of oars, they could only finish sixth.

The Cycling Team with No Bikes

The Ugandan cycling team arrived in New Zealand for the 1974 Commonwealth Games at Christchurch without any bikes. They thought that machines would be provided by the Games organisers and, on discovering that this was most definitely not the case, the Ugandans had to borrow some from local enthusiasts.

Late for the Match

The number one seed for the men's singles at Wimbledon in 1946, Australia's Dinny Pails, blew his chances when he got lost en route to SW19 for his quarter-final encounter with Yvon Petra of France. Arriving twenty minutes late for the match, Pails was so flustered and ill-prepared that he flopped to a shock defeat in four sets. Petra went on to win the title.

Hit by Cow

Belgian cyclist Jules Van Hevel was quietly fancied to become world professional road race champion for 1928 but his victory hopes were shattered when, while sharing the lead, he was knocked off his bike by a marauding cow.

Victory Trip

One of the great upsets in Davis Cup history was the United States' defeat by Ecuador in Guayaquil in 1967. After Miguel Olvera had beaten Arthur Ashe in four sets, Ecuador's jubilant captain, Danny Carrera, was so excited that he tried to jump the net to embrace his player. But in doing so, Carrera tripped on the net and broke an ankle.

Danger: Bad Marshalling Ahead

Incompetent marshalling at the 1988 Liège–Bastogne–Liège cycle race sent the entire field of 200 riders speeding down a hill straight into roadworks. Over fifty of the competitors were brought down in the ensuing pile-up.

A Paws in the Action

In April 1995 a black cat found its way on to Belfast greyhound track in the middle of a race. The dogs immediately focused on the cat rather than the hare but while the canny cat managed to escape over a fence, the distracted greyhounds piled into each other and ended up in an unseemly heap on the track. The race was abandoned.

Bibliography

Back Page Racing – George Plumptre (Aurora, 1996)

Barclays World of Cricket – ed. E. W. Swanton (CollinsWillow, 1986)

Bare Fist Fighters of the 18th and 19th Century – Dick Johnson (The Book Guild, 1987)

Benson and Hedges Golfers' Handbook – ed. Laurence Viney (Macmillan, 1989)

The Book of Heroic Failures – Stephen Pile (Futura, 1982)

Century of the Marathon – Riël Hauman (Human and Rousseau, 1996)

The Commonwealth Games: The First 60 Years – Cleeve Dheensaw (Queen Anne Press, 1994)

The Complete Book of the Olympics – David Wallechinsky (Aurum Press, 1992)

The Complete Book of the Winter Olympics – David Wallechinsky (Aurum Press, 1994)

Count Maggi's Mille Miglia – Peter Miller (Alan Sutton, 1988)

Cricket Facts and Feats – Bill Frindall (Guinness, 1996)

Curiosities of Cricket – Jonathan Rice (Pavilion, 1993)

Cycling Facts and Feats – Jeremy Evans (Guinness, 1996)

Daily Telegraph Chronicle of Cricket – ed. Norman Barrett (Guinness, 1994)

Daily Telegraph Chronicle of Horse Racing – ed. Norman Barrett (Guinness, 1995)

Golf Facts and Feats – Andrew Swales (Guinness, 1996)

The Golfers – ed. Peter Dobereiner (Collins, 1982)

Grand Prix Racing – Anthony Pritchard (Aston Publications, 1991)

Grand Prix Showdown – Christopher Hilton (Patrick Stephens Ltd, 1992)

The Guinness Book of Rallying – John Davenport (Guinness, 1991)

A History of Australian Cricket – Chris Harte (André Deutsch, 1993)

The History of the British Lions – Clem Thomas (Mainstream, 1997)

More Cricket Extras – David Rayvern Allen (Guinness, 1992)

Motor Sports: A Pictorial History – Raymond Flower (Collins, 1975)

The Oxford & Cambridge Boat Race – Christopher Dodd (Stanley Paul, 1983)

RAC Rally – Maurice Hamilton (Partridge Press, 1989)

A Race Apart: The History of the Grand National – Reg Green (Hodder & Stoughton, 1988)

Rugby Shorts – Chris Rhys (Guinness, 1990)

Stop The Game, I Want To Get On! – Jimmy Greaves with Norman Giller (Harrap, 1983)

The Story of the Davis Cup – Alan Trengrove (Stanley Paul, 1985)

Turf Accounts – Graham Sharpe (Guinness, 1990)

The Virgin Book of Golf Records – Rob Pegley (Virgin, 1998)

Wisden (various)

The World of Rugby – John Reason and Carwyn James (BBC Books, 1979)